Lecture Notes
in Business Information Processing

410

Series Editors

Wil van der Aalst
RWTH Aachen University, Aachen, Germany

John Mylopoulos
University of Trento, Trento, Italy

Michael Rosemann
Queensland University of Technology, Brisbane, QLD, Australia

Michael J. Shaw
University of Illinois, Urbana-Champaign, IL, USA

Clemens Szyperski
Microsoft Research, Redmond, WA, USA

More information about this series at http://www.springer.com/series/7911

Ilan Oshri · Julia Kotlarsky ·
Leslie P. Willcocks (Eds.)

Digital Technologies for Global Sourcing of Services

14th International Workshop
on Global Sourcing of Information Technology
and Business Processes, Global Sourcing 2019
Obergurgl, Austria, December 18–21, 2019
Proceedings

 Springer

Editors
Ilan Oshri 🄳
The University of Auckland
Auckland, New Zealand

Julia Kotlarsky 🄳
The University of Auckland
Auckland, New Zealand

Leslie P. Willcocks 🄳
London School of Economics
London, UK

ISSN 1865-1348   ISSN 1865-1356   (electronic)
Lecture Notes in Business Information Processing
ISBN 978-3-030-66833-4   ISBN 978-3-030-66834-1   (eBook)
https://doi.org/10.1007/978-3-030-66834-1

This Springer imprint is published by the registered company Springer Nature Switzerland AG
The registered company address is: Gewerbestrasse 11, 6330 Cham, Switzerland

Preface

This edited book is intended for use by students, academics and practitioners who take an interest in outsourcing and offshoring of information technology and business services. The book offers a review of the key topics in sourcing of services, populated with practical frameworks that serve as a toolkit for students and managers. The range of topics covered in this book is wide and diverse, offering various perspectives on the employment of digital technologies in the context of sourcing services. More specifically, the book examines sourcing decisions and management practices around digital platforms, robotic process automation and blockchain, giving specific attention to digital aspects of innovation in sourcing. Topics discussed in this book combine theoretical and practical insights regarding challenges that industry leaders, policy makers and professionals face or should be concerned with. Case studies from various organizations, industries and countries are used extensively throughout the book, giving it a unique position within the current literature.

The book is based on a vast empirical base brought together through years of extensive research by leading researchers in information systems and strategic management.

This book includes selected papers presented at the 14th Global Sourcing Workshop. (We decided to skip the 13th number because of superstition. Since the 12th workshop was in February 2018, and then the next one was almost -two years later – December 2019 – we decided to call it the 14th.)

November 2020

Ilan Oshri
Julia Kotlarsky
Leslie P. Willcocks

Organization

Global Sourcing Workshop is an annual gathering of academics and practitioners.

Program Committee

Julia Kotlarsky   The University of Auckland, Auckland, NZ
Ilan Oshri   The University of Auckland, Auckland, NZ
Leslie Willcocks   London School of Economics, London, UK

Contents

Gravitation of Blockchain in Shared Services: The Next Phase of Service Delivery Strategy

Vipin K. Suri[1], Marianne D. Elia[1], and Jos van Hillegersberg[2(✉)]

[1] Shared Services International Inc, Mississauga, Canada
[2] Faculty of Behavioral, Management and Social Sciences, Industrial Engineering and Business Information Systems, University of Twente, P.O. Box 217, 7500 AE Enschede, The Netherlands
j.vanhillegersberg@utwente.nl

Abstract. A Blockchain is an immutable, tamper-proof, shared ledger of state changes of a digital asset. It is an incorruptible digital ledger of economic transactions that can be programmed to record not just financial transactions but virtually everything of value. This digital ledger is managed via a distributed network across many nodes that can verify and confirm those transactions through consensus. The implications of the technology are far-reaching but there are conditions that should be met in order for Blockchain to be a viable solution. The purposes of this research are to (1) explore the current Blockchain use cases in Shared Services (2) understand the value created by Blockchain in Supply Chain Management and (3) study the tactical challenges in adopting a Blockchain strategy in Shared Services. In addition to a literature review conducted, we conducted in-depth interviews with selected Shared Services Leaders and experts. Results of our research indicate that Blockchain technology can deliver on expectations and implementation in Shared Services organizations will require simple steps. This study provides the data necessary for executives to build a business case for applying Blockchain technology in Shared Services and investigates the potential that Blockchain has to revolutionize industry and deliver gains in speed, security, transparency, traceability and accountability for a wide range of business processes.

Keywords: Blockchain · Data integrity · Hashing · Block · Encryption · Distributed ledger · Market maker · Industry group · Regulator · Node selection · Digital asset · Intermediaries

1 Introduction

Blockchain creates a ledger of all transactions in a given process. Each ledger entry is autonomous so can provide insights into cash flow and add extra security in exchanges involving cryptocurrency. Virtually incorruptible due to the fact that the data contained within a ledger entry cannot be copied, Blockchain is the backbone of cryptocurrency transactions. It can track any item of value, so is particularly useful in shipping as well as online retail, making it a powerful tool for business units with the vision to utilize this tool.

© Springer Nature Switzerland AG 2020
I. Oshri et al. (Eds.): Global Sourcing 2019, LNBIP 410, pp. 1–16, 2020.
https://doi.org/10.1007/978-3-030-66834-1_1

A Blockchain facilitates secure online transactions. It is a decentralized and distributed digital ledger that is used to record transactions across many computers so that the record cannot be altered retroactively without the alteration of all subsequent blocks and the collusion of the network. This allows the participants to verify and audit transactions. While the knowledge on Blockchain technology and applications is rapidly expanding, there is little insight on how Blockchain can enhance delivery of Shared Services.

Using a combination of available literature study and in-depth interviews with experts and practitioners we address the following research questions:

1. What are the key factors that facilitate adoption of Blockchain technology in Shared Services?
2. What are the challenges in adopting Blockchain technology in Shared Services?
3. What processes are ideal candidates for Blockchain technology?
4. What is the promise of Blockchain technology in Shared Services?

To develop a common understanding of the terms used in Blockchain technology, we offer the following definitions:

Hashing - Hashing is a form of cryptographic security.
Encryption - Encryption is a two-step process used to first encrypt and then decrypt a message, hashing condenses a message into an irreversible fixed-length value, or hash.
Public Key - A public identifier that can be freely shared with others; this is the identity on the Blockchain
Private Key - A key that must never be shared with anyone

This paper is organized in following sections: Sect. 1 has just provided an introduction to Blockchain technology and has set the stage for our study. Section 2 provides a summary of our literature review related to Blockchain technology and use cases in Shared Services for Blockchain. Section 3 presents our data collection methods. Section 4 provides findings and analysis of data collected and Sect. 5 outlines the conclusions and future research.

2   Literature Review

There is great confusion and debate about what a blockchain even is - some people argue it has become a meaningless buzzword - but the standard definition describes a shared, decentralized, cryptographically secure, immutable digital ledger. In the broadest terms, a blockchain allows a group of strangers to agree on a state-of-affairs and to proceed together on the basis of that covenant. Bitcoin's blockchain is meant to supplant the powerful middlemen called banks, but in theory a blockchain could replace any kind of institution - a credit agency, a social media service - that exists to safeguard a changing set of historical records. We pay these centralized entities handsomely for their custodial services, not only in the form of the rents they charge but in the control they exert over our lives. The blockchain, in theory, afford us new opportunities to solve complex coordination problems without letting the incumbent coordinators extract so much value in the process. This had, of course, been the initial premise of the internet itself. Its great collaborative potential, however, had been funneled into the leviathans of Amazon, Facebook, and Google - a new and massively powerful set of trusted third parties. The blockchain pointed the way to the sunlit uplands of a genuinely decentralized world. A loose culture of entrepreneurs and cyberpunks came together in what felt like a special moment of experimental ferment. Most of these early blockchain innovators just took the original cryptocurrency's source code, made their preferred changes, and launched their alternative versions as distinct cryptocurrencies, it was as if they'd modified the DNA of an existing species to create a new, reproductively isolated branch of the family tree [1].

Over the past couple of years, the emergence of Robotic Process Automation (RPA) tools ranging from desktop 'fixes' to server based, end-to-end driven process automation have been a major contributor towards real-time, digital, automated operations. However, flying somewhat under the radar, a novel business-to-business transaction network has been promising to fuel the next step change in the digital revolution. It's called blockchain and is defined as a 'peer-to-peer distributed ledger forged by consensus, combined with a system for 'smart contracts' and other assistive technologies, which together can be used to build a new generation of transactional applications that establishes trust, accountability and transparency at their core, while streamlining business processes and legal constraints.

Blockchain gets its name from blocks, a series of transactions (i.e. a bank statement); and a chain containing a sequential set of transaction records (i.e. blocks), in the order in which they occurred. The beauty of blockchain technology is that it works across a network and allows for instant, seamless business-to-business transactions based on pre-agreed and confirmed data nodes - effectively, 'an operating system for marketplaces, data-sharing networks, micro-currencies and decentralized digital communities with the potential to vastly reduce the cost and complexity of getting things done in the real world'. Blockchain's ability to track ownership without involving third-parties opens the door to decentralized transactions in a way that positively disrupts current business models.

Consider the many and various interactions a business has with the external markets: a key hurdle to transactions is the invariable slowdown that results from separate parties awaiting clearance for prescribed activities. In the world of blockchain, these kinds of interactions are pre-approved and take place instantly across networks based on Distributed Ledger Technology, which stores all the information needed to greenlight transactions in real-time.

To date, the financial services sector has been the most active - clearing houses, exchanges and the like have large volume, multiple transactions. Many have proof of concepts and pilots in quite advanced stages and some are already working with production systems and data. Within the Shared Services space, blockchain offers interesting opportunities for the P2P and Supply Chain process. E-invoicing, for example, could overcome some of its challenges, particularly with larger suppliers, as the technology removes the need for reconciliation. Supply chain is a natural fit, as there are lots of steps - electronic ordering, invoicing and acknowledgement - that can be broken down.

A shared ledger between a customer and all its suppliers would support optimization [2].

Digitalization of the accounting system is still in its infancy compared to other industries, some of which have been massively disrupted by the advances of technology. Some of the reasons may be found in the exceptionally high regulatory requirements in respect to validity and integrity.

The entire accounting system is built, such that forgery is impossible or at least very costly. To achieve this, it relies on mutual control mechanisms, checks and balances. This inevitably affects every day's operations. Among other things there are systematic duplication of efforts, extensive documentations and periodical controls. Most of them are manual, labor intensive tasks and far from being automated. To date, that seemed to be the sacrifice of revealing the truth. The recently emerged Blockchain is a trust-less, distributed ledger that is openly available and has negligible costs of use. The use of the Blockchain for accounting use-cases is hugely promising. From simplifying the compliance with regulatory requirements to enhancing the prevalent double entry book-keeping, anything is imaginable. Modern financial accounting is based on a double entry system. Double entry bookkeeping revolutionized the field of financial accounting during the Renaissance period; it solved the problem of managers knowing whether they could trust their own books. However, to gain the trust of outsiders, independent public auditors also verify the company's financial information. Each audit is a costly exercise, binding the company's accountants for long time periods. Stakeholders place their trust in the auditors retained by management to vouch for them. An obvious problem of agency is created by this arrangement (Fig. 1). Do auditors work for the managers who hire and pay them or for the public that relies on their integrity in order to make decisions? [3].

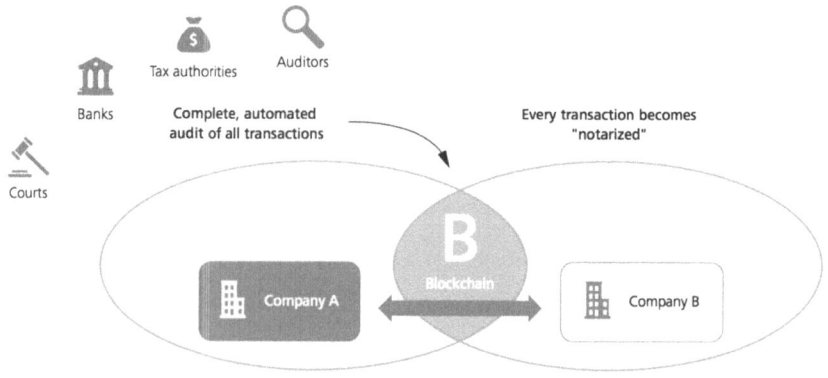

Blockchain entry serves in both companies' accounting

Fig. 1. Blockchain technology enables complete, conclusive verification without a trusted party [3]

By design, blockchains are inherently resistant to modification of any stored data. Functionally, a blockchain can serve as an open, distributed ledger that can record transactions between two parties efficiently and in a verifiable and permanent way. Blockchain can be used as a source of verification for reported transactions. An example might be where, instead of asking clients for bank statements or sending confirmation requests to third parties, auditors can easily verify the transactions on publically available blockchain ledgers. The automation of this verification process will drive cost efficiencies in the audit environment. The days of sample based substantive testing will soon be challenged, as auditors will resort to blockchain technology to test the whole population of transactions within the period under observation. This extensive coverage will drastically improve the level of assurance gained in affected audit engagements. In the Bitcoin blockchain, a transaction of low value currently takes approximately 10 min to be validated as a single block verification is deemed appropriate. The more blocks elapse before a transaction is considered as verified, i.e. the further in the chain, the more the related transactions are immutable. Typically, a high value transaction will take approximately 1 h to be verified (6 blocks). Contrast this with traditional financial transactions where information might take up to a month or more to be cleared. This pseudo real-time verification blockchain characteristic could also impact the audit process. Instead of assessments at year end (or interim), audit firms will be in a position to perform continuous on-line assessments throughout the period under audit [4].

The benefit of utilizing a blockchain in this manner is it would create a standardized record keeping process, which allows auditors to verify a large portion of the most important data behind the financial statements automatically. This would dramatically reduce the cost, labor and time necessary to conduct an audit, freeing up auditors to spend more time on areas where they can add value such as, working on very complex transactions or on internal control mechanisms (Fig. 2).

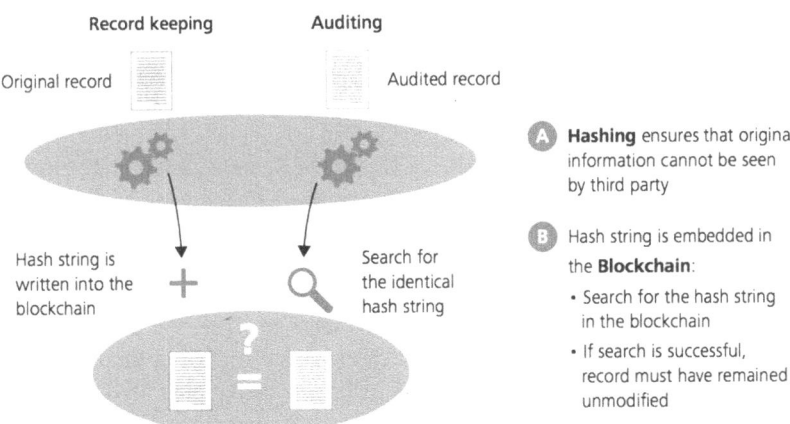

Fig. 2. One approach to verify the integrity of records using Blockchain [3].

There are many potential uses for HR that could benefit from blockchain technology. From a hiring perspective, access to academic credentials and certifications could reduce the amount of time recruiters spend verifying information. A wealth of information about potential candidates could be stored on blockchain making it easy for recruiters to find and verify everything from educational levels, postgraduate certifications and accomplishments. This would give a competitive edge to organizations that recruit based on verifiable credentials to find candidates that are overlooked by other organizations that only focus on traditional education and resumes. Once a credential is recorded to the blockchain, it can't be changed, deleted or faked. A fraudulent credential may look like an issued one, but it can be verified against the original blockchain record to confirm if it is valid or not. Digital credentials would remain secure, even if the company issuing them were to be hacked. Also, if schools or businesses shut down, a candidate's records would remain available. This means their records can be accessed no matter where in the world an individual decides to seek employment. The benefits for international employees are that a blockchain can process payroll faster and less expensively, avoiding international currency trade fees. By cutting out the intermediary, payments could come within hours rather than days - similar to cross-border payments [5].

Ireland-based global consulting firm Accenture and Italy-based insurance giant Generali Group's employee benefits unit have debuted a blockchain solution for employee benefits. The partnership was announced in a press release from the firms on April 16, 2019. Generali Employee Benefits (GEB) is an employee benefit solutions provider and global business line of Italy's largest insurance firm and 8th largest globally. The press release states that GEB operates the largest employee benefits solutions network worldwide. The blockchain solution will reportedly facilitate data sharing for parties involved in the reinsurance process for captive and pooling services. It will also reportedly improve procedures' reliability through the use of smart contracts and automated reconciliation. Captive insurance refers to underwriters who are wholly-owned by their insured clients, while reinsurance pooling services are a risk financing mechanism used by insurers to increase their ability to underwrite specific types of risks. The blockchain tool is designed to innovate and simplify GEB's existing employee benefits operating model for captive services, which spans policies such as life, disability, accident and healthcare insurance. The solution is reportedly supported by Generali and inspired by the work of the insurance industry collaborative blockchain initiative B3i. The solution's launch reportedly comes after the successful completion of a prototype in 2018, involving major agricultural firm Syngenta, as well as Spanish, Swiss and Serbian local insurers. The prototype was found to provide significant benefits for the employee benefits sector by establishing effective integration of systems, data and processes for all stakeholders, improving data quality and saving time and costs. GEB's CEO stated in the press release that in its provision of a seamless ecosystem, "blockchain will change not only our Network but the employee benefits industry as we know it". As reported, B3i Service AG - the Swiss blockchain startup founded by B3i in March of last year - expanded its group of investors this month as part of its ongoing funding round. The startup is focused on multi-company syndicated risk placement, accounting, and claims, and has developed a product based on R3 Corda's distributed ledger technology [6].

The advent of emerging digital technologies, such as robotic process automation (RPA), analytics, machine learning, cloud, and blockchain, is transforming the shared services landscape. Most large global businesses that use shared services models for a range of business functions, from finance and procurement to HR, are revamping the way they structure their support ecosystems. The convergence of a set of digital capabilities encourages organizations to abandon the individual or shared functional silos of the traditional shared services model. Instead, they are adopting a new integrated business services (IBS) model. When applied across functions such as finance, IT, HR, procurement, security, field operations, and others, it forms the basis of multi-functional integration. It has the power to transform business performance and become the gold standard of providing business services. Successful adoption ushers in savings through improved operational efficiency while also setting the stage for future growth and acquisition activity. The blockchain technology is transforming the way in which data is stored, verified, and accessed. Enabled by digital technology, a blockchain is a form of ledger that records data or transactions in a chronological order. The ledger is automatically replicated and maintained by each participant to create a decentralized, consensus controlled, tamper-proof public ledger of assets and transactions. Blockchain is set to revolutionize finance and accounting. Unlike current financial transactions, blockchain does not rely on any single party, middleman, or regulatory intermediary. Consensus authentication drives blockchain as the record of transactions is shared among all parties. The transaction becomes more secure and transparent. This transformation will be far reaching. According to Outlier Ventures, around 250 major corporations are active in blockchain, either through in-house developments or investment in start-ups, accelerators, and consortial. All major banks, as well as Visa, MasterCard, and NASDAQ, are working on blockchain. Dynamic startups such as Ethereum, Blockstream, Ripple, DAH, and Abra are likely to make a big impact as the opportunity evolves. One advancement that blockchain enables is a move to triple-entry bookkeeping. Triple-entry bookkeeping is a new development in accounting that will eradicate the need for expensive, time-consuming duplication of processes between two parties during a transaction. The existing accounting process is streamlined. The distributed ledger will do away with the exchange of invoices and receipts, and their manual entry into individual accounts. Instead of entering transactions separately into independent sets of books, they are automatically, reliably, and efficiently updated in a third ledger, shared between both parties. Using digitally signed receipts and cryptographic authentication, the third ledger is inherently approved by and accessible to both parties [7].

Blockchain has applications outside of F&A and is fast becoming a conduit for implementing an integrated business services model. The enhanced visibility the blockchain offers makes it much easier to oversee even complex supply chains. The ability to track and trace shipments can reduce errors and disputes, while the instant provision of digital letters of credit and bills of landing can revitalize logistics. Automated smart contracts reduce paperwork and delays, and improve cash flows throughout a supply chain. Platforms such as that offered by Skuchain or Hijro bring new levels of transparency and security to supply chains. They provide optimal planning and agility for downstream buyers and working capital relief for upstream suppliers. One area in which blockchain is clearly unifying disparate parts of businesses is in security and field operations. Every asset, device, and worker can be issued a blockchain-backed digital identity as part of an enterprise-wide trust network. This allows instant monitoring and authentication for every worker across every asset in the business, reducing the likelihood of security failure by removing any single point-of-failure [7].

As with all other business decisions, the decision to apply Blockchain technology involves a cost factor. Since it is designed to facilitate interactions between organizations, someone will have to act as the "host", at least for permissioned Blockchains. Beyond licensing the technology itself, the primary costs are infrastructure (hosting) and the energy required for computing. Many transactions are needed to validate blocks, and Blockchain is unlikely to be less expensive than slower, more traditional alternatives. When individual consumers benefit from the implementation of Blockchain, such as in supply chain traceability applications, B2C companies are expected to assume the cost, but when suppliers are the primary beneficiaries, Blockchain may become a new factor in invoice payment discounting. There is not one blockchain, but rather a number of companies and programmers experimenting with applications for distributed ledger technology. This has resulted in multiple competing standards with limited interoperability, diminishing the potential value to be gained by creating visibility all the way back through the supply chain and making it difficult to operate within individual industries.

There is an effort underway involving the International Organization for Standardization (ISO/TC 307) that would establish standards for terminology and concepts related to blockchain and distributed ledger technologies, but with the speed of development, companies may be faced with the need to make decisions before such a standard is accepted and put into practice. In a fully distributed blockchain, there is no need for a central administrator because the block-level cryptography makes the data stored in them immutable.

Cryptocurrency blockchains are always on the lookout for something they call a "51% attack." Under a 51% attack, a group of "miners" (programmers) would have a controlling interest in the blockchain, allowing them authority over all of the blocks seeking authorization. 13 in July of 2014, mining group ghash.io briefly went above the 50% point in the Bitcoin blockchain. The group voluntarily reduced its share of the network and put a plan in place to prevent them from going above 40% in the future. In a permissioned blockchain (such as we expect to see implemented in a B2B scenario) there might not be such altruism. If something goes wrong, there are no regulations to govern blockchain-based transactions [8].

A growing number of companies have expressed their will to enter the blockchain arena. But after some number of years in which their focus was mainly on the benefits of blockchain in various areas, in terms of speed, costs, streamline operations and increased efficiency, their attention is now turned to the various challenges and bottlenecks that are preventing widespread adoption. First of all, there is a reputation challenge. Blockchain is still very much connected to the crypto world in the mind of many. And that is seen as a world of bad actors, hackers, frauds and speculators. But more important are the technical ones such as immaturity (still slow and cumbersome), lack of scalability, lack of interoperability, stand-alone projects, difficult integration with legacy systems, complexity and lack of blockchain talent. What to think about the organizational challenges at corporates like lack of good governance, lack of awareness and understanding, lack of user experience and education, the attitude of incumbents, or the security and privacy challenges, including lack of regulation. And finally, but not unimportant other challenges such as culture, energy consumption/environmental cost [9].

Tracking down contaminated food has historically been a messy affair, sometimes taking retailers and food companies weeks to learn exactly what products they need to pull from store shelves. "Imagine if we could pinpoint with certainty within minutes, not days," mused Frank Yiannas, one of Walmart's top food safety executives, in a recent video published by the retailer. Thanks to technology originally designed to monitor cryptocurrency, Yiannas' vision is closer to becoming a reality—something that could put a significant dent in the number of foodborne illnesses that occur every year. It's part of a new program in which IBM is partnering with Walmart, Nestlé, Dole, Tyson Foods, Kroger, and others, to use blockchain technology to track food throughout the complex global supply chain. Massive companies putting pressure on suppliers to use blockchain will migrate a huge swathe of the food world into one organized system. That is no small feat when farmers, processors, distributors, and retailers are currently use different types of documentation to track their products - some of them still on paper. Under the new system, if a consumer falls ill from E.coli traced to a batch of lettuce, a food-safety investigator could conceivably scan a barcode on the packaging to quickly learn where it came from and where other lettuce from the same batch went. Retailers will be able to quickly remove contaminated products from shelves, thus stopping the spread of illnesses. Walmart has been using a pilot version of the technology, showing how blockchain can be expanded beyond the financial, health care, and natural resources sectors to be applied to the foods that consumers interact with every single day. Coupled with companies' efforts to stop food-borne illnesses early on, this could signal a major moment in how humans keep the food system in check [10].

Large companies are always battling with their legacy applications, because these can be anchors that drag them when new technologies arrive. Even when you thought corporate IT was safe with modern software environments that make use of modular cloud-based capabilities, container-based-technology to facilitate operations deployments, or continuous delivery with agile and rapid developments practices, the blockchain is yet another "modern technology" that will need to be absorbed and integrated into the technology toolset of any software development teams.

In addition to internal applications and use cases, there will be a number of new opportunities for creating shared blockchain services either at the vertical level (e.g., a particular financial services application), or at the horizontal level (e.g., a generic records verification service). Companies will need to decide what implementation approaches to choose, based on their own competencies and choice of external partnerships. You should not just see the Blockchain as a problem-solving technology. Rather, it is a technology that lets you innovate and target new opportunities [11].

Blockchain is often seen as a system of record that ensures data integrity through ledgers that are immutable distributed systems that cannot be deleted or updated. In other words, Blockchain ensures the integrity of the data. Whether it is the public Blockchain like Ethereum or a Hyperledger based private Blockchain system, they can easily work as a system of records. Even though it may fit well for certain uses, there are some limitations to using Blockchain as a system of records:

- A traditional database has Create, Read, Update and Delete options for managing data, often called CRUD. With Blockchain, only Create and Read functions are allowed. Update is done by creating a new record and Delete is not an option
- People are already using a system of records that is more versatile and data is a big issue in moving to a new system of records. An ideal scenario would be to use the existing system of records, with extra integrity provided by another layer

- Even though using Blockchain as a system of records builds integrity into the system, it comes with a performance hit, extra cost, scale concerns and other very real issues

A better approach is to use your existing business system and use Blockchain as a "system of integrity" for the data. With this approach, the limitations of blockchain as a system of record is overcome, while still ensuring the integrity of your data by taking advantage of the immutability of blockchain. Salesforce, database services in the cloud, cloud storage solutions like AWS S3, on-premises databases or even SaaS offerings can act as a system of record while blockchain can serve as the system of integrity. Traditional cryptographic fingerprinting techniques like Hashing or Checksums when used with Blockchain as the storage for these digital fingerprints, can serve as a battle tested way to ensure data integrity. In other words, blockchain is an additive to your existing system of record, not a replacement. When you create data, it is easy to add a digital fingerprint to the data that can be a marker to ensure the integrity of that data. This fingerprint is then stored in a safe place and can be called upon anytime to verify the original data integrity. Since blockchain is immutable and decentralized, it can safely store the fingerprints and act as a military grade data integrity platform. By using blockchain as the integrity layer, organizations can continue using their existing systems of record while also staying compliant with any data integrity requirements [12].

3   Data Collection Method

The purposes of this research are to (1) explore the current blockchain use cases in Shared Services (2) understand the value created by blockchain in Supply Chain Management and (3) study the tactical challenges in adopting a blockchain strategy in Shared Services. In addition to literature review, we conducted in-depth Interviews and/or sent questionnaires to Shared Services Leaders and experts.

3.1   In-Depth Interviews/Questionnaires

In addition to literature review, in-depth interviews were conducted with 13 executives and experts from 12 industries. In cases where the interviews couldn't be arranged, the questions were emailed to the participants. The demographics of the participants are shown in Table 1 below.

The purpose of the in-depth interviews/questionnaires was to seek answers to the following 14 questions:

1. What is your understanding about Blockchain technology?
2. Has your company adopted Blockchain technology in any functional area? If yes, which ones?
3. Some experts believe that Blockchain technology will be bigger than Robotic Process Automation for the Shared Services industry. What is your opinion?
4. In your opinion, what does this game-changing Blockchain technology mean for Shared Services?

5. What are the key characteristics that facilitate adoption of Blockchain technology in Shared Services?
6. What are the expected benefits of adopting Blockchain technology in Shared Services?
7. What are the potential areas in Finance Shared Services for adopting Blockchain technology in order to improve data integrity?
8. What are the potential areas in HR Shared Services for adopting Blockchain technology in order to streamline HR processes?
9. What are the potential areas in Procurement & Supply Chain Shared Services for adopting Blockchain technology in order to improve validation, authentication, traceability and transparency?
10. What are the potential opportunities in other areas of Shared Services for adopting Blockchain technology in order to improve visibility of business processes?
11. Are you familiar with the benefits achieved by Walmart with adoption of Blockchain technology? Can your company realize similar benefits?
12. What are the challenges you foresee or have encountered with the adoption of Blockchain technology in Shared Services?
13. Our research indicates that Blockchain technology is being used to replace paper trails, improve validation and authentication, and increase visibility and transparency. What is your opinion?
14. As part of our research, we will be providing business cases for adopting Blockchain technology. Are your executives open to adopting Blockchain technology in your company?

The answers to the questions received from 17 respondents (35% response rate) are summarized in Sect. 4 and analyzed to develop insights about the adoption of Blockchain technology in various areas of Shared Services.

Table 1. In-depth interviews/questionnaires: demographics of participants

S. No.	Industry	Location	Position	No. of participants
1	Health Services	Canada	N/A	1
2	Nonprofit Organization	Canada	Senior Director - People Services	1
3	Banking	Canada	Various	5
4	Pharmaceuticals	UK	FSSC Manager	1
5	IT	China	Various	3
6	Oil & Gas	China	Various	3
7	IT & Management Consulting	China	Various	3
8	IT	USA	Co-founder/CEO	1

(*continued*)

Table 1. (*continued*)

S. No.	Industry	Location	Position	No. of participants
9	Banking	Canada	N/A	1
10	Electricity Generation	Canada	Various	3
11	Telecommunications	Canada	Various	2
12	Insurance	Canada	N/A	1
13	Broadcasting	Canada	Various	3
14	Transportation/Delivery	Canada	Group Leader - Delivery Management	1
15	Health Care Provider	Canada	Various	2
16	Railways	Canada	Director - Network Services	1
17	Publishing	Canada	Director - SS	1
18	Consumer Retail	Canada	Assistant Treasurer	1
19	Financial Institution	USA	N/A	1
20	Federal Government	Canada	N/A	1
21	Audit & Consulting Services	Canada	N/A	1
22	Data Processing & Consulting	Canada	Global BPO Director	1
23	Supermarket Chain	Canada	N/A	1
24	Wholesale Bakery	Canada	N/A	1
25	Energy	USA	SVP - Global Human Resources	1
26	Management Consulting	USA	Managing Director	1
27	Construction	Canada	Various	2
28	Asset Management	Canada	CFO	1
29	Consumer Packaged Meats	Canada	CIO	1
30	Textile Manufacturing	China	Director - Logistics	1
31	Tax Advisory & Consulting	USA	Senior Manager - Process Automation	1

4   Results

Based on the analysis of data collected, key results are summarized as in this section.

4.1 Understanding of Blockchain Technology

Literature review and respondents' answers indicate that there is strong understanding from both a business use case and technology perspectives. From a technology perspective, Blockchain technology allows developers to build applications that have their code executed on a set of globally distributed computers.

From a business perspective, it allows removal of the requirement of trust between two parties. RPA will help reform the execution of business processes while Blockchain will help provide the support for executing these business process in a secured manner across various technologies and industries. Blockchain will have a bigger user group.

4.2 Application of Blockchain Technology to Shared Services

There are many potential applications across Shared Services where Blockchain could provide maximum benefit to the corporate Shared Services organization. Everything from immutable records, timestamps, cost, labor and time reductions to automation are all possible with a Blockchain solution. What is already happening right now is that plenty of organizations are testing Blockchain in their internal operations, often by commissioning Centers of Expertise. In fact, intra-company transactions offer plenty of pain points that present a perfect opportunity for Blockchain. Any place where there is pause for validation or authentication is where Blockchain can automate that need.

Any transaction where 'trust' might be an issue is an opportunity for Blockchain. One example is cross-border payments within an enterprise, which suffer all the same hurdles and loops "as if you are paying a third-party". And whether these transactions are large or small, they are plentiful enough that performance improvement can be achieved. While the value of Blockchain through internal application via Shared Services can be demonstrated, the true wins will accrue in leveraging Blockchain across external transactions, with third parties.

Blockchain technology allows seamless business-to-business transactions based on pre-agreed and confirmed data nodes, through a network. This capability of Blockchain technology empowers businesses, Shared Services in particular, to process decentralized transactions at a higher speed and lower cost essentially by automating the requirement for authentication or validation. Blockchain technology can help share more efficient connections between suppliers, customers, enterprise users and shared service centers. Through the identification of all parties on the authenticity of electronic data, combined with the automatic analysis of data flow, the automation efficiency of Shared Services business processing can be accelerated.

4.3 Potential Areas for Adopting Blockchain Technology in Shared Services

Based on our research, the following Table 2 shows potential areas for adopting Blockchain technology in Shared Services:

4.4 Key Characteristics that Facilitate Adoption of Blockchain Technology

Key characteristics that facilitate adoption of Blockchain technology include Transparency, Immutability, Audit Trail, Consensus, Finality and Multiple Nodes.

Table 2. Potential areas for adopting Blockchain in shared services.

Procurement and supply chain management	Human resources	Accounting
Ordering, Procurement, Invoicing, Acknowledgement Logistics Visualization: Track and Trace Shipments Letters of Credit Bills of Lading Custom Clearance Smart Procurement Contracts Stolen Goods/Counterfeit Products Inventory Replenishment Products Return Management Warranties Management	Employee Identification Recruitment Process Access to Academic Credentials and Certifications Payroll Process for International Employees Benefits Administration Employment Contracts Grievance Management Storage of Current and Past Performance Reviews	Bookkeeping Entries Exchange of Invoices and Receipts Approval of Documents Payment Automation Credit Control Auditing Process

Through the non-tampering of the Blockchain technology, the efficiency of Shared Services business processing can be accelerated. Other characteristics include improving business traceability, reducing business audit workload and reducing Shared Services audit risks by recording physical information.

Using Blockchain technology as a way of removing the reliance on trust between two parties (whether that's in sharing data between both parties or executing a certain business process that's built using code).

4.5   Expected Benefits of Adopting Blockchain in Shared Services

Any process requires authentication in order to proceed. Traditionally, this has taken the form of a centralized check effectively, a ledger that acts as a clear authority. Blockchain offers this ledger, but because there are so many partners it is distributed across, and validated by, all of them. Even better, no single party can manipulate or change it. So, this eliminates or limits the need for a central authority.

The expected benefits of adopting Blockchain technology in Shared Services are to improve the efficiency of business processing, improve the authenticity of business, reduce the risk of Shared audit, reduce the transmission of original parts, reduce the operating cost, and reduce repeated data entry. Other benefits include lower cost of executing shared software code without having to verify that it was done correctly.

4.6   Challenges with the Adoption of Blockchain Technology in Shared Services

Despite the obvious benefits, real implementations are still few. One problem is actually forming the business network and getting the relevant counterparts together. The challenge is that everyone has to sign up to a common contract and share data in the hyper ledger in order for it to work, so it requires industries to meet and agree application between themselves. The other challenge is to coordinate internal system transformation, supplier system transformation, determine what needs to be stored in the Blockchain, and whether to use the external chain or the internal chain. It is necessary to deal with the trust relationship between the company's self-built blockchain and the public network alliance, and there is no set of recognized authority alliance in the Internet at present.

Some of the other challenges include difficulty in defining and aligning standards between different parties, lack of talent, high implementation cost and complexity of future maintenance work. Education is also a challenge as lots of people don't fully understand Blockchain technology. Overinflating the value proposition, too much hype has gone into Blockchain technology that has not materialized or is flat out false. Many enterprises are interested in exploring Blockchain technology but not interested in deploying it fully within the next few years.

5   Conclusions and Future Research

5.1   Conclusions

Our research conducted indicates that Blockchain technology is being used within Shared Services to replace paper trails, improve validation and authentication and increase visibility and transparency. Blockchain creates a ledger of all transactions in a given process. Each ledger entry is autonomous so can provide insights into cashflow and add extra security. Virtually incorruptible due to the fact that the data contained within a ledger entry cannot be copied, Blockchain can track any item of value, so is particularly useful in shipping as well as online retail, making it a powerful tool for business units with the vision to utilize this technology.

The process of taking any piece of digital data of any size and chopping, mincing and mixing it until it is an unrecognizable string of digits and characters is called hashing. Hashing is one of the core concepts needed to understand blockchain. The other three are Public/Private key cryptography, decentralization and then the blockchain data structure itself. Hashing makes it easy to confirm the authenticity of data when comparing two or more versions. An extra cent in a ledger will be obvious instantly. A missing comma in a contract will make itself immediately apparent. Public-private key encryption, within the context of Blockchain, is what allows to keep track of virtual identities and signatures. A private key allows the owner to encrypt data. A public key allows everybody else to decrypt the data. A private key functions as a digital signature.

5.2   Future Research

This research paper introduces the potential for adopting blockchain in Shared Services. It offers the value proposition of introducing blockchain in various functions within Shared Services. The findings and analysis presented here will assist more companies to develop an over-arching strategy for adopting the blockchain technology. Future research is required in the areas of technology service providers and availability of implementation tools. Specifically, future research should focus on answering the following questions:

1. Which service provider organizations are providing services for digital transformation of Shared Services using blockchain and what investments will create meaningful results for them?
2. What service automation tools e.g. cognitive automation tools are available for automating Knowledge-Based Shared Services?
3. What industries are adopting the service automation strategy to automate their Expertise Services and what implementation approaches have proven to be effective?
4. What are the use cases and the associated challenges, risks and opportunities and how blockchain development and deployment can be managed?

References

1. Lewis-Kraus, G.: Inside the Crypto World's Biggest Scandal. In: Business, p. 41 (2018)
2. Hodge, B.: Blockchain is a Gamechanger. In: SSON, p. 7 (2018)
3. Andersen, N.: Blockchain Technology: A Game Changer in Accounting. In: Deloitte, p. 5 (2018)
4. Psaila, S.: Blockchain: A Gamechanger for Audit Processes. In: Deloitte (2018)
5. Perroser, R.: Are There Use Cases in Shared services for Blockchain. In: IQPC: Blockchain in Shared Services, p. 7, 18 March 2018
6. Huillet, M.: Accenture, Generali Launch Blockchain Solution for Employee Benefits. In: Cointelegraph, p. 1 (2019)
7. Gopal, V.: Using Emerging Technologies to Build NextGen Shared Services. In: Tata Consulting Services, p. 9 (2018)
8. Biju Mohan, B.K.V.N.: Blockchain in the Real World. In: Smart by GEP, p. 10 (2018)
9. De Meijer, C.R.W.: Remaining challenges of blockchain adoption and possible solutions. In: MIFSA (2020)
10. Purdy, C.: Supermarkets are Now Using Blockchain to Keep Food Fresh. In: Quartz, p. 2, 24 August 2017
11. Mougayar, W.: The Business Blockchain. Wiley, Hoboken (2018)
12. Chainkit: Continuous Data Integrity Using Blockchain (2019). [Online]

How Agility Can Be Increased in IT Sourcing and Contracting: Learnings from an Autonomous Driving Case

Daniel Gerster[1]([⊠]) and Christian Dremel[2]

[1] University of St. Gallen, 9000 St. Gallen, Switzerland
d.k.gerster@gmail.com
[2] University of Bamberg, 96047 Bamberg, Germany
christian.dremel@uni-bamberg.de

Abstract. New digital services and products rely heavily on digital technologies and need to be deployed in an ever-shorter timeframe in response to rapidly changing market demands. To address this challenge, companies review their sourcing strategies to shorten tender duration for large-scale IT initiatives and to increase flexibility in contracting of IT services. This study aims at revealing how the application of agile practices impacts the sourcing and contracting of IT services. As the automotive industry is especially affected by digital transformation, this revelatory case study shows how the German premium car manufacturer CarCo increased agility in sourcing and contracting of IT services for an autonomous driving development platform. Agile practices turned out to be essential in dealing with technological novelty and hurdles, regulatory uncertainty, and frequently changing requirements. We found that applying agile practices to the sourcing and contracting of IT services has two implications: First, agile practices aim at reducing tender duration, decreasing pre-contractual uncertainty, and therefore lead to an increase of speed and flexibility. Second, agile software development changes contract nature as comprehensive requirements are replaced by high-level specifications focusing on early results and business outcomes. We contribute to the extant body of knowledge on IT sourcing and contracting by providing managerial recommendations on how agile practices could reduce time-to-market and increase flexibility in the sourcing and contracting of IT services.

Keywords: IT sourcing · IT contracts · Agile sourcing · Agile contracts · Agile practices · Autonomous driving

1 Introduction

New digital services and products rely heavily on digital technologies [1, 2] and need to be deployed in an ever-shorter time in response to rapidly changing market environments [3, 4]. In consequence, more and more companies adopt agile practices to increase speed and flexibility [5, 6]. The adoption of agile practices has widespread implications on products, processes, technology, people, and structure that are just beginning to be

© Springer Nature Switzerland AG 2020
I. Oshri et al. (Eds.): Global Sourcing 2019, LNBIP 410, pp. 17–37, 2020.
https://doi.org/10.1007/978-3-030-66834-1_2

understood [7]. The sourcing and contracting of IT services is especially affected by the need to increase speed and flexibility as unclear or frequently changing requirements due to technical novelty are in conflict with well-defined, strict, and long-lasting contracts and detailly specified requirements [8]. Within this study we relate to IT services as IT application development or IT operations services for large-scale IT systems [9]. The pervasive usage of agile information systems development (ISD) significantly impacts IT contracts as comprehensive and well-defined requirements are replaced by lean specifications focusing on business outcomes. This change creates the need to secure capacities for agile feature teams with defined capacities while the exact specifications (i.e., user stories) will be detailed during a sourcing endeavor and the respective implementation. In consequence, companies have to review their sourcing strategies to reflect agile delivery, reduce tender duration, and to increase speed and contract flexibility [10, 11].

Against this backdrop, this study takes the sourcing and contracting of IT services as an example for a domain being especially affected by digital transformation. Extant research on sourcing and contracting of IT services deals primarily with large IT projects in a non-agile context [11], focuses on aspects of IT delivery or governance related to IT outsourcing [12, 13], aims at reducing contractual risks but does not look at project success or missed business opportunities [8], focuses at specific aspects of agile contracting, or lacks practical advice on how the overall tender duration can be reduced [14].

Therefore we aim at addressing these research gaps by extending the applicability of agile practices beyond ISD [15]. In doing so, we try to shed light on how agility could be increased in the sourcing and contracting of large-scale IT initiatives – in our case an IT platform for the development of autonomous driving capabilities – with the following research question: How can agility be increased in sourcing and contracting of large-scale IT initiatives?

To do so, we target the automotive industry as it is highly affected by digital transformation and technological innovations such as autonomous driving, connectivity, electromobility, and shared mobility [16, 17]. These four trends can be most easily remembered by the acronym ACES [18]. Our case study with CarCo, a German premium car manufacturer, is characterized by technological novelty (i.e., autonomous driving and machine learning) and technical hurdles (i.e., providing storage and computing capacities to analyze data volumes of up to 200 Petabyte) with frequently changing functional requirements or unclear regulatory requirements in target markets in combination with an ambitious timeline (i.e., begin of series production intended for 2021). With our exploratory research we aim at illuminating the far-reaching implications of adopting new digital technologies in context of an organization applying scaled agile practices according to the framework LeSS [19].

2 Background

This section introduces the extant literature related to the sourcing and contracting of IT services in an agile context. We briefly introduce agile and scaled agile practices in ISD and discuss potential risks and challenges for its adoption at enterprises. Furthermore, we address the disconnect between agile ISD and vendor management, summarize research on incomplete contracts, and introduce IT outsourcing as potential lever for innovation. Finally, we relate to the impact of agile ISD on IT contracts and how the application of agile practices to IT tenders could help in reducing overall tender duration, pre-contractual uncertainty and, thus, contractual risks, while simultaneously increasing flexibility.

2.1 Agile Practices and Related Challenges in ISD

Agile practices can be seen as a response to challenges resulting from the traditional way of ISD according to "Plan-Build-Run" [20] and the resulting separation between build and run [21]. Agile practices root in systems thinking and lean practices [19, 22, 23] where systems thinking aims at changing our perspective to solve problems in new and unexpected ways [24]. The Agile Manifesto is perceived as a practitioners' collection of best practices on agile ISD [25]. Agile practices can be exemplarily characterized by the formulation of value stories, removing complexity, shortening release cycles to incorporate customer feedback, and effort estimation with story points [15, 21, 26]. Agile practices aim, for instance, at clean code, pair programming and immediate customer feedback, test-driven development, automated testing, continuous deployment [27] and achieve their benefits through the synergistic combination of individual agile practices [28].

To pinpoint the key concepts relevant for our research, we do not include details on the composition of agile teams or their daily agile practices here and refer to the wide body of extant knowledge on agile ISD: Exemplarily, Kniberg [29] and Gonçalves and Lopes [30] explain the setup of agile teams with the case of Spotify. Recker [31], Przybilla [32], or Wang [26] present various insights into daily practices of agile teams like stand-ups, planning poker to estimate development efforts with function points, or retrospectives. Related to project management practices, McAvoy and Butler [33] highlight the changing role of the project manager in agile ISD as a devil's advocate where teams are empowered to decision making.

Practitioners made several attempts to scale agile practices to the enterprise level by adapting agile practices known from ISD and new agile structures [5]. To address the inherent challenges of implementing scaled agile practices at larger organizations, frameworks for scaled agile practices emerged [34]: Among others, LeSS (Large Scale Scrum) is a lightweight agile framework developed by Craig Larman and Bas Vodde for scaling Scrum to more than one team [19] and SAFe (Scaled Agile Framework) is another approach developed by Dean Leffingwell for lean agile thinking and more visibly incorporating of scalable DevOps [23, 35].

The adoption of agile practices does not come without challenges especially in the context of large and established organizations [5]. Some of the most frequently mentioned challenges of applying agile practices at scale include: (1) Communication issues as large and established enterprises usually do not consist of small and collocated teams [36–38], (2) a lack of flexibility, coordination, and cultural challenges such as trust, openness or willingness to transform [39, 40] – an often underestimated prerequisite for a successful implementation [41], (3) limited scalability and uncontrollable risks in case of the application of agile practices in a short timeframe without proper organizational change management [42, 43], (4) applying agile practices in a predominately non-agile environment limiting potential benefits [36], (5) challenges related to organization, teams, misconceptions regarding agile practices, sustainability, scaling and business value [37, 40].

2.2   The Disconnect Between Agile ISD with IT Vendor Management

The rich literature on IT sourcing is closely related to IT outsourcing which can be defined as "handing over the management of a function, assets, people, or activity to a third party for a specified cost, time and level of service" [44]. In consequence, IT outsourcing can be regarded as a specific form of IT sourcing. Topics of managing risks in IT contracts or governance and vendor management have a prominent take in the extant IT outsourcing literature [13, 45].

While few research on outsourcing in context of innovation exists [13], IT-outsourcing is increasingly perceived as an innovation lever [46, 47]. A collaborative, trustful environment between client and IT provider can be facilitated by applying agile practices like early involvement of the IT provider in solution design or an iterative approach in sprints [37]. Consequently, agile practices can help establishing a high-quality relationship between client and provider contributing to achieve innovation through outsourcing [48]. Furthermore, questions of how to reduce risks and uncertainty in the relationship between client and provider, e.g., by a restrictive control with service level agreements (SLAs) or a strict provider governance, play an important role [49]. According to Lacity and Willcocks (2014), innovation is rarely a one-time, big-bang project, but rather multiple innovation projects deliver substantial improvements over time and innovation does not automatically result from outsourcing per se [47]. Key innovation drivers in outsourcing projects are acculturation, i.e., "the process by which two or more cultures merge from a cohesive culture" [47], inspiration, a joint funding and benefiting from innovation, and successful cultural change management [47].

While IT outsourcing was in the past largely motivated by process optimization and cost efficiency [13], its focus has shifted towards innovation while mere offshoring activities have declined in importance [11]. The digitization of business processes, cloud computing, and cyber-security are supposed to have a similar disruptive potential in the upcoming years [10, 50].

2.3   Incomplete Contracts

Incomplete contracts are argued to explain various economic issues [51]. Incomplete contracts are usually preceded by an invocation of transaction costs and one or several of the following three ingredients: Unforeseen contingencies, cost of writing contracts, or cost of enforcing contracts [52]. A key rationale of the incomplete contracts literature is that contracts are incomplete by nature [52, 53] and result from information asymmetries between seller and buyer similar to principal-agent relationships and, thus, explain for a suboptimal level of sourcing [51, 54].

Since it is not feasible to include all contingencies into contracts, information asymmetries between buyer and seller may occur [53]. Consequently, contracts need to find a way to handle uncertainty by assuring cost-efficiency and contract reliability. Agile contracts are perceived as one way to address contract uncertainties and to increase manageability as they aim at an early incorporation of the IT provider into the solution design allowing for joint-learning and application of best practices [8, 55].

2.4   How Agile Practices Can Help Addressing Issues of Traditional ISD

Key issues inherent to traditional ISD are that developing complete functional specifications is usually (1) not economical since a considerable effort is required before implementation starts [56]; (2) not feasible since learnings of first iterations of feature development cannot be incorporated [57], and (3) not helpful since the client usually remains unable to express all requirements in sufficient complete and consistent detail up front [22]. Consequently, in situations of frequent changes or unclear requirements, endless re-negotiation of requirements may result when traditional approaches to ISD are applied [14].

Contrary, agile practices can help addressing some key issues of traditional ISD: (1) Focus on business priorities: Sprints are planned according to business priorities as specified by the product owner as a representative for the client's priorities [26]. This procedure ensures that only features of value to the customer are developed, thus, allowing for a clear prioritization of business objectives and customer value. (2) Focus on workable solutions: Agile practices aim at an early provisioning of prototypes to be used for early client discussions and, thus, allowing for an early incorporation of customer feedback for further improvements in subsequent iterations [58]. (3) Simple design: The recognized lack of helpfulness of complete up-front specification of functional requirements has led to the rise of agile ISD methods such as Scrum [59] where voluminous specifications are replaced by lean specifications [56]. (4) Small releases are deployed in short, iterative sprint cycles: By this approach, simple functionality is deployed quickly in sprint cycles of two to three weeks [26, 60]. Short sprint cycles ensure that new features can be deployed early, shipped iteratively, and improved gradually [61]. Furthermore, changing requirements can be considered within a reasonably short timeframe [62]. (5) Continuous testing and integration: New features will be tested and deployed instantaneously without waiting for big release bundles [27]. (6) Pair programming: Pair programming ensures a quality check already during coding as one developer codes while another programmer checks quality simultaneously [27]. (7) Self-organizing teams: Distributed leadership and decision-making speed up implementation and ensure that required information is readily available [60]. (8) Complementing agile management practices: Daily stand-ups and retrospectives serve as supporting organizational culture as they facilitate team communication on sprint status and foster learning and continuous improvement [31, 60].

It may be argued that applying these agile practices to ISD has three implications: First, time-to-market for important features can be reduced as features with high business impact can be prioritized [62]. Second, product quality can be increased due to early and automated testing, incorporated quality checks due to pair programming, communication and mutual feedback [27]. Third, flexibility for deployment of changing features can be increased due to short, iterative sprint cycles and lean requirements specification [63]. Furthermore, applying short and iterative sprint cycles allows for short term changes of features as specification takes place instantaneously in subsequent sprints.

An agile and iterative approach to ISD can therefore – by design – decrease risk and uncertainty and can protect clients from things they may not know [8]. Furthermore, an agile approach limits both the scope of the deliverable and extent of the payment and allows for inevitable change, and focuses negotiations on the neglected area of delivery [8].

2.5 The Impact of Agile Practices on IT Contracts

Incorporating agile practices into IT contracts significantly impacts both, fixed price and time and material (T&M) contracts as large and precisely specified contract volumes will be replaced by modules sourced in small and iterative packages [55]. Consequently, specific challenges occur for both, fixed price and T&M contracts: Related to fixed-price contracts, challenges exist regarding contract negotiation caused by lean requirements specifications: The overall project scope is defined only high level causing difficulties in finding an agreement of whether the requirements are fulfilled or not [55]. Furthermore, project scope and solutions materialize only gradually and prototyping implies performing a considerable amount of work that does not make it into the final project [56] making it difficult to reach a fixed-price agreement in an agile setting [55].

Similarly, T&M contracts face challenges regarding agile contract elements: While T&M contracts seem fairer at first glance as the payment corresponds exactly to the delivered work, they incentivize the provider to increase development efforts and neglect quality control [56]. In consequence, implementation risks are almost fully with the client [14].

To summarize, closing contracts is a challenging undertaking especially in the context of technological novelty and uncertainty like ISD and digital technologies [55]. Most importantly, successful contracts result from relationships that rely on trust, collaboration, and transparency [8]. Agile contracts acknowledge the fact that all contracts are incomplete by nature, thus setting up mutually agreed-upon frameworks that explicitly address the management of contingencies [8].

3   Research Approach and Case Study Context

3.1 Research Approach

This study applies an inductive qualitative research approach to explore the need to increase agility in IT sourcing and contracting caused by new digital technologies. We conduct a revelatory single case study because of the lack of extant knowledge and to get rich, in-depth empirical insights [64]. This case study is revelatory for two reasons: First, we provide access to a phenomenon of interest that has been largely inaccessible to previous research due to its novelty (i.e., sourcing of a technological innovation like autonomous driving). Second, researchers have usually limited exposure to real-world cases applying agile practices (1) at large-scale in an entire department, or (2) to the sourcing and contracting of a complex IT endeavor leveraging new digital technologies as both in combination are rather new and rare instances. In consequence, we opt for a revelatory case study design to maximize the chances of credible novelty [65].

To obtain in-depth qualitative data, exploratory interviews with managers, experts, and sourcing advisors involved in the tender were used as primary source for data collection. Interviews were conducted between September 2018 and March 2019 in either English or German based on a semi-structured interview guideline following the recommendations of Schultze and Avital [66] and Strauss and Corbin [67] to ground the interviews in the participants' own experiences and to allow the theory to emerge from data. Questions were formulated open-end to allow the interviewees the possibility to explore their experience and views in detail [64, 67]. Follow-up questions were formulated for further clarification purposes. Each interview had a duration of approximately 50–75 min and was carried out personally in face-to-face meetings. The interview results were documented in detail in form of interview notes and, if permitted, in form of recorded interviews. The interview documentations were reviewed for consistency and completeness by another researcher that has not participated at the interviews. Table 1 provides an overview of the conducted interviews.

Table 1. Overview of case study interviews.

Organization/department	Interviewees	No. of interviews
Car development (business unit)	Executive sponsor or manager; Team leads; Experts	5
Corporate IT (IT department)	IT-Manager; Experts	4
Purchasing (incl. legal and cost engineering)	Team lead; Sourcing/cost experts; Sourcing legal advisor	3
Consulting (external sourcing advisors)	Consultants; Project manager	4
Provider involved in the tender	Bid manager; Commercial/legal lead	2

3.2   Case Study Context: Autonomous Driving Development System Overview and Resulting Challenges for IT Sourcing

This case study examines the challenging task of sourcing and contracting of an IT platform for the development of autonomous driving capabilities at CarCo to examine the implications of applying agile practices to IT sourcing and contracting. CarCo is a leading German premium car manufacturer with more than 130,000 employees and in business for more than 100 years. As an innovation leader and pioneer in electromobility, CarCo decided to bundle its engineering resources to develop autonomous driving capabilities in a centralized unit in 2017 and intended to establish a centralized IT platform scalable to cover all levels of autonomous driving. CarCo's autonomous driving engineering department consists of approximately 1,100 full-time employees at the time of our research and has been established as fully agile unit applying the scaled agile framework LeSS [19, 68].

CarCo seeks to develop own autonomous driving capabilities related to high and full autonomous driving (level 4 and 5) according to SAE's definition [69, 70] with intended deployment in serial production in 2021 for level 3. The IT platform for the development of autonomous driving capabilities will be used for programming, simulation and testing of the autonomous driving code to be deployed productively in cars.

CarCo intended to outsource the development and operations of this IT platform to a proficient provider to benefit from joint innovative expertise on new digital technologies such as artificial intelligence, business analytics and machine learning. Figure 1 provides an overview of the business processes required for the development of the autonomous driving capabilities. As the deployed autonomous driving code improves with the amount of driven test kilometers, the collection of real driving data is essential. CarCo assumed at the time of research that two million of driven test kilometers will be sufficient to secure the autonomous driving code for productive usage.

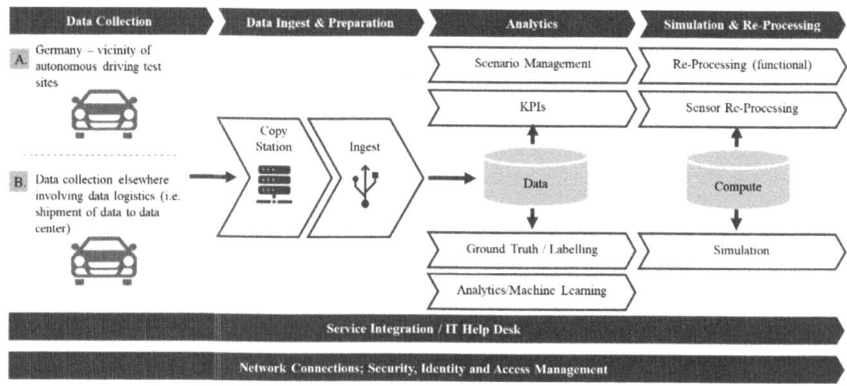

Fig. 1. Overview of business value streams and related autonomous driving IT capabilities.

Data collection takes place with the help of a test fleet covering a full range of representative driving scenarios in more than 20 countries. Collected data consist of camera, lidar, radar and other sensor as well as related driving meta data. Data collected by a test fleet driving in the vicinity of CarCo's Autonomous Driving Campus is directly ingested from the car to the data center with the help of a copy station. Contrary, data collected during test drives in remote locations such as other countries are physically transported to the data center involving complex physical data logistics processes (i.e., shipment of disks storing up to 64 TB of recorded data from test drives) and are directly ingested into the data center. As part of the ingest process, data is checked for completeness and consistency to ensure that the data can be further processed. Once ingested, data is stored in a centralized data lake where it will be categorized according a predefined set of KPI and autonomous driving scenarios once automated and manual labelling took place. The data is then used for simulation and training of the autonomous driving algorithm (functional re-processing) and for validating new sensor set-ups (sensor re-processing). Services integration and a help desk is provided centrally for the autonomous driving development system along with network connectivity, security, identity and access management.

Contrary to traditional large-scale IT projects, three aspects of this setting are especially noteworthy as they highlight why traditional approaches to IT sourcing and contracting would not be suitable: First, despite of its strong technology focus, the lead for specification, selection, and implementation of the autonomous driving development platform is with CarCo's car development unit and not with its IT department. Resources from CarCo's IT department contributed with subject-matter expertise in an advisory role only. Consequently, resources from CarCo's car development department had neither a profound knowledge and experience in sourcing of large IT projects, nor a decent market knowledge of IT providers being capable of delivering an EUR 200 million IT project involving new digital technologies such as machine learning, big data, or online video gaming required for simulation purposes. Second, the corresponding car development business unit consists of approx. 1,100 employees and is organized according to LeSS [19]. The rationale for this setting was that traditional approaches to ISD were perceived as not suitable to cope with unclear or frequently changing functional requirements resulting from technical novelty or unclear regulatory requirements. Third, CarCo cooperates for the development of autonomous driving capabilities with other car manufacturers and original equipment suppliers (OES) in a joint development setting implying that each cooperation partner contributes with different feature teams working on the same code basis where area product owners coordinate feature development across feature teams of the different cooperation partners. This setting creates specific challenges as technical compatibility needs to be ensured between cooperation partners (one centralized code basis and code repository) and as potential cultural differences between cooperation partners from different parts of the world might occur.

The following challenges resulted from the necessity to find alternatives to traditional approaches to ISD and particularly for IT sourcing and contracting:

1. An ambitious timeline as the autonomous driving development platform needed to be available in spring 2019 to secure start of serial production in cars as of 2021. This timeline resulted in roughly one year lead time between intended go-live and the initial project start where neither details of the functionality, nor required high-level quantities and platform key parameters were available.
2. Technological novelty as neither CarCo, nor IT providers had previous experience in establishing an autonomous driving development IT platform of this scale and scope as core platform technology components like machine learning, big data or online video gaming are comparably new digital technologies where providers lack a profound experience.
3. Technical hurdles due to exceptionally high data volumes caused by high and full autonomous driving where an hour of test drive results in approx. 12–15 Terabyte of camera, lidar, radar, other sensor and meta data. Consequently, due to the need to secure proper functionality of new code or code changes, roughly 200 Petabyte of test data need to be stored and reprocessed in case of code or sensor/lidar data changes. To avoid delays in deployment of new code, the platform needs to have a computing capacity allowing the reprocessing of all stored date (i.e., 200 Petabyte) within a sprint's length of two weeks.
4. Unclear or not fully specified legal framework for operations of autonomous driving cars in intended markets – Europe, Japan, and the US as policy makers have not yet

decided about the local legal minimum requirements for certification of autonomous driving solutions. Consequently, it can be assumed that car manufacturers aim at fulfilling higher standards as legally required to avoid significant changes to their development systems as soon as stricter legal requirements are published by local policy makers.

5. Unclear or frequently changing requirements due to the novelty of autonomous driving. As already mentioned, detailed technical specifications or quantities could not have been specified initially for the establishment of the autonomous driving development system. This circumstance resulted in high uncertainly requiring flexibility regarding changing technology components or key parameters making a traditional "waterfall approach" almost impossible.

6. Multi-partner setting with other car manufacturers and suppliers engaging in a cooperation for joint development of autonomous driving capabilities. As the automotive industry is faced by four major disruptions known as "ACES", car makers increasingly cooperate to share investments in new technologies. Like electromobility, autonomous driving involves significant investments [71, 72]. These new cooperations require new technical infrastructure as for instance code development has to take place on a joint code base that can be accessed by developers from different cooperation partners. Furthermore, the coordination of feature teams across different car manufacturers and suppliers results in organizational complexity and high coordination effort.

4   Results

Based on the case study findings, we observed that agility plays an important role for IT sourcing and contracting as agile ISD services need to be contracted differently compared to traditional ISD services. We refer to agile practices applied during the request for proposal (RFP) as 'agile sourcing' whereas to sourcing of agile ISD services as 'sourcing agile'. The subsequent section presents our case study findings.

4.1   'Agile Sourcing' to Reduce Tender Duration and Time-to-Market

A backwards calculation revealed that the autonomous driving development platform would need to be established in March 2019 to ensure a seamless start of serial production in 2021. To achieve this ambitious goal, contract signature with the IT provider for the development platform had to take place in November 2018. Consequently, a time frame of roughly nine months for defining the tender scope including volumes, services, functionality, technical concepts, and for vendor selection including contract negotiation resulted. The high-level timeline is displayed in Fig. 2.

Our empirical data revealed six levers to increase agility in IT sourcing: (1) Focusing on business outcomes without specifying the means of realization, (2) lean requirements specification, (3) using a services catalogue to describe IT services in a standardized and structured way, (4) engaging in a detailed discussion between client and provider during the tender, (5) communicating the tender schedule in advance and (6) conducting an request for information (RFI) before launching an RFP. In detail, the following findings could be derived from the interviews at CarCo:

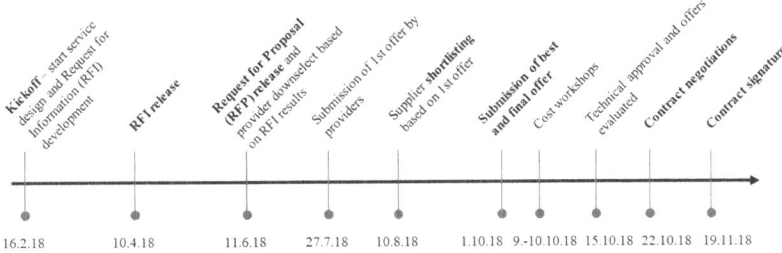

Fig. 2. Timeline for the autonomous driving IT development platform.

1. Focus on business outcomes ("value stories") without specifying the means of realization. To achieve this objective, desired business features were defined only high-level and details of the realization were left up to the provider. This approach follows the agile practice of focusing on business outcomes and to create freedom for the feature teams to decide about the realization [22, 25]. Consequently, different technologies or means of realization could have been selected by the provider based on their expertise. This approach significantly differs from traditional ISD using comprehensive statements of work often not only specifying expected deliverables but also related technologies or means of realization for desired functionalities reducing the degree of freedom for providers significantly. Examples for business services described high-level include the collection of camera, lidar, radar, and sensor data of test drives, the ingestion of collected test data to the data center, or the simulation of the autonomous driving code based on new sensor set-ups. In line with extant knowledge on agile sourcing, the freedom of providers to decide on details of realization can be perceived as lever to shorten tender duration as they are free to apply technologies of their preference [55].

2. Lean requirement specifications describing features only high-level was applied for three reasons: First, to shorten the duration for requirements specification, second, because of the lack of details for specification provisioning due to uncertainty or frequently changing requirements, and third, to include providers in the solution design at an early stage to leverage their ideas and creativity in resolving technical hurdles and challenges. Consequently, only platform key parameters like intended target volumes for available storage or computation time for specific operations like reprocessing of a defined data set within a given time were specified. This approach follows the recommendations of the Agile Manifesto that best architecture and requirements designs emerge from self-organizing teams [25] and reduces overall tender duration [8].

3. A service catalogue has been used to describe business services in a structured, standardized, and comprehensive way. A service catalogue describes required services in a formal structure and links them with service levels and quantities [73, 74]. The service catalogue turned out to be especially beneficial in reducing tender duration: To speed up the process of provider proposal development, providers submitted just a pricing matrix corresponding to the services requested in the services catalogue stating prices along with provider-specific assumptions. To avoid the review of lengthy, non-standardized proposals, only the completed pricing sheet responding

to the requested services and the provider's assumption list were subject to negotiations. Provider-specific assumptions were then reviewed and discussed between the client and the provider in so called "walk-through-sessions". The documentation of accepted changes in a separate document became part of the contract along with the pricing sheet. This process ensured that the original contract text including all exhibits and attachments remained unchanged and needed not to be reviewed for potential changes made by the provider. Consequently, the resulting negotiations and review of contract documents could be significantly reduced resulting in a reduced tender duration.

4. As part of the RFP, a detailed discussion between the client and providers on the intended solution took place in workshops. Workshops were organized according to different streams of the tender reflecting key business processes of the development platform for autonomous driving complemented by a commercial and legal stream taking on responsibility for contract negotiation. The approach of detailed discussions between client and providers in workshops ensured that providers could gain a profound understanding of the required functionality and gave the client the possibility to get familiar with the intended technical solution proposed by the provider. This process had three implications: First, providers had the opportunity to really understand the client's requirements and to get familiar with client key personnel present in the workshops. Second, due to the early involvement, providers had the opportunity to make suggestions for specific solutions and, thus, to find superior ways for technical realization related to innovation or novelty. Finally, the teams of the client and providers had the opportunity to get each other to know in detail allowing for an assessment of potential fit of team cultures for a potential cooperation after contract signature. Consequently, this approach contributed in reducing inherent uncertainty before contract signature, and, thus, avoiding potential conflicts between client and provider after contract signature. In line with agile practices, solution design defined in mutual workshops between client and providers was like sprints for solution design in iterative cycles to immediately incorporating customer feedback [57].

5. The tender schedule has been clearly defined and communicated in advance by the client. This approach was necessary to stick to the tight timeline resulting from an intended go-live for the IT platform for the development of autonomous driving capabilities as of 1.3.2019. To do so, the number of workshops in each tender phase was clearly defined and communicated. Consequently, both, client and providers were forced to bring required senior stakeholders for decision making on behalf of either party to the workshops due to the lack of the possibility to postpone decisions to subsequent meetings. This could have been achieved since providers participating in the tender had to commit in advance to the communicated tender procedure and timeline.

6. To conduct a profound vendor selection and to increase confidence in the future provider, an RFI has been initially launched for provider pre-screening and qualification before starting the RFP. Despite of consuming almost two months, the RFI turned out to be very valuable for the following reasons: First, the ability to address a potentially wider range of providers with the option for a vendor pre-qualification before entering the RFP. Second, the possibility to launch the RFI at an earlier point

in time as – contrary to the RFP – even not all high-level requirements needed to be defined to place an RFI. Third, to incorporate learnings on innovative solutions made by as many as possible providers including specialized niche-providers with only a limited chance to get qualified in the subsequent RFP. Fourth, to give providers the possibility to understand the client's requirements and tender scope at an earlier stage before entering the RFP enabling them to make more profound assumptions regarding expected tender effort, cost and likelihood for bid winning.

4.2 Contractual Agility to Increase Flexibility While Maintaining Cost-Efficiency

Our empirical data revealed three levers to increase contractual agility: (1) Specifying only initial quantities while defining quantities for subsequent quarters successively, (2) contracting agile ISD with 'T-shirt sizes' for reference teams, and (3) applying an agile fixed-price contract and lean SLAs. In detail, the following findings could be derived from the interviews at CarCo:

1. An 'investment board' approach where only initial quantities for the first quarter after contract signature were specified: This has been done for two reasons: First, a lack of the possibility to specify detailed quantities for subsequent quarters and second, the option to have maximum flexibility regarding the quantities in subsequent quarters in case of changes in demand. To cope with this situation, client and provider agreed on establishing a so-called 'investment board', a monthly meeting of client and provider representatives reviewing system utilization in the previous month and deciding on quantities for the next quarter as well as updating the rolling forecast for quantities in subsequent quarters. To reflect lead times for ordering hardware, the provider had three months for deploying agreed capacities. Consequently, all remaining quantities following the first quarter after go-live for the total contract duration of five years would be specified during the course by the 'investment board'. This approach aimed at ensuring maximum flexibility regarding ramp-up of the system's key parameters like computing power or storage. Simultaneously, the provider had enough time to provide requested capacities within sufficient lead time. To ensure that deployed capacities will not be cancelled by the client before the usual lifetime, the parties agreed that quantity flexibility was limited with respect to two conditions: First, a ramp-down of already deployed capacities would be reimbursed by the client with the anticipated cost for the remaining contract lifetime of the respective component. Second, the ramp-up of capacities would be limited to a maximum of 20% exceeding the already deployed capacity to ensure that the ordered capacity increase can be feasibly deployed without within a quarter's time frame. In case of disputes, an agreed governance with defined escalation mechanisms would apply.
2. To significantly increase flexibility in contracting of application development services, only a rough indication of the required skills and quantities was defined initially: To secure provider resources availability, the client committed on initial quantities for application development according to so-called 'T-shirt sizes'. 'T-shirt sizes' ranked from XS to XL describing an average person day effort for feature development ranging from T-shirt size XS (equaling one person-day) to XL (equaling 21 person days). Furthermore, the client specified the shoring mix for each ordered

T-shirt size to allow planning of regional availability of application development resources as requested. Quantities for desired volumes of sprint teams according to a defined T-shirt size and shoring mix were reviewed and adapted by the 'investment board' as well.

3. Cost-efficiency was intended with the following two measures: First, the client aimed at a fixed price agreement despite of the flexible scope in a fully agile setting: A fixed price has been agreed based on the scope, quantities, and assumptions made as specified in the pricing sheet. Only deviations from the quantities stated in the pricing sheet and approved by the 'investment board' were subject to a separate remuneration by the client. Second, cost-efficiency has been achieved by focusing SLAs on business process impact, e.g., interruption of business processes and not the availability of single system components. This approach ensured that only SLAs of relevance for business impact were negotiated and monitored which in turn facilitated a swift contract negotiation of SLAs and a resource-efficient SLA monitoring after go-live.

5 Discussion

Agile practices contribute to reducing time to market, increasing flexibility, or reducing uncertainty and, thus, reducing contractual risks in IT sourcing and contracting. Table 2 provides an overview of the different agile practices observed, resulting implications (i.e., on how the measures contribute to sourcing, contracting, and operations), and applying agility levers.

Related to increasing agility in IT sourcing and contracting, we found that speed can be increased by either reducing tender duration or reducing time to market of critical features. While reducing tender duration by itself reduces time to market (i.e., required features are available earlier), some agile practices contribute to a reduced time to market immediately. For instance, agile practices may reduce the time required for feature specification, development, testing and deployment as it is the case for instance with a lean requirements specification. This can be achieved by agile ISD in small feature teams taking care of the entire software lifecycle from specification, development, testing, integration, deployment, and operations. As feature teams are – unlike project teams – standing, they are already familiar with the topic and can immediately start working productively.

Some agile practices can also contribute to an increased flexibility while allowing focusing on business outcomes or a lean requirements specification: Both measures reduce time required for feature specification and focus on specification of features of relevance for clients only [75]. Consequently, a more detailed specification will be done as part of the implementation. In doing so, the decision which features should be prioritized can be made at a later point and, thus, increases flexibility allowing to implement new features on short notice. However, due to the limited research time frame for this study, it cannot be excluded that initial time savings are not partly lost in later stages when more details have to be specified successively as prerequisite to feature implementation.

Furthermore, agile practices aim at reducing contractual uncertainty: This can be achieved with an early engagement in discussions between the client and provider on

Table 2. Overview applied agile practices, implications and resulting agility lever.

Agile practice	Implications			Agility lever
	Sourcing	Contracting	Operations	
I. Agility in IT sourcing/tender process				
1. Focus on business outcomes ("value stories") without specifying the means of realization	Tender duration ↓		Time to market ↓	Speed
2. Lean requirements specification with only high-level feature description	Tender duration ↓	Flexibility ↑	Time to market ↓	Speed: Flexibility
3. Use a services catalogue for feature description in a structured and standardized way		Contractual uncertainty ↓	Time to market ↓	Speed: Risk reduction
4. Conduct a detailed discussion between client and provider in walk-through sessions		Contractual uncertainty ↓		Risk reduction
5. Communicate the tender schedule clearly in advance	Tender duration ↓	Contractual uncertainty ↓	Time to market ↓	Speed: risk reduction
6. Conduct an RFI before launching an RFP		Contractual uncertainty ↓		Risk reduction
II. Contractual agility				
1. Specify only initial quantities and conduct a monthly 'investment board' for review and revised future quantities	Tender duration ↓	Flexibility ↑	Time to market ↓	Speed: Flexibility
2. Contract agile ISD with 'T-shirt sizes' for feature teams of a defined size and shoring mix	Tender duration ↓	Flexibility ↑		Speed: Flexibility
3. Apply an agile fixed-price contract and lean SLAs	Tender duration ↓	Contractual uncertainty ↓	Time to market ↓	Speed: Risk reduction

feature realization. By this, the provider engages well in advance in discussion of the intended features like which functionality is important to the client, what parameters need to be considered or which technologies and realization options to choose. With this measure, client and provider likewise can get each other to know well in advance before the realization starts and can discuss and align on potentially critical points related to the realization of features.

Related to the IT contract, we found that agility can be increased by the same levers like in the IT sourcing process – increasing speed and flexibility and reducing contractual uncertainty. Tender duration and time to market can be reduced by only specifying initial quantities and defining the quantities for subsequent quarters after contract signature according to a defined process as it is for instance the case with a monthly 'investment board'. Likewise, flexibility in the resulting IT contract can be increased with contracting for external feature teams according to defined 'T-shirt sizes' for teams of a defined skill level, shoring mix, and team size. Pre-defined 'T-shirt sizes' ranging from XS to XL avoid lengthy discussions on specifications for provider feature teams. Finally, contractual uncertainty can be reduced by negotiating an agile fixed price contract based on high-level specifications of the required business outcomes. By this approach, the provider has no incentive for spending more time on feature development as it is the case with T&M contracts. Likewise, the client has no commercial risks as the price for a defined set of business outcomes is predefined before development starts.

As a result of this study's setting (i.e., a single case study with a limited time frame for research), we can only assume long-term success of applying agile practices to the sourcing and contracting. Following the Standish Group's definition of project success, a project is claimed to be successful if it is completed on-time and on-budget, with all features and functions as initially specified [76]. Related to this definition, respondents confirmed initial project success as the IT development platform went online on time, with all initially required features and in budget.

Besides of applied agile practices, the success factors identified by Lacity and Willcocks (2014) for dynamic innovation in business process outsourcing could be observed as well and support CarCo's rationale to outsource the autonomous driving development platform: The early involvement of providers in the tender process allowed for an early acculturation between client and provider. This involvement together with jointly developing and further optimizing systems specifications in an agile, iterative approach in sprints fostered inspiration and resulted in jointly-developed innovative ideas. As requirements specification focused on business outcomes rather than means of realization, the provider was incentivized to drive innovation and further optimization as both parties would benefit from innovation mutually. Finally, change management has been taken seriously with a well-prepared transition and transformation phase considering cultural and organizational aspects.

This study contributes to theory and practice likewise by extending extant knowledge on IT sourcing and contracting with agile practices. Related to theory, we reveal that theory to IT sourcing and contracting should be enhanced regarding two dimensions. First, if the subject matter of sourcing is agile ISD, relevant measures for sourcing agile software development services need to be applied. For instance, comprehensive statements of work should be replaced by high-level functional requirements and development capacities will be sourced according to fixed capacities – feature teams of a defined size according to 'T-shirt sizes', skill- and shoring mix. Second, we show how applying agile practices in the tender process can significantly reduce tender duration and can contribute in reducing pre-contractual risks and uncertainty by involving providers early in the tender process and benefit from their experience regarding the solution design.

Related to practice, this study shows how managers can speed up the process for large-scale IT tenders by applying agile practices into the sourcing process.

6   Conclusion

Companies increasingly adopt agile practices to foster innovation and performance in rapidly changing market environments [77]. While agile practices are widespread at startups or born digital companies like Amazon or Google [78], established companies started to adopt agile practices just recently [5, 7].

This study aims at revealing the implications and potential benefits of applying agile practices to the sourcing and contracting of large-scale IT endeavors. Accordingly, our research is motivated by the lack of empirical evidence on how agility can be increased in the sourcing and contracting of IT services by referring to a revelatory case study with CarCo in the context of autonomous driving. We contribute to the rich body of knowledge on IT sourcing and contracting with examples on how to reduce the duration of large-scale IT tenders and to increase the flexibility at IT contracts. For practitioners, this case study reveals insights on how the application of selected agile practices to the domain of IT sourcing and contracting can help in reducing the duration of large-scale IT tenders and pre-contractual uncertainty while flexibility of the resulting IT contract can be increased.

This study does not come without limitations: The case of CarCo might not be transferrable to companies of other industries or sizes. Specifically, prestige projects involving technological innovation like autonomous driving significantly increase the likelihood that providers engage in new or uncommon contract types and incur related contractual risks. Furthermore, due to topic novelty, only the time frame related to the sourcing of IT development platform for autonomous driving capabilities could have been considered. A longitudinal perspective of how the agile principles formulated in the contract come into live after contract start seems to be especially worthwhile.

Our future research will cover the following aspects: First, a longitudinal observation examining how agile contract components work in practice after contract signature seems required to validate of whether the intended contract flexibility could have been achieved. Second, due to the focus on the time span before contract signature, aspects of provider management or governance in a fully agile setting have not been considered. As this contract makes use of comparably new contractual elements like a monthly 'investment board' for reviewing and adapting system utilization and deciding on quantity changes in the subsequent quarters, we would expect specific challenges resulting from this contract feature. Third, as CarCo started to establish a cooperation with other car manufacturers and suppliers to share investments in autonomous driving development systems, specific aspects of the cooperation (i.e., how to coordinate feature teams from cooperation partners) should be reflected. Finally, the perspective of providers has not been sufficiently addressed by this study. As providers are vital for service delivery, we feel that this important perspective of the contractual partner should be considered.

Despite of the novelty of the content and the significant challenges imposed by the adoption of agile practices to IT sourcing and contracting, agility seem to be more than a short-term, transitory trend and is likely to play an important role as companies seek to increase speed and flexibility in response to rapidly changing market environments. It remains striking to learn how agility can be increased in sourcing and contracting of large-scale IT projects.

References

1. Ross, J.W., et al.: Designing and executing digital strategies. In: Thirty Seventh International Conference on Information Systems, Dublin, Ireland (2016)
2. Weill, P., Woerner, S.L.: Thriving in an increasingly digital ecosystem. MIT Sloan Manag. Rev. **56**(4), 27–34 (2015)
3. D'Aveni, R.A., Dagnino, G.B., Smith, K.G.: The age of temporary advantage. Strateg. Manag. J. **31**(13), 1371–1385 (2010)
4. Overby, E., Bharadwaj, A., Sambamurthy, V.: Enterprise agility and the enabling role of information technology. Eur. J. Inf. Syst. **15**(2), 120–131 (2006)

5. Gerster, D., et al.: How enterprises adopt agile forms of organizational design: a multiple-case study. ACM SIGMIS Database: the DATABASE for Advances in Information Systems **51**(1), 84–103 (2020)
6. Highsmith, J.A.: Adaptive Leadership - Accelerating Enterprise Agility (2013). https://assets.thoughtworks.com/articles/adaptive-leadership-accelerating-enterprise-agility-jim-highsmith-thoughtworks.pdf
7. Gerster, D., Dremel, C., Kelker, P.: "Agile meets non-agile": implications of adopting agile practices at enterprises. In: Twenty-fourth Americas Conference on Information Systems, New Orleans, USA (2018)
8. Arbogast, T., Larman, C., Vodde, B.: Agile contracts primer (2012). http://www.agilecontracts.org/agile_contracts_primer.pdf. Accessed 16 Oct 2018
9. Bardhan, I.R., et al.: An interdisciplinary perspective on IT services management and service science. J. Manag. Inf. Syst. **26**(4), 13–64 (2010)
10. Demirbas, U., Gewald, H., Moos, B.: The impact of digital transformation on sourcing strategies in the financial services sector: evolution or revolution? In: Twenty-Fourth Americas Conference on Information Systems, New Orleans, USA (2018)
11. Gewald, H., Schäfer, L.: Quo vadis outsourcing? a view from practice. J. Global Oper. Strat. Sourcing **10**(1), 2–17 (2017)
12. Dibbern, J., et al.: Information systems outsourcing: a survey and analysis of the literature. ACM SIGMIS Database: the DATABASE for Advances in Information Systems **35**(4), 6–102 (2004)
13. Lacity, M.C., Khan, S.A., Willcocks, L.P.: A review of the IT outsourcing literature: Insights for practice. J. Strateg. Inf. Syst. **18**(3), 130–146 (2009)
14. Pries-Heje, L., Pries-Heje, J.: Agile contracts: designing an agile team selection guideline. In: Information Systems Research Seminar in Scandinavia (2014)
15. Conboy, K.: Agility from first principles: reconstructing the concept of agility in information systems development. Inf. Syst. Res. **20**(3), 329–354 (2009)
16. Dremel, C., et al.: How AUDI AG established big data analytics in its digital transformation. MIS Q. Executive **16**(2), 81–100 (2017)
17. Dremel, C., et al.: Actualizing big data analytics affordances: A revelatory case study. Information & Management (2018)
18. Heineke, K., Kampshoff, P.: The trends transforming mobility's future. McKinsey Quarterly (2019) https://www.mckinsey.com/industries/automotive-and-assembly/our-insights/the-trends-transforming-mobilitys-future, 15 Sep 2019
19. Larman, C., Vodde, B.: Less.works (2017). https://less.works/less/framework/index.html. Accessed 19 Apr 2018
20. Royce, W.W.: Managing the development of large software systems: concepts and techniques. In: Proceedings of the 9th International Conference on Software Engineering. IEEE Computer Society Press, Monterey (1987)
21. Rigby, D.K., Sutherland, J., Takeuchi, H.: Embracing Agile. Harvard Bus. Rev. **94**(5), 40 (2016)
22. Kulak, D., Li, H.: The Journey to Enterprise Agility: Systems Thinking and Organizational Legacy. Springer, Heidelberg (2017). https://doi.org/10.1007/978-3-319-54087-0
23. Leffingwell, D.: Scaling Software Agility: Best Practices for Large Enterprises. Pearson Education, Upper Saddle River (2007)
24. Deming, W.E.: Out of the Crisis, vol. 1st MIT Press ed. The MIT Press, Cambridge (2000)
25. Fowler, M., Highsmith, J.A.: The agile manifesto. Softw. Dev. **9**(8), 28–35 (2001)
26. Wang, X., Conboy, K., Pikkarainen, M.: Assimilation of agile practices in use. Inf. Syst. J. **22**(6), 435–455 (2012)
27. Fitzgerald, B., Stol, K.-J.: Continuous software engineering: a roadmap and agenda. J. Syst. Softw. **123**, 176–189 (2017)

28. Fitzgerald, B., Hartnett, G., Conboy, K.: Customising agile methods to software practices at Intel Shannon. Eur. J. Inf. Syst. **15**(2), 200–213 (2006)
29. Kniberg, H.I.: Anders. Scaling Agile @ Spotify with Tribes, Squads, Chapters & Guilds (2012). https://creativeheldstab.com/wp-content/uploads/2014/09/scaling-agile-spo tify-11.pdf
30. Gonçalves, E., Lopes, E.: Implementing scrum as an IT project management agile methodology in a large scale institution. In: European Conference on Research Methodology for Business and Management Studies. Academic Conferences International Limited (2014)
31. Recker, J., et al.: How agile practices impact customer responsiveness and development success: a field study. Project Manag. J. **48**(2), 99–121 (2017)
32. Przybilla, L., Wiesche, M., Krcmar, H.: The influence of agile practices on performance in software engineering teams: a subgroup perspective. In: Proceedings of the 2018 ACM SIGMIS Conference on Computers and People Research. ACM (2018)
33. McAvoy, J., Butler, T.: The role of project management in ineffective decision making within Agile software development projects. Eur. J. Inf. Syst. **18**(4), 372–383 (2009)
34. Dyba, T., Dingsoyr, T.: What do we know about agile software development? IEEE Softw. **26**(5), 6–9 (2009)
35. ScaledAgile. Essential SAFe 4.5 (2017). http://www.scaledagileframework.com/. 29 Oct 2017
36. Gregory, P., et al.: The challenges that challenge: engaging with agile practitioners' concerns. Inf. Softw. Technol. **77**, 92–104 (2016)
37. Gregory, Peggy., Barroca, Leonor., Taylor, Katie., Salah, Dina, Sharp, Helen: Agile challenges in practice: a thematic analysis. In: Lassenius, Casper, Dingsøyr, Torgeir, Paasivaara, Maria (eds.) XP 2015. LNBIP, vol. 212, pp. 64–80. Springer, Cham (2015). https://doi.org/10.1007/978-3-319-18612-2_6
38. Dahlberg, T., Lagstedt, A.: There is still no "fit for all" is development method: business development context and IS development characteristics need to match. In: Proceedings of the 51st Hawaii International Conference on System Sciences (2018)
39. Schnitter, J., Geppert, J.: Agile software development: what is left to do? In: Brunetti, G., Feld, T., Heuser, L., Schnitter, J., Webel, C. (eds.) Future Business Software. PI, pp. 93–104. Springer, Cham (2014). https://doi.org/10.1007/978-3-319-04144-5_8
40. van Hillegersberg, J., Ligtenberg, G., Aydin, M.N.: Getting agile methods to work for cordys global software product development. In: Kotlarsky, J., Willcocks, L.P., Oshri, I. (eds.) Global Sourcing 2011. LNBIP, vol. 91, pp. 133–152. Springer, Heidelberg (2011). https://doi.org/10.1007/978-3-642-24815-3_8
41. Conboy, K., Carroll, N.: Implementing large-scale agile frameworks: challenges and recommendations. IEEE Softw. **36**(2), 44–50 (2019)
42. Paasivaara, M., Lassenius, C., Heikkilä, V.T.: Inter-team coordination in large-scale globally distributed scrum: do scrum-of-scrums really work? In: Proceedings of the ACM-IEEE International Symposium on Empirical Software Engineering and Measurement. ACM (2012)
43. Cram, W.A.: Agile development in practice: lessons from the trenches. Inf. Syst. Manag. **36**(1), 2–14 (2019)
44. Willcocks, L., Oshri, I., Rottman, J.: Forword to MISQEs special theme book on outsourcing. MIS Quarterly Executive Special Theme Book on Outsourcing, pp. 3–5 (2015)
45. Liang, H., et al.: IT outsourcing research from 1992 to 2013: a literature review based on main path analysis. Inf. Manag. **53**(2), 227–251 (2016)
46. Whitley, E.A., Willcocks, L.: Achieving step-change in outsourcing maturuty: toward collaborative innovation. MIS Q. Executive **10**(3), 95–107 (2011)
47. Lacity, M., Willcocks, L.: Business process outsourcing and dynamic innovation. An International Journal, Strategic Outsourcing (2014)

48. Oshri, I., Kotlarsky, J., Gerbasi, A.: Strategic innovation through outsourcing: the role of relational and contractual governance. J. Strateg. Inf. Syst. **24**(3), 203–216 (2015)
49. Wu, S.P.-J., Straub, D.W., Liang, T.-P.: How information technology governance mechanisms and strategic alignment influence organizational performance: Insights from a matched survey of business and IT managers. MIS Q. **39**(2), 497–518 (2015)
50. IDG. Studie Sourcing 2017. (2017). https://shop.computerwoche.de/fileserver/files/1715/208 364044222138/idg_studie2017_4_sourcing_web_leseprobe.pdf. Accessed 22 Oct 2018
51. Tirole, J.: Incomplete contracts: where do we stand? Econometrica **67**(4), 741–781 (1999)
52. Hart, O., Moore, J.: Foundations of incomplete contracts. Rev. Econ. Stud. **66**(1), 115–138 (1999)
53. Hart, O., Moore, J.: Incomplete contracts and renegotiation. Econometrica J. Econometric Soc. **56**, 755–785 (1988)
54. Guston, D.H.: Principal-agent theory and the structure of science policy. Sci. Public Policy **23**(4), 229–240 (1996)
55. Opelt, A., et al.: Agile contracts: creating and managing successful projects with Scrum (2013). Wiley
56. Book, Matthias., Gruhn, Volker, Striemer, Rüdiger: adVANTAGE: a fair pricing model for agile software development contracting. In: Wohlin, Claes (ed.) XP 2012. LNBIP, vol. 111, pp. 193–200. Springer, Heidelberg (2012). https://doi.org/10.1007/978-3-642-30350-0_15
57. Kim, G., et al.: The DevOps Handbook: How to Create World-Class Agility, Reliability, and Security in Technology Organizations. IT Revolution (2016)
58. Rizvi, B., Bagheri, E., Gasevic, D.: A systematic review of distributed Agile software engineering. J. Softw. Evol. Process **27**(10), 723–762 (2015)
59. Schwaber, K., Beedle, M.: Agile software development with Scrum, vol. 1. Prentice Hall, Upper Saddle River (2002)
60. Hekkala, R., et al.: Challenges in transitioning to an agile way of working. In: Proceedings of the 50th Hawaii International Conference on System Sciences, Hawaii, USA (2017)
61. Austin, R.D., Devin, L.: Research commentary—weighing the benefits and costs of flexibility in making software: toward a contingency theory of the determinants of development process design. Inf. Syst. Res. **20**(3), 462–477 (2009)
62. Ågerfalk, P.J., Fitzgerald, B., Slaughter, S.A.: Introduction to the special issue—flexible and distributed information systems development: state of the art and research challenges. Inf. Syst. Res. **20**(3), 317–328 (2009)
63. Coram, M., Bohner, S.: The impact of agile methods on software project management. In: Engineering of Computer-Based Systems, 2005. ECBS'05. 12th IEEE International Conference and Workshops on the Engineering of Computer-Based Systems. IEEE (2005)
64. Yin, R.K.: Case Study Research - Design and Methods, vol. 5. Sage (2009)
65. Langley, A., Abdallah, C.: Templates and turns in qualitative studies of strategy and management, in Building methodological bridges. Emerald Group Publishing Limited, pp. 201–235 (2011)
66. Schultze, U., Avital, M.: Designing interviews to generate rich data for information systems research. Inf. Organ. **21**(1), 1–16 (2011)
67. Strauss, A., Corbin, J.: Basics of Qualitative Research, vol. 15. Sage, Newbury Park (1990)
68. Larman, C., Vodde, B.: Practices for Scaling Lean and Agile Development: Large, Multisite and Offshore Projects with Large-Scale Scrum. Addison-Wesley, Reading (2008)
69. Herrmann, A., Brenner, W., Stadler, R.: Autonomous Driving: How the Driverless Revolution will Change the World. Emerald Publishing Limited, Bingley (2018)
70. SAE. Taxonomy and Definitions for Terms Related to On-Road Motor Vehicle Automated Driving Systems (2018). https://www.sae.org/standards/content/j3016_201401/. Accessed 28 Oct 2018

71. Heineke, K., et al.: Development in the mobility technology ecosystem—how can 5G help? McKinsey Quartlerly (2019). 31.05.2020. https://www.mckinsey.com/industries/automo tive-and-assembly/our-insights/development-in-the-mobility-technology-ecosystem-how-can-5g-help?cid=other-eml-alt-mip-mck&hlkid=7c09a3884716492da20e7b325aa32297& hctky=10293075&hdpid=cba7c3e9-b5e5-4eb3-8e6f-4c91049bbcc4. Accessed 13 Aug 2019

72. Mohr, D.M., Nicolai, Krieg, A., Gao, P., Kaas, H.-W., Krieger, A., Hensley, R.: The road to 2020 and beyond: What's driving the global automotive industry? (2019). https://www.mckinsey.com/~/media/mckinsey/dotcom/client_service/Automotive% 20and%20Assembly/PDFs/McK_The_road_to_2020_and_beyond.ashx. Accessed 8 July 2019

73. Mendes, C., da Silva, M.M.: Implementing the service catalogue management. In: 2010 Seventh International Conference on the Quality of Information and Communications Technology. IEEE (2010)

74. Arcilla, M., Calvo-Manzano, J.A., San Feliu, T.: Building an IT service catalog in a small company as the main input for the IT financial management. Comput. Stand. Interfaces **36**(1), 42–53 (2013)

75. Turk, D., Robert, F., Rumpe, B.: Assumptions underlying agile software-development processes. J. Database Manag. (JDM) **16**(4), 62–87 (2005)

76. Group, T.S.: Chaos Report (2015). https://www.standishgroup.com/sample_research_files/ CHAOSReport2015-Final.pdf. Accessed 31 May 2020

77. Sambamurthy, V., Bharadwaj, A., Grover, V.: Shaping agility through digital options: reconceptualizing the role of information technology in contemporary firms. MIS Q. **27**(2), 237–263 (2003)

78. Tumbas, S., Berente, N., vom Brocke, J.: Born digital: growth trajectories of entrepreneurial organizations spanning institutional fields. In: Proceedings of the Thirty Eighth International Conference on Information Systems, Seoul, Korea (2017)

IT Infrastructures Sourcing Challenges and Practices of Exploration-for-Exploitation in Public Sector Organizations: A Delphi Study

Dragos Vieru[1]([⊠]), Simon Bourdeau[2], Thibaut Coulon[2], and Élodie Boissières[1]

[1] TÉLUQ University, 5800 Rue Saint-Denis, Montréal, QC H2S 3L5, Canada
{dragos.vieru,elodie.boissieres}@teluq.ca
[2] Université du Québec à Montréal, 405 Rue Sainte-Catherine Est, Montréal,
QC H2L 2C4, Canada
{bourdeau.simon.2,coulon.thibaut}@uqam.ca

Abstract. Managing information technology infrastructures (ITI) in an effective manner represents a major challenge for any organization and even more for public sector organizations (PSOs) that often lack IT resources and are constrained by tight budgets. Despite the importance of these challenges for practitioners, there is a limited number of studies in this field. Applying the organizational ambidexterity (AO) lens to analyze IT managers' practices of ITI in public sector, with a specific emphasis on sourcing practices, the present study seeks to fill this gap. We present the outcomes of a Delphi study that involved 40 ITI experts from three sectors: public, private, and academic. Public sector practices of exploration-for-exploitation sourcing are discussed in this paper.

Keywords: Information technology infrastructures · Public sector organizations · Organizational ambidexterity · Sourcing practices · Delphi study

1 Introduction

Since the dawn of the 21st century, public sector organizations (PSOs) have undergone many changes, not only in their governance structures and managerial approaches, but also in the sourcing models of their information technologies infrastructures (ITI). For most practitioners and scholars, an ITI refers to "the composite of hardware, software and connectivity of an organizational system" [66, p. 1747] and "provides services to a range of applications and users, and it is usually managed by the IT-group" [60, p. 203].

Managing IT infrastructures represents one of the biggest concerns in PSOs due to the growing financial resources invested in IT projects each year [53]. However, compared to private organizations, PSOs face several other challenges such as the transparency and efficiency required in their IT-related sourcing, the lack of expertise in IT, and the fact that they must trade on public markets and follow governmental regulations [15, 41].

While most public ITI is still provided in-house, to overcome the aforementioned challenges, more and more PSOs are choosing external suppliers in order to: 1) develop,

© Springer Nature Switzerland AG 2020
I. Oshri et al. (Eds.): Global Sourcing 2019, LNBIP 410, pp. 38–68, 2020.
https://doi.org/10.1007/978-3-030-66834-1_3

purchase, maintain, and upgrade their ITI, both the hardware and software dimensions [14, 42]; and 2) evaluate, adopt, and implement emerging/new technologies [23, 56]. Since ITI are increasingly complex, the management and sourcing of these infrastructures have become a major problem for public sector IT managers [16, 17]. Despite their importance, the activities and practices related to the managing and sourcing of ITI in PSOs have been scarcely studied and documented in both academic and professional literatures [41]. It appears to be a significant lack of knowledge on the challenges faced by PSOs regarding the decisional process for the management and sourcing of their IT infrastructures.

Governments around the world are struggling to provide efficient and effective public services in order to meet the increasing expectations of citizens while dealing with decreased public resources and budgets at the same time [56]. To address this major problem, governments have initiated IT projects to open their data, which in turn can be used to create transparency and involve the public [35]. For instance, the emergence of cloud computing technologies has opened up new possibilities for many governments that want to implement e-government platforms [32, 56] that would enable a government to evolve from being an internal driven organization to being open by providing transparency and accountability, and engaging the public [37]. Another example is the blockchain technology and its application, the distributed ledger, that has the capability to deliver a new kind of trust to a wide range of public services [23]. Rapid advances in digital information across many government functions such as "big data" [13] and machine learning [4], will provide better measures of public service outputs that will generate insights into how public agencies perform and use resources. Initiatives to assess and eventually implement these technologies reflect the need to transform and explore new ways to accomplish openness, transparency, accountability and engagement.

There are relentless pressures on IT managers in public services to bring up-to-date their ITI in order to increase the quality of their services. Facing tight budgets, the idea of 'more with less' has become a slogan as IT managers seek improve the quality of service delivery [27]. This phenomenon is pervasive – an international trend from which there is no escape for public service managers. This global interest has attracted the attention of key world institutions such as the OECD [e.g., 34] on how modern ITI are the drivers of productivity and efficiency of public services. Some of the identified success factors are 1) implementing digital government strategies; 2) fostering an environment conducive to innovation, and 3) understanding better the effect of budgeting and government regulatory practices. New approaches should consider the inherent trade-offs between existing, known technologies and emerging or new technologies [34]. To accomplish all of this, there is a clear need for public sector IT managers to keep up-to-date existing ITI (*exploitation*) and at the same time, explore opportunities to implement new technologies (*exploration*) while aligning their sourcing strategies with the various human resources and budgeting restrictions, and procurement regulations.

There is a general consensus that organizations need to both explore and exploit successfully to survive and thrive [3, 5, 24]. Ambidexterity embodies the idea that enduring success of a firm depends on its ability to exploit current capabilities while concurrently exploring new opportunities as it reconfigures its resources to obtain competitive advantage [5]. *Exploitation* focuses on efficiency, increasing productivity, and extending operational processes, while *exploration* concentrates on building emerging capabilities and creating workable business options for the future [39]. It has been suggested that organizations need to both explore and exploit successfully to survive and thrive [3, 5, 24]. *Organizational ambidexterity* (OA) embodies the idea that enduring success of a firm depends on its ability to exploit current capabilities while concurrently exploring new opportunities as it reconfigures its resources to obtain competitive advantage [39, 63]. In their seminal article Tushman and O'Reilly (1996) propose the metaphor of a juggler (an ambidextrous person) to suggest that managers who are capable to integrate and reconcile both exploratory and exploitative activities can continuously produce innovations that would incorporate both incremental and radical innovations. Organizational ambidexterity is about doing both by providing the ability to mitigate the tension between exploration and exploitation in pursuit for competitiveness [29, 63].

In this study we use one of the several applications of the organizational ambidexterity construct, in the sense that we adopt Rothaermel and Alexandre's (2009) view of ambidexterity as a firm's "ability to simultaneously balance different activities in a trade-off situation" (54, p.759). In this vein, March (1991) indicates that the "essence of exploration is experimentation with new alternatives," whereas the "essence of exploitation is the refinement and extension of existing competences" (p. 85). In the context of public sector ITI management and sourcing, we conjecture that IT managers must develop the ability to resolve antinomies or to accommodate apparently opposite or conflicting practices. They will need to either engage in exploitation (refine and extend existing technology), in exploration (search for broader knowledge that helps the organization to acquire and implement new technology), or in a mix of both [54]. We infer that a PSO IT manager will probably source the ITI (known or new technology) either internally (insourcing) or externally (outsourcing).

This exploratory study has a two-fold goal:

1) *to identify the main challenges PSOs IT managers face when engaging in ITI sourcing practices*; and
2) *how do IT managers engage in ITI management and sourcing exploration and/or exploitation.*

Attempting to achieve this goal, our study draws on the organizational ambidexterity concept. We first engage in a systematic literature review of the ITI sourcing challenges in public sector, then provide a description of our conceptual foundation. We further explain the methodological approach used in our Delphi study that involved 40 ITI experts from three different sectors: private, public and academic. The outcomes of this study, a list of organizational practices identified by these experts, was analyzed by building on Rosenkopf and Nerkar's (2001) matrix that provides relevant criteria when sourcing for ITI [52]. We focus on two dimensions: 1) insourcing vs. outsourcing and 2) known vs. new technology sourcing. A discussion of the results followed by the presentation of the implications for both scholars and practitioners conclude the paper. Conceptually we identified a specific instance of contextual ambidexterity, – manifested as exploration to (continuously) improve exploitation and as such, we label it *exploration-for-exploitation*. Thus, the present study's goal is to provide the illustration of an instantiation of organizational ambidexterity.

It must be noted that data used in this article is part of a larger research project that had a broader scope and sought to shed light on the issues related to the management of technological and application infrastructures in public organizations, as well as the practices deployed to optimize the management of these infrastructures. In our analysis, we focus only on the IT sourcing issues and their related practices undertaken by IT managers as two of the several components of the ITI management process in public sector.

2   Literature Review: ITI Sourcing Challenges in Public Sector

Following Paré et al.'s (2015) recommendations [48], we identified three main categories of challenges related to ITI sourcing faced by IT managers in a public sector context: 1) Strategic-related ITI evolution challenges; 2) ITI sourcing business model challenges; and 3) Emerging technologies adoption issues.

2.1   Strategic-Related ITI Evolution Challenges

The extant literature shows four organizational strategy-related challenges that PSOs face: 1) challenges related to hardware and software infrastructures (mostly related to tight budgets and cost cuts); 2) challenges related to internal operational processes (differences in department-based procurement strategies and regulations and policies) [9]; 3) challenges related to e-government policies and the necessary infrastructures to align to those policies [10]; and 4) challenges stemming from the citizens/users' feedback that push public institutions to becoming smart cities or smart governments [33].

These important issues involve significant ITI transformations [22]. It has been suggested that in order to effectively address these challenges, IT managers in public institutions need a consistent strategic alignment of their ITI and business goals in order to increase the quality of public services and meet stakeholders' expectations [33].

2.2   ITI Sourcing Business Model Challenges

During the last decade, the topic of how sourcing of ITI supposed to be done became more and more prevalent since governments saw a rapid evolution of technologies and a sharp rise in service quality expectations from their respective citizens/users. According to Lember et al. (2018), PSOs prefer private sector tailor-made technologies for their core tasks to the insourced tailor-made solutions. The latter come with considerable transaction costs and are often difficult to implement on time. A recent study suggests that PSOs are forced to adopt new models of business because information technologies are nowadays the essence of up-to-date organizations and that their evolution is occurring at an uncontrollable pace [19]. To address this issue PSOs need to look at outsourcing as an important step in their development since this approach will bring in new technologies faster than the insource approach [12]. Indeed, it has been found that IT managers in static PSOs are slower in implementing changes in their technological routines and therefore struggle to deliver minimum services to their citizens [36].

The extant literature suggests that outsourcing partially, or all of public IT services would provide benefits to the public sector. A first benefit has been identified as being a relief in the maintenance of ITI for the organization that in the same time would also allow to cut on IT overhead expenses while allowing internal and external flexibility [6]. Another benefit would be the ability of public sector IT managers to better achieve strategic goals involving the access to essential or rare resources that would otherwise be more difficult or slower to acquire if insourced [21].

2.3 Emerging Technologies Adoption Challenges

Recently we have witnessed the emergence of a new kind of economy: the sharing economy [20]. An annual industry report forecasts an exponential growth of the sharing economy from an estimated 15$bn in 2014 to an expected 335$bn in 2025 [49]. In this context, the emerging technologies can be seen has an important means to achieve new goals identified in the sharing economy. One of the most promising emerging technology, blockchain, has the potential to solve the issue of the necessary changes in how governments maintain administrative control in a digital world [25]. Blockchain technology is an efficient solution to store persistent objects and assets (such as certificates and licenses, etc.) that will enable strong data security and efficient privacy [45]. It makes possible to have contracts that are embedded in digital code and stored in transparent (increases the public trust) databases, where they are sheltered from deletion and altering. In the public sector, some authors consider blockchain as "an institutional technology of governance that competes with other economic institutions of capitalism, namely firms, markets, networks, and even governments" [11, p. 16].

While it looks like a panacea, several issues must be addressed by IT managers in order to have this technology implemented and adopted by organizations: first, there is an important cost associated with the acquisition and implementation of the blockchain infrastructure; second, IT managers must ensure that their IT specialists are trained to use the technology; third, there will be a need for developing applications for blockchain [25]. However, the most important challenge PSOs will face when adopting this technology is how governments will address the impact that blockchain will have on the governance of the transactions. Whereas conventional systems have a relatively direct control, the distributed nature of blockchain technology entails important changes in responsibilities and new governance approaches [45].

While not an emergent technology per se, cloud computing (CC) is an emerging IT outsourcing model and it is considered amongst the five most influential technologies in the last decade [28, 58, 65]. Analyzing the benefits of CC technology, Sallehudin et al. (2015) found five factors that can impact its adoption by the PSOs: 1) the potential lack of compatibility (similar objectives with the organizations' work behavior, values, experience and practice); 2) the complexity (perception of the technology as being complex and difficult to use); 3) the potential lack of ability to try, test, or experiment; 4) IT personnel characteristics (lack of knowledge of the technology and power of persuasion); 5) lack of openness to new technology. Information security and privacy were also identified as significant challenges to adopt cloud computing [18].

In sum, the extant literature on ITI sourcing in public sector suggests that IT managers in PSOs need to adapt to a faster and constant technological evolution driven by: 1) performance/capacity enhancements, new functionalities, and frequent new software releases [40]; 2) opportunities to outsource some of their IT infrastructures installation and maintenance [12]; 3) growing importance given to citizens/users' feedback about their needs [36]; 4) unavoidable changes in the traditional organizational governance models [45].

3 Organizational Ambidexterity

The concept of organizational ambidexterity (OA) represents a firm's ability to simultaneously explore and exploit, enabling a firm to succeed at adaption over time rather than pursuing one of the two activities exclusively [29, 44].

Structural Ambidexterity. The concept of structural ambidexterity advances the idea that organizational structures should divide exploitative and explorative practices into separate organizational units, each with distinct competencies, processes, and cultures, while at the same time implementing a process of integration between exploration and exploitation [29, 63]. In other words, this implies that successful ambidexterity is conditioned by the capability of an organization to have different business units able to focus on operation activities, while others focus on adaptation [5].

Contextual Ambidexterity. Unlike structural ambidexterity, contextual ambidexterity is an approach that enables organizations to balance exploitative and explorative tasks without separating them [2, 29]. In this perspective, ambidextrous organizations enable an organizational context that foster and encourages the flexibility of employees to use their own judgment in how and when they will efficiently divide their time between the conflicting demands of exploitation and exploration across the same business unit [5, 24]. In this way, contextual ambidexterity enables firms to avoid going in a direction of change without regard to its bottom line [39]. The contextual approach supports O'Reilly and Tushman's (2013) argument that a firm that is capable of exploring and exploiting simultaneously is likely to realize superior performance compared to firms that favor one over the other. A successful implementation of this philosophy is Toyota. Adler et al.'s (1999) case study examines the contextual factors that contribute to ambidexterity between firm flexibility and efficiency. The authors found that reconciling the contextual factors of support, training and trust, increased the organization's capacity for flexibility at a given level of efficiency, and created capabilities that served to improve efficiency [1].

The literature on OA suggests the path from ambidexterity to organizational performance presents implementation challenges, particularly related to the need to and achieve flexibility in the allocation of company resources across alignment and adaptability activities [44, 63]. While some ambidexterity researchers assume that in general resources are available and that managers across the organization have equal access to them [44, 59], others suggest that this assumption is not always valid [31]. The amount of human capital required favors larger businesses' efforts to create and sustain ambidexterity. Ambidextrous organizations invest heavily in their pool of human resources so that employees are well-trained, skilled, motivated, and empowered to efficiently balance exploitation and exploration practices [38, 50]. Most theories regarding ambidexterity assume that organizations are large enough to allocate sufficient resources managers to fostering and maintaining an ambidextrous environment [24, 38]. However, in our context, the ideal route for an IT manager in a public sector organization with fewer resources and constrained by tight budgets and governmental regulations to pursue ITI sourcing ambidexterity requires more analysis.

4 Research Design: Delphi Method

Our literature review shows that PSOs face important challenges. However, the literature is relatively limited regarding how these challenges are overcome by ITI managers. Thus, to better understand how ITI manages overcome these challenges, and more specifically, to better understand the sourcing practices deployed, a Delphi study was conducted [43, 47]. The objectives are, first to identify the management and sourcing practices deployed by IT managers to overcome the challenges and second, to have a better understanding how IT managers balance their sourcing practices, in terms of exploitation and exploration, in order to generate ambidexterity.

The Delphi method allows a panel of experts to communicate and exchange, in an interactive and structured way, to identify, select and classify different ideas such as problems, key success factors or good practices [47, 55]. We chose the Delphi method because it has been used successfully in complex areas requiring expert conclusions [e.g., 55]. We followed the suggested steps to conduct a Delphi study [57] as well as the recommendations formulated by experts [47] in the elaboration of the methodological design.

In the present study, out of the 62 IT infrastructure management experts that were contacted, 40 accepted to participate in the study. In order to have a complementary perspective IT infrastructure, managers from private organizations as well as IT researchers from the academia were invited to participate in the study. During the Delphi study, experts had to identify and classify practices deployed to manage their ITI in terms of: 1) **exploitation**, e.g., practices deployed to extend the sustainability of their existing IT infrastructure and 2) **exploration**, e.g., the practices deployed to seize the opportunities related to the constant and rapid technological evolution. To do so, data collection process followed the three main phases underlying the Delphi method: 1) brainstorming; 2) narrowing; and 3) ranking [47].

4.1 Experts Selection

Choosing the right experts is one of the most, if not the most important step in the Delphi process. Indeed, an important relation exists between the selection and the quality of the results generated [47]. We followed Okoli and Pawlowski's (2004) and Paré et al.'s (2013) recommendations on experts selection. The experts selected had to have: 1) knowledge and expertise related to the management of ITIs in private or public organizations and/or 2) conducted studies (e.g. scholars) in the field of IT. Recruitment of the ITI experts was based on the authors' professional networks. The 40 experts that agreed to participate in the Delphi study were divided into three groups of experts: public, private and academic sectors. Table 1 illustrates the main demographic data of the expert panel. Due to the extended length (4 months) of the Delphi process, 6 experts had quit the study at different moments along the 3 phases: 4 practitioners, 1 academic, and 1 from public sector. Thus, at the end of the last phase (ranking), the panel had 34 experts.

Table 1. Demographics in the Delphi study

	Sectors			
	Public	Private	Academic	Total
Number of respondents	14 (13)	15 (11)	11 (10)	*40 (34)*
Age (avg.)	48	48	46.3	*47.1*
Professional experience (years)	25.3	23.3	20.2	*23.15*
IT Professional experience (years)	19	18.2	15	*17.6*

4.2 Step#1: Brainstorming and Validation

The questionnaires sent to the experts in the first step, brainstorming, was divided in three sections: 1) demographic; 2) a question on the exploitation practices related to the management of ITI and 3) a question on the exploration practices related to the management of ITI. Our two questions focused on the ITI managerial practices in general rather than only on the sourcing practices. By asking the experts to focus on managerial practices in general rather than only on sourcing one, the objective was to ensure that they would take a general perspective on the practices deployed to overcome the challenges of managing ITI. By asking the experts to focus only on one underlying dimension of ITI management, e.g., the sourcing practices, we would have had a partial perspective. Thus, we conducted a Delphi study that focused on the managerial practices to exploit and explore ITI. However, in this paper, our analysis focused on the practices related to ITI sourcing. Thus, the questions on exploitation and exploration practices were:

Exploitation-Focus Question: *What are the practices/strategies that can be used by organizations in general to extend the sustainability of their existing IT infrastructure, e.g. those currently deployed? These practices/strategies can be technical, strategic, organizational, human, etc.*

Exploration-Focus Question: *What are the practices/strategies used by organizations to overcome the challenges and seize the opportunities related to the constant and rapid technological evolution?*

Each expert was asked to provide a minimum of 6 answers (practices) per question. For each response, the experts had to provide a label describing the identified practice as well as a short description. The questionnaire was pre-tested with three IT experts (non-participants) to assess the clarity of the question, the design of the questionnaire and the approximate time required to complete it.

The experts identified 180 different practices for the exploitation-focused question and 198 different practices for the exploration-focused question. Data were compiled using MS Excel. The experts' answers and explanations were analyzed first individually, and then collectively by the first three authors. The purpose of this analysis was to group and synthesize all of these responses. Analogous and overlapping responses were grouped under the same label and, for each of these labels, a description was written based on the descriptions provided by the experts. A total of 45 labels were identified for the exploitation-focused question. To facilitate the interpretation, those labels were grouped into 5 categories: 1) knowledge management and competencies, 2) governance, 3) partnership, 4) strategic, and 5) technology. A total of 42 labels were identified for the exploration-focused question. To facilitate the interpretation, those labels were grouped into 6 categories: 1) employees, 2) technology, 3) architecture, 4) strategy, 5) collaboration, and 6) monitoring. Afterwards, a validation round was conducted to confirm the consolidated list of the identified practices in terms of meaning and representativeness. Thus, the experts were given the possibility to add, if needed, practices that they might have missed or forgot during the first round as well as to validate all the labels and definitions. The final lists are presented in Appendix 1 (for the exploitation-focused practices) and in Appendix 2 (for the exploration-focused practices).

4.3   Step #2. Narrowing and Step #3. Ranking

In the second step, narrowing, the experts were provided with the two lists and were asked to select, in each of them, the 10 most important practices, based on their respective effectiveness, without ranking them. For this steps and the following ones, the practices identified as important by each experts' group, private, public, and academic, were treated separately. For the questionnaires received, a selection rule was established following the recommendations of Delphi experts [43, 47], and applied to narrow the list of the most important practices. Thus, to be selected and incorporated in the lists used in the ranking step, a specific practice had to be identified by at least by 40% of the experts.

In the third and last step, ranking, the participants received two lists: one of the most important exploitation-focused practices and another of the exploration-focused practices as identified by the experts in step 2. In that last steps, the experts were asked to rank them in order of the level of their effectiveness (1 to N, where 1 = the most important/effective and N was the least important/effective). Appendix 3 (exploitation-focused practices) and Appendix 4 (exploration-focused practices) present the final rankings.

4.4   Consensus Creation

Afterwards, the ranking of each practices, as well as the Kendall W coefficient, were calculated [30]. The Kendall W coefficient was used to establish the level of consensus between the participating experts. It should be noted that a Kendall coefficient of W = 1.0 would mean that all the participating experts would perfectly agree with one another regarding the ranking of the practices [18]. It has been suggested that a consensus level $W < 0.3$ is considered low, between 0.3 and 0.5, it is considered moderate, between 0.5 and 0.7 it is considered good, and greater than 0.7 is considered strong [8]. Since all consensus coefficients (W) were less than 0.3 in the first round, a second ranking round was conducted. In the second round, the experts received a list presenting the organizational practices to be ranked accompanied by the average results obtained during the first ranking round. As it can be observed in Table 2, the consensus levels between the first and second rounds improved significantly.

Table 2. Kendall W coefficient level

Panels	Kendall's W	
	Round #1	Round #2
Experts from the academic sector	0.06	0.44
Experts from the public sector	0.13	0.54
Experts from the private sector	0.19	0.51

5 Coding and Results

The first step taken to analyze the Delphi data was to identify and extract all the practices related to sourcing from the two complete lists, the exploitation-focused and the exploration-focused practices. We also defined what sourcing will entail for us. In general sourcing represents the process of choosing or procuring IT resources, e.g., materials, software and services from an external or internal service provider. Sourcing may also focus on practices that could play a strategic role such as supplier management, contract development, supplier selection, contract negotiation, etc. Sourcing could also be related to the practice of identifying and recruiting talent for specific processes and/or functions. It has been found that "technology-sourcing decisions" are central to any organization and focuses on an organization's "decisions to broaden their technological portfolios through licensing agreements, a form of market contract, or acquisition" [61, p. 272].

Thus, organizations acquire technological know-how by either: (1) developing their technology independently, (2) acquiring other organizations which possess the desired ITI, or (3) entering into a technology sourcing agreement. Oshri et al. (2015) provide a more clear and encompassing definition of sourcing: "Sourcing is the act through which work is contracted or delegated to an external or internal entity that could be physically located anywhere. IT encompasses various insourcing (keeping work in-house) and outsourcing arrangements such as offshore outsourcing, captive offshoring, nearshoring and onshoring" (46, p. 7). We used this definition to assess and classify the complete list of exploitation and exploration practices identified in the Delphi study.

First, each of the practices listed in Appendices 1 and 2 were classified as sourcing-related or not. Second, we tried to characterize each of the sourcing-related practices according to the two dimensions adapted from Rosenkopf and Nerkar's (2001) framework: 1) ITI sourcing approach (insourcing vs. outsourcing), and 2) type of sourced technology (known vs. new technology). This classification was done in two steps. First, the practices listed in Appendices 1 and 2 were separately classified by two of the authors using Oshri et al.'s (2015) sourcing definition. The practices were grouped by categories (5 categories for the exploitation and 6 categories for the exploration practices).

The second step was to compare the two classifications and discuss the differences between the two classifications. The outcome was that about 10% of the identified practices were not classified the same way by the first two authors. In order to resolve the differences and reach consensus, the authors met to discuss gaps and yield a common classification. Because the classification was based on the interpretations of each practice description and that these descriptions were not always clear regarding the underlying ITI sourcing approach and/or the type of sourced technology (new vs. known), some of the sourcing practices have been classified into more than on class. Tables 3 and 4 present the sourcing practices identified during the narrowing and ranking phases and categorized by sector (public, private, and academic), while Table 5 presents the practices that can be described as instances of ambidexterity manifested as exploration to (continuously) improve exploitation (exploration-for-exploitation).

Table 3. Exploitation-focused sourcing practices ranked by the experts

# (App.1)	EXPLOITATION-Focused Sourcing Practices	Ranking		
		Public	Private	Academic
33.	Acquire reliable technological equipment	2		
44.	Virtualize servers	3	7	
42.	Ensure redundancy of critical components	5		
43.	Virtualize infrastructure	6	6	
37.	Implement a Service Oriented Architecture	7	5	
28.	Develop and monitor maintenance and replacement plans	10		
7.	Transfer and duplicate IT Skills	13	11	
26.	Develop a strategic vision of technological infrastructure		1	1
45.	Virtualize storage		3	10
27.	Develop and document the business architecture plan (including technology infrastructure)	14	4	
5.	Establish a continuous improvement program	4	12	3
9.	Adopt a modular approach			6

To identify the ambidexterity instances, for each of the exploitation-focused sourcing practice identified, we provided its 'twin' in the list of exploration-focused practices (Table 5). In order to perform the 'matching', we read and interpret each practice description identified at the end of the ranking phase (Appendices 3 and 4).

The identification numbers (#) presented in the first column are those ones identified in Appendix 1 (for Table 3) and Appendix 2 (for Table 4). Since no matching was perfect, the exploitation-exploration pairs of practices presented in Table 5 were matched only when a significant overlap was present. Six (6) public sector exploration-for-exploitation sourcing practices were identified (pairs #5/30, 27/20, 28/21, 33/9, 43/12, 44/12).

Table 4. Exploration-focused sourcing practices ranked by the experts

# (App.2)	EXPLORATION-Focused Sourcing Practices	Ranking		
		Public	Private	Academic
9.	Adopting reliable and evolutive technologies	1		
35.	Develop collaboration between IT and business units	2	3	1
30.	Implement mechanisms for continuous improvement	4	9	5
20.	Define a corporate architecture framework	5		
29.	Assess internal and external technological risks	10		
16.	Reuse of IT assets	13		9
31.	Outsource	14		15
21.	Define life cycle and design a roadmap		4	
42.	Use of external experts		8	
12.	Migrate to cloud computing	3	10	11
15.	Use of business and artificial intelligence		12	12
33.	Develop collaboration between development and operation teams			3
34.	Develop collaboration between IT and external partners			8

Table 5. Exploration-for-exploitation sourcing practices based on ranking

# (App.1)	EXPLOITATION – Focused Practices		EXPLORATION – Focused Practices	# (App.2)
5.	Establish a continuous improvement program	←→	Implement mechanisms for continuous improvement	30.
9.	Adopt a modular approach	←→	Adopt an architecture in micro-services and modules	18.
16.	Establish and monitor the evolution of the portfolio of the components of the technological infrastructure	←→	Adopt a portfolio management approach	25.
19.	Establish inter-organizational partnerships	←→	Develop collaboration between IT and external partners	34.
		←→	Develop partnership	36.
22.	Use of external consultants specialized in the management of the technological infrastructure	←→	Use of external experts	42.
23.	Use of external services (e.g. outsourcing)	←→	Outsource	31.
25.	Develop an organizational policy on "Bring your own devices (BYOD)"	←→	Adopt a "bring your own devices" approach (BYOD)	24.
27.	Develop and document the business architecture plan (including technology infrastructure)	←→	Define a corporate architecture framework	20.
28.	Develop and monitor maintenance and replacement plans	←→	Define life cycle and design a roadmap	21.
31.	Establish a service offer	←→	Expand the IT service offering	28.
33.	Acquire reliable technological equipment	←→	Adopting reliable and evolutive technologies	9.
37.	Implement a Service Oriented Architecture	←→	Adopt a service-oriented architecture (SOA)	19.
43.	Virtualize infrastructure	←→	Migrate to cloud computing	12.
44.	Virtualize servers	←→	Migrate to cloud computing	12.
45.	Virtualize storage	←→	Migrate to cloud computing	12.

6 Discussion

We conducted a Delphi study with 34 experts from three sectors: public, private, and academic, to identify various ITI sourcing practices. In order to analyze these practices, we adapted Rosenkopf and Nerkar's (2001) framework that provides important criteria when sourcing for IT and focuses on two dimensions: 1) ITI sourcing approach (insourcing vs. outsourcing); and 2) Type of sourced technology (known vs. new technology).

Focusing on sourcing exploitation practices, more than half of the practices suggested by the experts (14 out of 24) were related to both internally and externally sourcing approaches (insourced and outsourced), which indicates a certain flexibility in their application (see Appendix 1). Several practices (7 out of 24) involved a purely outsourcing approach, which shows an important interest towards this type of sourcing approach. For instance, practices such as establishing inter-organizational partnerships, or renegotiating contracts for extension have been suggested. In addition, although a majority of exploitation practices oriented towards sourcing known technologies were expected, the results show that the practices put in place target both the sourcing of known technologies and also new ones.

Similarly, several sourcing exploration practices (9 of 22) were related to both internally and externally sourcing approaches (insourced and outsourced). In total, 17 of the 22 exploration practices have an outsourcing approach, while 14 have an insourcing approach (see Appendix 2). On the other hand, exploration practices were, for the most part, oriented towards new technologies (20 out of 22) compared to known technologies (8 out of 22).

Further, out of the 46 sourcing practices (24 in exploitation – see Appendix 3; 22 in exploration – see Appendix 4), 15 (5 in the public sector), were identified as exploration-for-exploitation (instances of contextual ambidexterity) which represents an interesting and important preliminary result. These 5 practices not only allow PSOs to exploit their ITI but also explore new opportunities. For example, adopting reliable and scalable technologies is the most important practice, according to the PO experts' ranking, and this practice not only allows PSOs to better exploit their ITI, but also enable them to cope with the rapid evolution of technologies. Among the other important ambidextrous practices, we found server virtualization, classified as a major exploitation practice but also having an impact on exploration, the implementation of continuous improvement mechanisms (rank 4 of exploration practices and also having an impact on exploitation), or the definition of an architectural framework (rank 14 of exploration practices and allowing organizations to keep up-to-date their existing ITI). The identification of these 5 contextual ambidextrous practices is an important starting point for PSOs wishing to efficiently allocate resources while being limited by tight budgets.

When comparing the exploitation ITI sourcing practices (see Table 5, left column) with the exploration ITI sourcing practices (see Table 5, right column), we observe that these practices are very similar in the way they were labeled by the experts. An obvious question raises: Is this a methodological error that has generated these results or rather those pairs are complementary? There is a possibility that these outcomes are caused by the fact that the same respondents identified both the exploitation and the exploration ITI sourcing practices. However, to minimize this possible error, two distinct questions, focusing on ITI management in general and not only on sourcing practices, where asked: one related to practices to extend the sustainability of their existing IT infrastructure (exploitation), and the other one related to practices to overcome challenges and exploit the opportunities related to the constant and rapid technological evolution (exploration).

Thus, we suggest that we identified several prominent practices of cross-over, i.e. complementary practices that we label them exploration-for-exploitation practices. Overall, a complex relational pattern and virtuous cycle has emerged. We conjecture that exploitation and exploration ITI sourcing practices feed or influence each other in the sense that the decisions made in terms of exploitation ITI (known or new) sourcing will constraint or orientate the avenues to explore in terms of exploration ITI (known or new) sourcing practices [51]. The exploitation decisions put an organization, especially a PSO that has tight budgets and human resources, on a certain path and thus the exploration ITI sourcing practices are path depend of the exploitation decisions [62]. Furthermore, the decision to engage in specific exploration ITI sourcing practices will feed or influence exploitation ITI sourcing practices in the sense that these decisions will generate new possibilities, new avenues in terms of sourcing practices which may not have been considered when engaged in previous exploitation ITI sourcing practices.

Thus, we suggest that exploitation and exploration ITI sourcing practices are interrelated and could be illustrated in terms of a continuous lifecycle [26, 64]. When deploying exploitation sourcing practices, managers should think about the durability of the ITI but simultaneously be mindful of how the ITI could or will evolve in the future since exploration practices will have an important impact on exploitation practices.

7 Conclusion

With the rapid and constant technological evolution, public sector organizations face important challenges regarding the decisional process of sourcing their IT infrastructures. Because of the extant academic and practitioner literatures' lack of pertinent studies on this important topic, this study is a first step to fill this gap by conducting a systematic review of the literature and a Delphi study. We have empirically identified ambidextrous ITI sourcing practices and proposed a contextualized view on challenges and related responses in three different sectors (public, private, and academic), with a specific focus on the public sector in this article.

Our main theoretical contribution is thus a sector specific instantiation of ambidexterity, which highlights specifically the benefits of exploration-for-exploitation practices. Our findings – as expected – are highly contextualized and contingent on the organizations (PSOs). From a practitioner's point of view, the study should help IT managers better react when confronted with new emerging technologies. It should also be beneficial for practitioners to learn how their colleagues from other sectors, especially the ones from the private sector, adopt and implement various organizational actions to face technological evolution and better source and manage their ITI. The results should also help public sector officials to identify cross-sectoral differences with private sector organizations and help them eventually better collaborate with private sector partners. Facing tight budgets and relentless pressures from the public, IT managers in public institutions must bring up to date their infrastructures in order to increase the quality of their services. The experts in our study suggested that reliable technological infrastructures are the raison d'être of their PSOs trying to keep in touch with the present reality of the digital world.

The closer you look, the more the distinction between quality delivery on one hand, and continuous improvement, creativity, and innovation on the other hand, becomes blurred (cross-over between exploration and exploitation). We have identified and evidenced an instance of contextual ambidexterity: exploration-for-exploitation, in other words, continuous improvement of the IT infrastructures that has become honed as integral part of the ambidextrous practices of the IT managers involved in our Delphi study.

Some limitations of the present study need to be acknowledged. First, even if the organizational actions were identified by 40 ITI experts and that a rigorous Delphi study was used, caution must be exercised before generalizing the results and systematically apply them in any organizational context. Second, the cross-sectional nature of the data collection limits the ability to explore how organizational actions might have interacted with one another throughout time.

We hope that the results of this study will guide and assist practitioners in their decision making as well as researchers in their investigation of issues related to the management of technological infrastructures. In this sense, we propose several avenues for future research. First, it would be noteworthy to assess the impact of sourcing practices identified in this study on organizational performance. Another research avenue would be to evaluate to what extent each of the identified sourcing practices would be easy or not to implement. Finally, it would also be interesting to analyze to what extent the proposed sourcing practices would increase the capacity and flexibility of the IT infrastructures [7, 66].

Acknowledgments. This research project was funded by and realized with the collaboration of the Center for Interuniversity Research and Analysis of Organizations - CIRANO (https://cirano. qc.ca/en).

Appendix #1 - Complete List of the EXPLOITATION-Focused Practices Identified in the Delphi Study

#	Labels	Descriptions	Nature of practices Sourcing-related Related	Not-rel.	Sourcing Approach Insourcing	Outsourcing	Type of Technology Known	New
	EXPLOITATION – Category #1 KNOWLEDGE MANAGEMENT and COMPETENCIES							
1.	**Knowledge of business needs**	Ensure that business units are able to evaluate, formulate and communicate their needs and that IT employees understand these business needs, that their knowledge is up to date, so that technology infrastructure is aligned with business needs.		X				
2.	**Foster collaboration between development teams and business units (Agile and DevOps)**	Deploying technology infrastructure development and delivery approaches, such as Agile or DevOps, which foster close collaboration between development teams and business units.		X				
3.	**Involvement in communities of practice**	Engage in communities of practice to share and collect experience and knowledge of management of technology infrastructure.		X				
4.	**Maintain IT skills**	Support IT employees in updating their IT skills and knowledge by providing in-house training and/or by financing specialized external training, conferences, etc. These competencies must be aligned with organizational needs and the evolution of IT in the marketplace.		X				
5.	**Establish a continuous improvement program**	Deploy a continuous improvement program of the technological infrastructure that involves both IT employees as well as internal and external users.	X		X		X	X
6.	**Establish a knowledge management system**	The implementation of a knowledge management system increases the efficiency and level of expertise of the resources responsible for ensuring the sustainability of the IT infrastructure.		X				
7.	**Transfer and duplicate IT Skills**	Ensure constant and ongoing transfer of IT skills between internal employees and, where possible, between external resources (e.g. consultants) and internal employees. In the case of critical IT skills, ensure a duplication of these IT skills.	X		X	X	X	X
8.	**Develop technological watch**	Put in place practices and a culture that fosters the monitoring of technological developments, to learn from other organizations, to discover new tools or approaches, etc.		X				
	EXPLOITATION – Category #2– GOVERNANCE		Related	Not-rel.	Insourcing	Outsourcing	Known	New
9.	**Adopt a modular approach**	Adopt a modular approach by establishing a strong technological infrastructure foundation that can be developed with additional modules.	X		X	X	X	X
10.	**Centralize IT and data center management**	Centralize the management of IT and data centers to reduce the size, overall cost, complexity and needs of technological infrastructure.		X				
11.	**Consolidate and standardize the**	Consolidate and standardize the development and support practices, e.g. guidelines, architecture standards,		X				

#	Practice	Description	Related	Not-rel.	Insourcing	Outsourcing	Known	New
	development and support practices	technologies, programming languages, approaches, methods, tools, etc., to enable reuse, valorization and optimization of the existing technological infrastructure.						
12.	Establish a technological infrastructure governance framework	Establish a technological infrastructure governance framework, e.g., IT orientations, values, guidelines, objectives, RACI matrix, decision-making processes, etc., for all employees involved in the development, maintenance, and evolution of the technological infrastructure.		X				
13.	Establish a data governance framework and IT utilization guidelines	Establish a data governance framework that encompasses the processes, policies, practices, and structures needed to orchestrate the people, processes, and use of technologies within an organization and optimize the collection, storage, use and dissemination of IT and data.		X				
14.	Establish a licensing and purchase of hardware / software policy	Setting objectives, guidelines, guidelines, a RACI matrix, etc. to oversee the purchase and renewal of licenses, hardware and software.	X		X	X	X	X
15.	Establish standards and performance norms for the technological infrastructure	Define technical standards and performance norms in terms of speed, volume, safety, risks, etc. to ensure that the technological infrastructure's performance and capacity planning are optimally managed.		X				
16.	Establish and monitor the evolution of the portfolio of the components of the technological infrastructure	Establish a portfolio of technology infrastructure components and track their evolution including internal developments, external vendors, as well as hardware, software.	X		X	X	X	
17.	Assess and monitor the capabilities of the technological infrastructure components	Establishment of a governance structure, e.g. processes and committees, to evaluate, monitor, and control of the capacity of the technological infrastructure components.		X				
18.	Promote the use of standardized technologies	Promote the use of standardized technologies (avoid over-tailoring) that are compatible and mastered by the organization and whose reliability and performance have been demonstrated.		X				
	EXPLOITATION – Category #3 – PARTNERSHIP		Related	Not-rel.	Insourcing	Outsourcing	Known	New
19.	Establish inter-organizational partnerships	Engage in partnerships with external organizations facing similar technological infrastructure challenges / issues in order to share resources, expertise, knowledge, costs, and risks related to the development and delivery of technology solutions	X			X	X	X
20.	Renegotiate contracts for extensions	Renegotiate with external service providers to extend SLA (service level agreement) beyond the scheduled end date.	X			X	X	X
21.	Do business with local service providers	Sign service agreements with local providers because proximity can facilitate communication and collaboration.	X			X	X	X
22.	Use of external consultants specialized in the management of the technological infrastructure	Use external consulting services specializing in the management of technology infrastructure, e.g. development, maintenance and evolution.	X			X	X	X

			Related	Not-rel.	Insourcing	Outsourcing	Known	New
23.	Use of external services (e.g. outsourcing)	Use external services by transferring the support, maintenance, evolution and/or development of some or all the technological infrastructure components to a service provider with performance obligations stipulated in a SLA.	X			X	X	X
24.	Establish a contract management structure and policy	Establishment of a specialized team and a policy (e.g. orientation, guidelines, objectives, strategy) for bid management and contract management, e.g., negotiation, drafting, follow-up, etc.	X		X	X	X	X
	EXPLOITATION – Category #4 – STRATEGY		Related	Not-rel.	Insourcing	Outsourcing	Known	New
25.	Develop an organizational policy on "Bring your own devices" (BYOD)	Develop a policy and provide an environment, e.g. networking, applications, support, security, web services, etc., to support the "Bring your own device" approach.	X		X	X	X	X
26.	Develop a strategic vision of technological infrastructure	Develop a vision of the technological infrastructure and the IT function, with all stakeholders of the organization to meet current needs, anticipate future needs and prioritize investments. It is important to establish an IT strategic plan, e.g., objectives, roles, impacts, risks, etc., aligned with the organization's strategic objectives to prioritize IT investments and the delivery of technological infrastructure components.	X		X	X	X	X
27.	Develop and document the business architecture plan (including technology infrastructure)	Develop and document a business architecture plan, including the technological infrastructure components, to meet future needs and to ensure that new and / or outsourced components are consistent and fit into the business architecture plan.	X		X	X	X	X
28.	Develop and monitor maintenance and replacement plans	Establish and monitor the maintenance and replacement plan for the technological infrastructure components in order to anticipate changes, budget these changes, spread the replacement of certain components, avoid breakage or obsolescence, minimize impacts on users, etc.	X		X	X	X	X
29.	Use reliable software	Ensure that the software developed (or configured) is as reliable as possible as soon as it goes into production, making sure that it has been rigorously tested and passed through a business approval cycle		X				
30.	Establishing an IT Strategic Plan	Establish an IT strategic plan, e.g. objectives, roles, impacts, risks, etc., aligned with the organization's strategic objectives to prioritize IT investments and the delivery of technological infrastructure components	X		X	X	X	X
31.	Establish a service offer	Establish and IT services offer that meets the needs of the organization's stakeholders in order to make the technological infrastructure in place profitable and help the organization to operate, evolve, and transform itself.	X		X	X	X	
32.	Evaluate the added value of the components of the tech. infra.	Evaluate and demonstrate the added value of the different components of the technological infrastructure for the organization and its stakeholders		X				
33.	Acquire reliable technological equipment	Acquire "quality" technological hardware and equipment that can be more expensive to purchase in the short term, but more reliable and durable in the long term.	X			X		X

		Related	Not-rel.	Insourcing	Outsourcing	Known	New
34.	**Set up shared services** — Set up shared services to share costs, centralize tenders, consolidate acquisitions and standardize technology infrastructure.	X		X		X	X
35.	**Optimize and reuse technological components** — Optimize and reuse technology components from some business units in other units with smaller needs or in development environments (R&D).		X				
	EXPLOITATION – Category #5 – TECHNOLOGY						
36.	**Analyze the operating data of the tech. infra. using artificial and business intelligence tools** — Use business intelligence tools such as machine learning, data analysis, etc. to better understand, for example, energy consumption curves, break patterns, etc. and support the maintenance and evolution of the tech. infra.		X				
37.	**Implement a Service Oriented Architecture** — Use web services, e.g., software (SaaS), infrastructure (IaaS) and/or platform (PaaS), through public, private and / or hybrid clouds.	X		X	X		X
38.	**Automate and digitize monitoring and maintenance tasks** — Automate and digitize certain technology infrastructure monitoring and maintenance activities, such as automatic computer shutdown or automatic updates, to reduce manual tasks, improve identification and problem solving, optimizing the use of resources, etc.		X				
39.	**Create and publish API** — Create and publish APIs (application programming interface) to facilitate the exchange of information between different software		X				
40.	**Establish a policy for energy efficiency of the technological infrastructure** — Establish a policy, e.g., goals, guidelines, directions, levels, etc., to ensure that new technology devices deployed during upgrades or replacements meet pre-established energy efficiency criteria and minimize environmental impacts.		X				
41.	**Use of Open Source** — Use open source software to operate and evolve the technology infrastructure and to gain the benefits of flexibility (avoid the "lock-in" of proprietary software vendors) on the evolution or potential removal of software		X				
42.	**Ensure redundancy of critical components** — Ensure redundancy of the technology infrastructure's critical components, e.g. server, data, expertise, etc. in order to protect key organizational operations and data.	X			X	X	
43.	**Virtualize infrastructure** — Virtualize all components of the technological infrastructure and network to separate the hardware and software layers to extend the life of physical equipment and simplify the physical infrastructure.	X		X	X		X
44.	**Virtualize servers** — Virtualizing some applications and workstations (VDI - Virtual Desktop Infrastructure) on servers will significantly reduce the cost of power, heating / cooling, human resources, nr. of workstations, data center, etc.	X		X	X		X
45.	**Virtualize storage** — Virtualizing storage technologies will provide longer amortization for older and less efficient storage technologies.	X		X	X		X

Appendix #2 – Complete List of the EXPLORATION-Focused Practices Identified in the Delphi Study

#	Labels	Descriptions	Nature of practices Sourcing-related		Sourcing Approach		Type of Technology	
			Related	Not-rel.	Insourcing	Outsourcing	Known	New
		EXPLORATION – Category #1 – EMPLOYEES						
1.	Development of transversal skills	Develop IT employee cross-functional skills in relation with the organization's strategy. At the technological level, it involves hiring or training employees on different technology platforms and programming languages to bridge old with new technological infrastructures, identify areas for improvement, facilitate integration of technological changes, etc. There is also a need to develop a good understanding of the issues related to organization's strategy such as the evolution of the IT infrastructure.		X				
2.	Implication of IT experts	Involve internal technology expertise in the identification of and decisional process related to the evolution of technological infrastructures in order to better position the organization, to identify solutions in line with the existing IT, to prepare employees for the change (minimize resistance), etc.		X				
3.	Establishment of working conditions favoring the retention of employees	Create working conditions that encourage retention, collaboration and knowledge sharing between employees in order to cope with technological developments, such as appointing a "Chief happiness officer", promote the reconciliation work-private life, etc. It is also important to assess and manage the risks related to employee frustration that that stem from factors such as changing assignments, perceived cumbersome bureaucracy, etc.		X				
4.	Plan for continuous development skills	Plan the development of employees' IT skills on an ongoing basis by offering coaching, involving them in internal training, sending them to seminars, etc. to ensure up-to-date skills, cope with the emergency of new technologies and enable technological change readiness.		X				
5.	Implement an innovation policy and internal contests	Developing incentive mechanisms that encourage internal innovation e.g., innovation contests on a regular basis to stimulate thinking, sharing ideas, testing new technologies and finding solutions to overcome organizational challenges associated with technological evolution.		X				
6.	Nurture an open mindset culture	Promote an organizational culture of open mindset with regard to the management of technology infrastructure and IT in general in the organization.		X				
7.	Use of internship and hire young graduates	Use interns to introduce new ideas, new knowledge, new work practices, new technologies, etc.		X				
8.	Using crowd creativity (Crowdsourcing)	Use the creativity of external resources to learn about new trends, concepts, and opportunities related to technological developments.		X				

			Related	Not-rel.	Insourcing	Outsourcing	Known	New
EXPLORATION – Category #2 – TECHNOLOGY								
9.	Adopting reliable and evolutive technologies	Adopt components in the technology infrastructure that are "flexible" and scalable, for example, components that can be updated, enhanced and / or extended; promote open standards and cloud computing; continuously test and adopt new components, etc.	X					X
10.	Automate technological services in a standardized way	Automate technological services using market standards (e.g., SDDC, Software-defined data center) to separate organizational processes from technological infrastructures and thus promote the evolution of infrastructure by minimizing the impacts on the organizational processes.		X				
11.	Create spaces of creativity	Create spaces for employees to be creative, for example, "sandboxes" to develop and test prototypes, to "play" with new technologies, to explore, and so on.		X				
12.	Migrate to cloud computing	Migrate "on premise" systems to cloud computing platforms in order to have greater flexibility, to respond to unanticipated high demands, to ease the scalability of systems, avoid in-house the management of systems development.	X		X	X		X
13.	Openness and transparency	Promote the use of open standards, open API and open data to capitalize on IT communities to achieve systems interoperability and better cope with technological evolution.	X	X				
14.	Use of standards	Promote the use of standards when acquiring, developing and maintaining technological infrastructures in order to standardize practices, facilitate the interoperability of systems and ease the integration of emerging technologies.		X				
15.	Use of business and artificial intelligence	Use artificial intelligence tools, such as machine learning, to exploit the data generated by technological infrastructure (e.g. energy consumption, speed, number of errors, etc.) and thus be better prepared to cope with technological change.	X		X	X		X
16.	Reuse of IT assets	Reuse and adapt, where possible, existing technological infrastructure components when implementing technological innovations to optimize the use of existing technological resources.	X		X		X	
17.	Use of performance indicators to evaluate infrastructure performance	Develop and use indicators to assess the performance of the components of the technology infrastructure, e.g., costs, volume, downtime, maintenance, etc. and thus identify, the components to be replaced.		X				
EXPLORATION – Category #3 – ARCHITECTURE			Related	Not-rel.	Insourcing	Outsourcing	Known	New
18.	Adopt an architecture in micro-services and modules	Adopt a technological architecture of micro-services and modules in order to promote a flow between applications and hardware, to reuse micro-services, to facilitate the extension, the elasticity and the evolution of the technological infrastructure.	X		X	X		X
19.	Adopt a service-oriented architecture (SOA)	Adopt a service-oriented architecture to enable a more flexible and easier way to evolve technology infrastructure.	X		X	X		X
20.	Define a corporate architecture	Define an enterprise architecture framework and evaluate all	X		X	X		X

#	Name	Description	Related	Not-rel.	Insourcing	Outsourcing	Known	New
	framework	elements of this architecture, e.g. processes, data, technologies, applications, services, standards, structures, etc. to meet organization's business objectives, guide transformation, and sustainably manage technological changes and infrastructure.						
21.	Define life cycle and design a roadmap	Define the life cycle of the components of the technological infrastructure and design a road map of future components replacement to anticipate technological developments and investments, optimize technological changes, adapt these technological evolutions to the organizational environment and avoid obsolescence.	X		X	X		X
22.	Establish architectural teams	Creation of a "business architecture" team responsible for establishing the enterprise architecture framework, (e.g. determining standards and guidelines) and an "operating architecture" team responsible for determining - based on the 'AE' - the products / services / methods to put in place a roadmap based on the various major areas of the technological infrastructure.		X				
23.	Create a committee for IT monitoring and prioritization	Creating a committee to identify and monitor technology needs, technological change and technology advancement to align with the organization's enterprise architecture framework and to raise organization's awareness of technological infrastructure's roles.		X				
	EXPLORATION – Category #4 - STRATEGY		**Related**	**Not-rel.**	**Insourcing**	**Outsourcing**	**Known**	**New**
24.	Adopt a "bring your own devices" approach (BYOD)	Adopt a "bring your own devices" approach, while setting rules of supervision, to transfer to employees the responsibility of anticipating, planning and managing the evolution of technologies according to their needs.	X		X	X	X	X
25.	Adopt a portfolio management approach	Adopt a portfolio management of all technology projects to be able to identify complementarity and balance between technology infrastructure projects and digital transformation projects.	X		X	X	X	X
26.	Adopt Agile methodologies	Adopt agile and iterative development methods, e.g. Scrum, DevOps, etc., to have the ability to improve continuously, to deliver more frequently and quickly (to improve time-to-market ratio), to adapt quickly to changes, to involve business units, to have a better understanding of business needs and to constantly readjust to technological developments.		X				
27.	Development of business cases	Develop business cases to demonstrate importance and relevance (e.g. cost savings, productivity improvement, etc.) to invest in new infrastructures technologies as well as the risks and impacts on the organization of not investing in these technologies	X		X	X	X	X
28.	Expand the IT service offering	Expand the IT service offerings and the technology infrastructure required to provide these services by merging or acquiring the technology services of external organizations	X			X	X	X

#	Item	Description	Related	Not-rel.	Insourcing	Outsourcing	Known	New
29.	Assess internal and external technological risks	Evaluate the probability of technology risks (internal and external) and their potential impacts, to identify Infrastructure components to be updated, extended or replaced, to mitigate those risks.	X		X	X	X	X
30.	Implement mechanisms for continuous improvement	Establish mechanisms for continuous improvement of the technological infrastructure in order to improve, simplify, and anticipate technological developments, e.g., conducting recurrent technological infrastructure evaluation by having an interdisciplinary monitoring committee.	X		X	X	X	
31.	Outsource	Engaging in outsourcing practices to take advantage of suppliers' expertise, innovation, and IT infrastructure.	X			X	X	X
	EXPLORATION – Category #5 – COLLABORATION		Related	Not-rel.	Insourcing	Outsourcing	Known	New
32.	Collaborate with specialized firms and research center	Developing collaborations with research centers (university centers or research groups) as well as technology firms, e.g. Forrester, Gartner, etc. to share knowledge / experience and maintain an up-to-date look at technology trends and developments.	X		X	X		X
33.	Develop collaboration between development and operation teams	Facilitate the collaboration between the technological and application infrastructure development teams and the operation / maintenance teams in order to facilitate knowledge sharing, and the identification of trends, needs, ideas, etc. in connection with the evolution of technological infrastructure.	X		X			X
34.	Develop collaboration between IT and external partners	Collaborate regularly with external partners, e.g. clients and suppliers, to identify their needs, their expectations, their vision (including the technological aspect); co-develop technological solutions; implement a common technology watch, etc.	X			X		X
35.	Develop collaboration between IT and business units	Collaborate regularly with users, business units and internal decision-makers to identify their needs, develop a common strategy, maintain appropriate alignment of evolution efforts, develop and test new functions, share knowledge.	X		X			X
36.	Develop partnership	Develop partnership with other organizations to co-develop technology solutions, share employees, etc. (e.g., pool IT services, share technology infrastructures).	X			X		X
37.	Involvement in communities of practice	Engage in communities of practices to share knowledge, lessons learned, ideas, issues, challenges, practices, trends, etc. related to the evolution of technological infrastructures.	X			X		X
	EXPLORATION – Category #6 – MONITORING		Related	Not-rel.	Insourcing	Outsourcing	Known	New
38.	Consult reports and professional studies	Continuously consult studies and reports published by technology firms, for example, Gartner, McKinsey, etc., to track technological developments, predict trends, and identify approaches / strategies to prepare for them.		X				
39.	Create an organizational culture and implement a structure to foster technology watch	Establish a technology watch culture and structure to continually monitor technological developments; changing practices, trends, ways of doing things, assessing their relevance to the organization; to anticipate and prepare for technological challenges, etc.		X				

40.	Establish a center of excellence	Set up a center of excellence to share knowledge, projects, expertise, anticipate changes and prepare for challenges related to the evolution of technological infrastructure		X		
41.	Participation to practitioner conferences	Encourage employees' participation to practitioner conferences to have access to new trends and ideas, share experiences and best practices, etc.		X		
42.	Use of external experts	Use external experts / consultants to gain access to new knowledge, assist the organization in planning the evolution of the technology infrastructure, have expert assistance to make specific IT choices, facilitate digital transformations, have an external evaluation of the internal work practices.	X		X	X

Appendix #3 – EXPLOITATION-Focused Sourcing Practices - Final Ranking

#	EXPLOITATION-focused practices	Ranking		
		Public	Private	Academic
33.	Acquire reliable technological equipment	2		
44.	Virtualize servers	3	7	
42.	Ensure redundancy of critical components	5		
43.	Virtualize infrastructure	6	6	
37.	Implement a Service Oriented Architecture	7	5	
28.	Develop and monitor maintenance and replacement plans	10		
7.	Transfer and duplicate IT Skills	13	11	
26.	Develop a strategic vision of technological infrastructure		1	1
45.	Virtualize storage		3	10
27.	Develop and document the business architecture plan (including technology infrastructure)	14	4	
5.	Establish a continuous improvement program	4	12	3
9.	Adopt a modular approach			6
14.	Establish a licensing and purchase of hardware/software policy			
16.	Establish and monitor the evolution of the portfolio of the components of the technological infrastructure			
19.	Establish inter-organizational partnerships			
20.	Renegotiate contracts for extensions			
21.	Do business with local service providers			
22.	Use of external consultants specialized in the management of the technological infrastructure			
23.	Use of external services (e.g. outsourcing)			
24.	Establish a contract management structure and policy			
25.	Develop an organizational policy on "Bring your own devices (BYOD)"			
30.	Establishing an IT Strategic Plan			
31.	Establish a service offer			
34.	Set up shared services			

Appendix #4 – EXPLORATION-Focused Sourcing Practices - Final Ranking

#	EXPLORATION-focused practices	Ranking		
		Public	Private	Academic
9.	Adopting reliable and evolutive technologies	1		
35.	Develop collaboration between IT and business units	2	3	1
30.	Implement mechanisms for continuous improvement	4	9	5
20.	Define a corporate architecture framework	5		
29.	Assess internal and external technological risks	10		
16.	Reuse of IT assets	13		9
31.	Outsource	14		15
21.	Define life cycle and design a roadmap		4	
42.	Use of external experts		8	
12.	Migrate to cloud computing	3	10	11
15.	Use of business and artificial intelligence		12	12
33.	Develop collaboration between development and operation teams			3
34.	Develop collaboration between IT and external partners			8
18.	Adopt an architecture in micro-services and modules			
19.	Adopt a service-oriented architecture (SOA)			
24.	Adopt a "bring your own device" approach (BYOD)			
25.	Adopt a portfolio management approach			
36.	Develop partnership			
37.	Involvement in communities of practice			
27.	Development of business cases			
28.	Expand the IT service offering			
32.	Collaborate with specialized firms and research center			

Appendix #5–Ambidextrous Sourcing Practices – Complete List

ID	EXPLOITATION – Focused Practices	A-Dex*	EXPLORATION – Focused Practices	ID
5	Establish a continuous improvement program	←→	Implement mechanisms for continuous improvement	30
7	Transfer and duplicate IT Skills			
9	Adopt a modular approach	←→	Adopt an architecture in micro-services and modules	18
14	Establish a licensing and purchase of hardware/software policy			
16	Establish and monitor the evolution of the portfolio of the components of the ITI	←→	Adopt a portfolio management approach	25
19	Establish inter-organizational partnerships	←→	Develop partnership	36
20	Renegotiate contracts for extensions			
21	Do business with local service providers			
22	Use of external consultants specialized in the management of the ITI	←→	Use of external experts	42
23	Use of external services (e.g. outsourcing)	←→	Outsource	31
24	Establish a contract management structure and policy			
25	Develop an organizational policy on "Bring your own devices (BYOD)"	←→	Adopt a "bring your own devices" approach (BYOD)	24
26	Develop a strategic vision of technological infrastructure			
27	Develop and document the business architecture plan (including technology infrastructure)	←→	Define a corporate architecture framework	20
28	Develop and monitor maintenance and replacement plans	←→	Define life cycle and design a roadmap	21
30	Establishing an IT Strategic Plan			
31	Establish a service offer	←→	Expand the IT service offering	28
33	Acquire reliable technological equipment	←→	Adopting reliable and evolutive technologies	9
34	Set up shared services			

(*continued*)

(continued)

ID	EXPLOITATION – Focused Practices	A-Dex*	EXPLORATION – Focused Practices	ID
37	Implement a Service Oriented Architecture	←→	Adopt a service-oriented architecture (SOA)	19
42	Ensure redundancy of critical components			
43	Virtualize infrastructure	←→	Migrate to cloud computing	12
44	Virtualize servers	←→	Migrate to cloud computing	12
45	Virtualize storage	←→	Migrate to cloud computing	12
			Use of business and artificial intelligence	15
			Reuse of IT assets	16
			Development of business cases	27
			Assess internal and external technological risks	29
			Collaborate with specialized firms and research center	32
			Develop collaboration between development and operation teams	33
			Develop collaboration between IT and business units	35
			Involvement in communities of practice	37

*A-Dex = Ambidextrous relationship between exploitation-focused and exploration-focused sourcing practices

References

1. Adler, P.S., Goldoftas, B., Levine, D.I.: Flexibility versus efficiency? A case study of model changeovers in the Toyota production system. Organ. Sci. **10**(1), 43–68 (1999)
2. Andriopoulos, C., Lewis, M.W.: Exploitation-exploration tensions and organizational ambidexterity: managing paradoxes of innovation. Organ. Sci. **20**(4), 696–717 (2009)
3. Alves, M., Galina, S., Dobelin, S.: Literature on organizational innovation: past and future. Innov. Manag. Rev. **15**(1), 2–19 (2018)
4. Armstrong, H.: Machines that learn in the wild: Machine learning capabilities, limitations and implications. NESTA, London (2015). https://media.nesta.org.uk/documents/machines_that_learn_in_the_wild.pdf. Accessed 07 Jan 2020
5. Birkinshaw, J., Gibson, C.B.: Building an ambidextrous organization. MIT Sloan Manag. Rev. 47–55 Summer 2004
6. Burnes, B., Anastasiadis, A.: Outsourcing: a public-private sector comparison. Supply Chain Manag. Int. J. **8**(4), 355–366 (2003)

7. Bush, A.A., Tiwana, A., Rai, A.: Complementarities between product design modularity and IT infrastructure flexibility in IT-enabled supply chains. IEEE Trans. Eng. Manag. **57**(2), 240–254 (2010)
8. Cafiso, S., Di Graziano, A., Pappalardo, G.: Using the delphi method to evaluate opinions of public transport managers on bus safety. Saf. Sci. **57**, 254–263 (2013)
9. Campbell, J., McDonald, C., Sethibe, T.: Public and private sector IT governance: identifying contextual differences. Australas. J. Inf. Syst. **16**(2), 5–18 (2010)
10. Cordella, A., Iannacci, F.: Information systems in the public sector: the e-Government enactment framework. J. Strateg. Inf. Syst. **19**(1), 52–66 (2010)
11. Davidson, S., De Filippi, P., Potts, J.: Disrupting governance: The new institutional economics of distributed ledger technology (2016). SSRN 2811995
12. Duhamel, F., Gutierrez-Martinez, I., Picazo-Vela, S., Luna-Reyes, L.: IT outsourcing in the public sector: a conceptual model. Transforming Gov. People Process Policy **8**(1), 8–27 (2014)
13. Dunleavy, P.: Public sector productivity. OECD J. Budgeting **17**(1), 1–28 (2017)
14. Edberg, D., Ivanova, P., Kuechler, W.: Methodology mashups: an exploration of processes used to maintain software. J. Manag. Inf. Syst. **28**(4), 271–304 (2012)
15. Edler, J., Georghiou, L.: Public procurement and innovation - resurrecting the demand side. Res. Policy **36**(7), 949–963 (2007)
16. Edler, J., Yeow, J.: Connecting demand and supply: the role of intermediation in public procurement of innovation. Res. Policy **45**(2), 414–426 (2016)
17. Edquist, C., Hommen, L.: Public technology procurement and innovation theory. In: Edquist, C., Hommen, L., Tsipouri, L. (eds.) Public Technology Procurement and Innovation. Economics of Science, Technology and Innovation, vol. 16, pp. 5–70. Springer, Boston (2000). https://doi.org/10.1007/978-1-4615-4611-5_2
18. El-Gazzar, R., Hustad, E., Olsen, D.H.: Understanding cloud computing adoption issues: a delphi study approach. J. Syst. Softw. **118**, 64–84 (2016)
19. Ferreira, M.J., Moreira, F., Seruca, I.: Enterprise 4.0: the next evolution of business? In: New Perspectives on Information Systems Modeling and Design, pp. 98–121. IGI Global (2019)
20. Ganapati, S., Reddick, C.G.: Prospects and challenges of sharing economy for the public sector. Gov. Inf. Q. **35**(1), 77–87 (2018)
21. Gantman, S.: IT outsourcing in the public sector: a literature analysis. J. Global Inf. Technol. Manag. **14**(2), 48–83 (2011)
22. Gil-Garcia, J.R., Helbig, N., Ojo, A.: Being smart: emerging technologies and innovation in the public sector. Gov. Inf. Q. **31**, I1–I8 (2014)
23. Government Office for Science: Distributed Ledger Technology: beyond block chain: A report by the UK Government Chief Scientific Adviser, Government Office for Science, London (2016). www.gov.uk/government/uploads/system/uploads/attachment_data/file/492972/gs-16-1-distributed-ledger-technology.pdf. Accessed 07 Jan 2020
24. Gibson, C.B., Birkinshaw, J.: The antecedents, consequences, and mediating role of organizational ambidexterity. Acad. Manag. J. **47**(2), 209–226 (2004)
25. Iansiti, M., Lakhani, K.R.: The truth about blockchain. Harvard Bus. Rev. **95**(1), 118–127 (2017)
26. Howard-Grenville, J.A., Rerup, C.: Handbook of Process Organizational Studies. Sage, Thousand Oaks (2017)
27. Ho, A.T.K.: From performance budgeting to performance budget management: theory and practice. Public Adm. Rev. **78**(5), 748–758 (2018)
28. Kappelman, L., McLean, E., Luftman, J., Johnson, V.: Key issues of IT organizations and their leadership: the 2013 SIM IT trends study. MIS Q. Exec. **12**(4), 227–240 (2013)
29. Kauppila, O.-P.: Creating ambidexterity by integrating and balancing structurally separate interorganizational partnerships. Strateg. Organ. **8**(4), 283–312 (2010)

30. Kendall, M., Gibbons, J.: Rank Correlation Methods (Charles Griffin Book Series). Oxford University Press, Oxford (1990)
31. Kyriakopoulos, K., Moorman, C.: Tradeoffs in marketing exploitation and exploration strategies: the overlooked role of market orientation. Int. J. Res. Mark. **21**(3), 219–240 (2004)
32. Kuiper, E., Van Dam, F., Reiter, A., Janssen, M.: Factors influencing the adoption of and business case for Cloud computing in the public sector. In: eChallenges e-2014 Conference Proceedings, pp. 1–10. IEEE (2014)
33. Laita, A., Belaissaoui, M.: Information technology governance in public sector organizations. In: Rocha, Á., Serrhini, M., Felgueiras, C. (eds.) Europe and MENA Cooperation Advances in Information and Communication Technologies. AISC, vol. 520, pp. 331–340. Springer, Cham (2017). https://doi.org/10.1007/978-3-319-46568-5_34
34. Lau, E., Lonti, Z., Schultz, R.: Challenges in the measurement of public sector productivity in OECD countries. Int. Prod. Monitor **32**, 180–195 (2017)
35. Lee, G., Kwak, Y.H.: An open government maturity model for social media-based public engagement. Gov. Inf. Q. **29**(4), 492–503 (2012)
36. Lember, V., Kattel, R., Tonurist, P.: Technological capacity in the public sector: the case of Estonia. Int. Rev. Admin. Sci. **84**(2), 214–230 (2018)
37. Lourenço, R.P.: An analysis of open government portals: a perspective of transparency for accountability. Gov. Inf. Q. **32**(3), 323–332 (2015)
38. Lubatkin, M.H., Simsek, Z., Ling, Y., Veiga, J.F.: Ambidexterity and performance in small-to medium-sized firms: the pivotal role of top management team behavioral integration. J. Manag. **32**(5), 646–672 (2006)
39. March, J.G.: Exploration and exploitation in organizational learning. Organ. Sci. **2**(1), 71–87 (1991)
40. Moe, C.E., Päivärinta, T.: Challenges in information systems procurement in the public sector. Electron. J. e-Gov. **11**(1), 307–322 (2013)
41. Moe, C.E.: Research on public procurement of information systems: the need for a process approach. Commun. Assoc. Inf. Syst. **34**, 1335–1391 (2014). Article no. 78
42. Moe, C.E., Newman, M., Kyaw Sein, M.: The public procurement of information systems: dialectics in requirements specification. Eur. J. Inf. Syst. **26**(2), 143–163 (2017). https://doi.org/10.1057/s41303-017-0035-4
43. Okoli, C., Pawlowski, S.D.: The Delphi method as a research tool: an example, design considerations and applications. Inf. Manag. **42**(1), 15–29 (2004)
44. O'Reilly, C.A., Tushman, M.L.: Organizational ambidexterity: past, present, and future. Acad. Manag. Perspect. **27**(4), 324–338 (2013)
45. Ølnes, S., Ubacht, J., Janssen, M.: Blockchain in government: benefits and implications of distributed ledger technology for information sharing. Gov. Inf. Q. **34**, 355–364 (2017)
46. Oshri, I., Kotlarsky, J., Willcocks, L.P. (eds.): The Handbook of Global Outsourcing and Offshoring. Palgrave Macmillan UK, London (2015). https://doi.org/10.1007/978-1-137-437 44-0_9
47. Paré, G., Cameron, A.-F., Poba-Nzaou, P., Templier, M.: A systematic assessment of rigor in information systems ranking-type Delphi studies. Inf. Manag. **50**(5), 207–220 (2013)
48. Paré, G., Trudel, M.C., Jaana, M., Kitsiou, S.: Synthesizing information systems knowledge: a typology of literature reviews. Inf. Manag. **52**(2), 183–199 (2015)
49. PricewaterhouseCoopers: The sharing economy: Consumer intelligence series (2015). https://www.pwc.com/us/en/technology/publications/assets/pwc-consumer-intelligence-series-the-sharing-economy.pdf. Accessed 07 Jan 2020
50. Prieto, I., Santana, P.: Building ambidexterity: the role of human resource practices in the performance of firms from Spain. Hum. Resour. Manag. **51**, 189–212 (2012)
51. Rerup, C., Feldman, M.S.: Routines as a source of change in organizational schemata: the role of trial-and-error learning. Acad. Manag. J. **54**(3), 577–610 (2011)

52. Rosenkopf, L., Nerkar, A.: Beyond local search: boundary-spanning, exploration, and impact in the optical disk industry. Strateg. Manag. J. **22**(4), 287–306 (2001)
53. Rosacker, K.M., Rosacker, R.E.: Information technology project management within public sector organizations. J. Enterp. Inf. Manag. **23**(5), 587–594 (2010)
54. Rothaermel, F.T., Alexandre, M.T.: Ambidexterity in technology sourcing: the moderating role of absorptive capacity. Organ. Sci. **20**(4), 759–780 (2009)
55. Rowe, G., Wright, G.: The Delphi technique as a forecasting tool: issues and analysis. Int. J. Forecast. **15**(4), 353–375 (1999)
56. Sallehudin, H., Razak, R., Ismail, M.: Factors influencing cloud computing adoption in the public sector: an empirical analysis. J. Entrepreneurship Bus. **3**(1), 30–45 (2015)
57. Schmidt, R.C.: Managing Delphi surveys using nonparametric statistical techniques. Decis. Sci. **28**(3), 763–774 (1997)
58. Schneider, S., Sunyaev, A.: Determinant factors of cloud-sourcing decisions: reflecting on the IT outsourcing literature in the era of cloud computing. J. Inf. Technol. **31**(1), 1–31 (2016)
59. Simsek, Z., Heavey, C., Veiga, J.F., Souder, D.: A typology for aligning organizational ambidexterity's conceptualizations, antecedents, and outcomes. J. Manage. Stud. **46**(5), 864–894 (2009)
60. Sirkemaa, S.: IT infrastructure management and standards. In: Proceedings of the International Conference on Information Technology: Coding and Computing (ITCC 2002) (2002)
61. Steensma, H.K., Corley, K.G.: Organizational context as a moderator of theories on firm boundaries for technology sourcing. Acad. Manag. J. **44**(2), 271–291 (2001)
62. Sydow, J., Schreyögg, G., Koch, J.: Organizational path dependence: opening the black box. Acad. Manag. Rev. **34**(4), 689–709 (2009)
63. Tushman, M.L., O'Reilly, C.A.: Ambidextrous organizations: managing evolutionary and revolutionary change. Calif. Manag. Rev. **38**(4), 8–29 (1996)
64. Van de Ven, A.H., Poole, M.S.: Explaining development and change in organizations. Acad. Manag. Rev. **20**(3), 510–540 (1995)
65. Wyld, D.C.: Moving to the cloud: An introduction to cloud computing in government. IBM Center for the Business of Government (2009)
66. Zardini, A., Rossignoli, C., Ricciardi, F.: A bottom-up path for IT management success: from infrastructure quality to competitive excellence. J. Bus. Res. **69**(5), 1747–1752 (2016)

Digital Maturity: A Survey in the Netherlands

Erik Beulen[✉]

TIAS School for Business and Society, Tilburg University, Tilburg, The Netherlands
e.beulen@tias.edu

Abstract. Digital transformations facilitate the need for speed. However, how the required digital maturity to manage transformation is not well-understood. This Dutch research examines inhibitors for digital maturity and is focusing on the business as well as the information technology side. Using a literature review and survey research of managers from national and global firms based in the Netherlands; we present a research model and empirically test the hypothesized relationships. The results show the inhibitors for digital maturity including the capability limitations for both the Chief Information Officer and the business representatives. In the research also the balance between achieving the digital business and information technology maturity has been measured: number of months required to achieve digital maturity. There is support for the hypothesis that information technology and business digital maturity are balanced.

Keywords: Architecture · Chief digital officer · Chief information officer · Digital strategy · Digital transformations · Governance

1 Introduction

Digital (Business) Transformations can be defined as "the process of exploiting digital technologies and supporting capabilities to create a robust new business model" [1]. In this collaboration defining a digital transformation strategy is essential. This strategy covers the corporate, operational and functional strategy, which includes the information technology strategy [2]. On the technology side, new digital technologies, SMACIT (social, mobile, analytics, cloud and Internet of Things) technologies, open new doors [3]. The use of technologies is essential [4], however a strategy is more important than the technology [5]. This technology push fuels the business by enabling new products and services (digital service backbone) and improving existing processes (operational backbone) – [6]. These definitions indicate that digital transformations take two to tango: business and IT.

Organization will potentially have different digital transformation maturities. In order to be successful both the business and the IT digital maturity needs to be balanced. This doesn't mean that organization need to be mature right here, right now. Organizations need to have an aligned digital maturity roadmap. In order to achieve alignment and to improve the digital maturity some organizations appoint a Chief Digital Officer (CDO). The CDO is a catalyst for achieving digital maturity [7]. However, some organizations

© Springer Nature Switzerland AG 2020
I. Oshri et al. (Eds.): Global Sourcing 2019, LNBIP 410, pp. 69–81, 2020.
https://doi.org/10.1007/978-3-030-66834-1_4

might not be convinced on the need to embark on a digital transformation (Myth #5: executives are hungry for digital transformations [8]).

Digital mature organizations can be characterized by 1. having a board of management that lives and breathes digital [9–11], 2. embedding digital in the DNA of their organisation [12–14], 3. setting priorities for digital adoption considering an innovation focus on processes and on existing and/or new services [15, 16], 4. experiment with new technologies, including artificial intelligence and machine learning [17–19], 5. accomplish seamless cooperation between business representatives and digital leaders [20, 21], 6. collaborate with start-ups, scale-ups, tech giants and universities [22–25], 7. embed digital governance by recalibrating business and information technology roles and by integrating the digital unit in the organisation [26, 27] and 8. implement architecture by design and a thorough data strategy [28, 29].

Only a very small percentage will not be impacted by disruption, most organizations need to decide on their Digital Transformation roadmap, ranging from making low risk moves to making bold steps [30]. What is stopping organizations from Digital Transformation success?

2　Literature Review

Successful digital transformation requires digital business and digital information technology maturity [31–33]. The digital business maturity is hindered by 1. capabilities of the business representatives [5, 34, 35], 2. poor digital strategy [36–38], 3. budget constraints [39, 40], 4. poor change management capabilities [8, 41], 5. poor governance [26, 42] and 6. poor enterprise architecture [43, 44].

The digital business maturity is hindered by 1. capabilities of the chief information officer [45, 46], 2. lack of ability to centrally manage the core data [47, 48], 3. lack of trust in information technology department [49, 50], 4. technical debt [51–53], 5. IT legacy platforms [54, 55] and 6. governance frameworks [26, 56].

Finally, the digital maturity is hindered by the capabilities of the chief digital officer [57]. There is a lively debate if this is a digital business maturity or a digital information technology maturity [7, 58–60]. The chief digital officer is a catalyst for both the business and information technology [61].

3　Hypothesis

Successful digital transformation requires both digital business and digital information technology maturity. Organizations need to resolve inhibitors. Prior to testing the hypothesis, the impact of the in the literature identified inhibitors will be explored by a survey (Likert scale 1-10–1 is low and 10 is high). This provides guidance on where organizations need to focus to achieve digital maturity.

The data for this research is collected by a survey. The survey was submitted to ICT Media, a Dutch organization that facilities IT decision makers in the Netherlands. The members of this community are Chief Information Officers and their direct reports. The response rate was 1.5% (57 responses, including two not completed responses to 3,500 invitations). The survey was an anonymous survey; therefore, it is not possible to conclude the representativeness of the sample. However, the spread over the different sectors and spread of the size of the organizations the respondents represent do not indicate that the respondents are not representative for the community, which was also confirmed by ICT Media.

Furthermore, this research explores the Pearson correlation between the time required for organizations to achieve digital business and digital information technology maturity; Pearson correlation [62–65]. The hypothesis test if the digital business maturity in terms of the time required for organizations to achieve maturity equals to the time required for organizations to achieve digital information technology maturity. The survey respondents provide their insight and understanding for both digital business and digital information technology maturity timeline (already achieved, <12 months, 13 to 24 months, 25–36 months, 37 to 60 months and >60 months – each value represents a numerical value in this research, ranging from "already achieved" representing the value "0" tot ">60 months" representing the value "5").

The expectation is that the organization will have an equal timeline for achieving/achieved digital business and digital information technology maturity. The 95% critical values (two-tales) of the correlation coefficients decide if r is significant or not. This will provide insides in the expected balance of the timeline for achieving/achieved digital business and digital information technology maturity.

ρ = achieving/achieved digital business and digital information technology maturity timeline balance

H_0 (achieving/achieved digital business maturity timeline – achieving/achieved digital information technology maturity timeline): $\rho = 0$

H_A (achieving/achieved digital business maturity timeline – achieving/achieved digital information technology maturity timeline): $\rho > 0$

4 Data Collection

The data for this research is collected by a survey. The survey was submitted to ICT Media, a Dutch organization that facilities IT decision makers in the Netherlands. The members of this community are Chief Information Officers and their direct reports. The response rate was 1.5% (57 responses, including two not completed responses to 3,500 invitations). The survey was an anonymous survey; therefore, it is not possible to conclude the representativeness of the sample. However, the spread over the different sectors and spread of the size of the organizations the respondents represent do not indicate that the respondents are not representative for the community, which was also confirmed by ICT Media.

The survey was conducted in Dutch. The participants completed their response via a portal. The responses were collected from 16 January to 2 February 2018. The potential participants received one friendly reminder the second week the survey was introduced.

5 Survey Population Characteristics

The participating organizations include all sectors. Over 10% of the participating organizations are in the sectors manufacturing, healthcare, government and financial services (see Fig. 1).

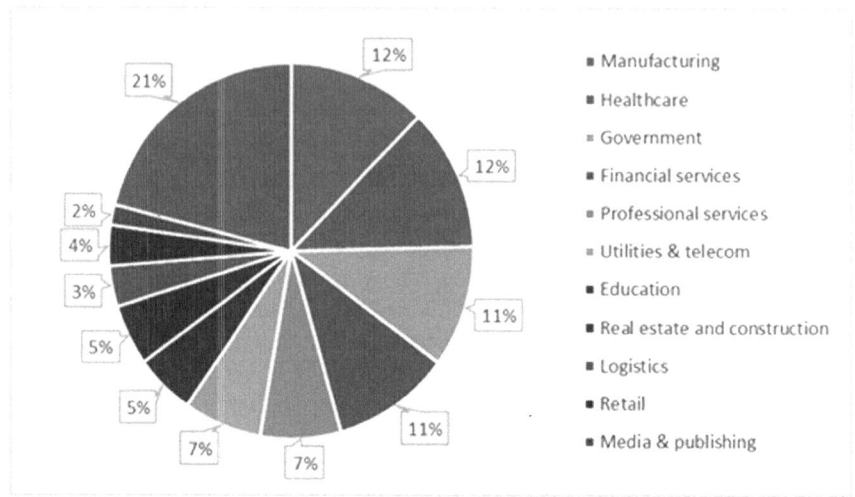

Fig. 1. Overview of sectors of participating organisations (N = 57)

The participating organizations are predominantly larger organizations, revenue/budget larger than €250 m (see Fig. 2).

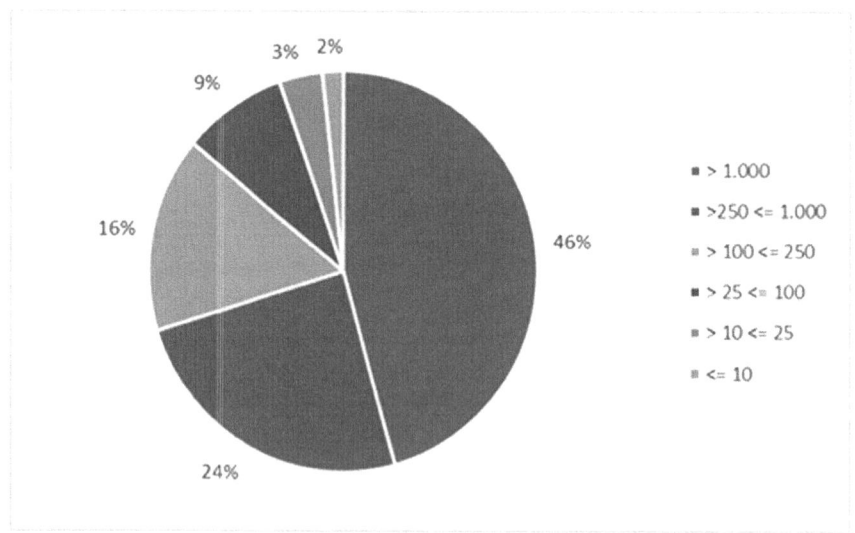

Fig. 2. Overview of annual revenue/budget in million Euro (N = 57)

The participating organizations operate predominantly in the Netherlands, over 50% of the participating organizations generates over 75% of their revenue or spends over 75% of their budget in the Netherlands (see Fig. 3).

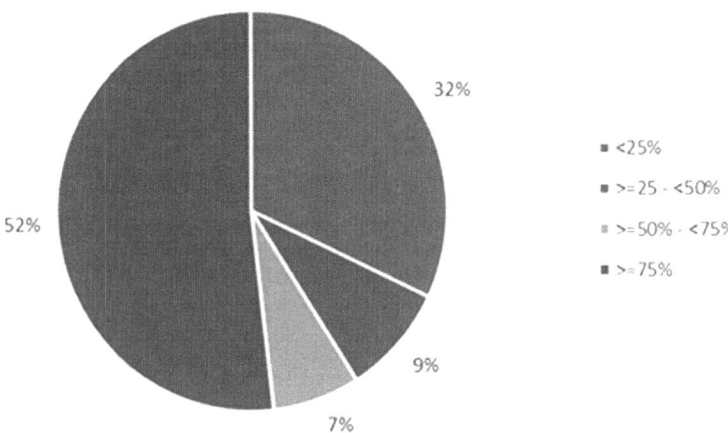

Fig. 3. Overview of % revenue/budget in the Netherlands (N = 57)

6 Data Analysis

Respondents also assessed the importance of improvement areas (see Fig. 4). This is mixture of improvement areas for both Digital Business Maturity and Digital Information Technology Maturity. The capabilities of business representatives (7.6 out of 10) and the chief information officer (7.1 out of 10) together with a poor digital strategy (7.1 out of 10) turn out to be the areas requiring most attention. Respondents also made clear that identifying, maintaining and recruiting qualified staff is important. In addition, the chief digital officer (6.8 out of 10) and change management capabilities (6.7 out of 10) received high scores. The outcome of the survey set a clear agenda for improving digital maturity.

The survey also addressed digital maturity, differentiating between digital maturity with respect to business and information technology. Most organisations do not see themselves as digitally mature yet: only four organisations out of the 55 surveyed consider themselves as digitally mature in business and information technology (see Fig. 5). The other respondents expect they need up to 60 months or more to become digitally mature. The survey outcome might be impacted by the survey respondents' profiles, predominantly chief digital officers, chief information officers and information managers, but undoubtedly there is room for improving maturity. What capabilities, processes, and tooling are required? This is essential input for the digital strategy and will support organisations in adopting digital in accordance with their digital strategy.

The number of responding organizations taken into account was 55 organizations (N = 55 − 2 incomplete responses). The preferred minimal number of responses is 25 [62]. The number of responses is sufficient for reliable testing.

The hypothesis test if the digital business maturity in terms of the time required for organizations to achieve maturity equals to the time required for organizations to

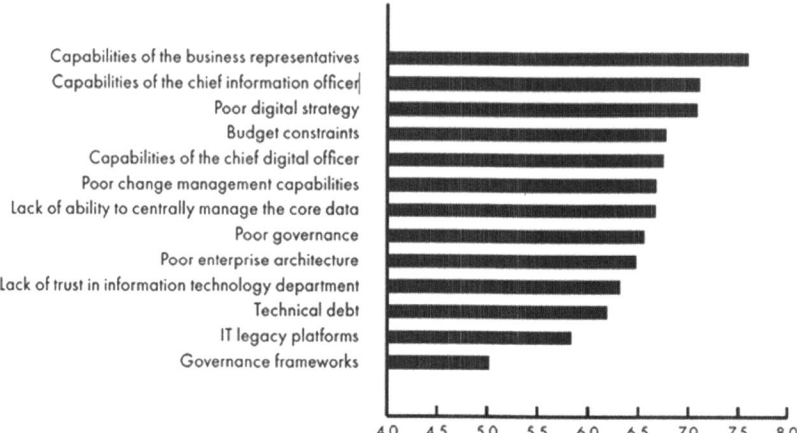

Fig. 4. Overview blockers for Digital Maturity. Overview Importance of improvement areas for Digital Maturity – 10-point scale, 10 is highest importance, and 0 is lowest importance (N = 57)

achieve digital information technology maturity. The 95% critical values (two-tales) of the correlation coefficients decide if r is significant or not. The Ho is accepted (see below text box).

ρ = achieving/achieved digital business maturity timeline – achieving/achieved digital information technology maturity timeline

H_0 (achieving/achieved digital business maturity timeline – achieving/achieved digital information technology maturity timeline) : $\rho = 0$

H_A (achieving/achieved digital business maturity timeline – achieving/achieved digital information technology maturity timeline) : $\rho \neq 0$

Mean (achieving/achieved digital business maturity timeline – achieving/achieved digital information technology maturity timeline) $= 0.76364$

Std dev (achieving/achieved digital business maturity timeline – achieving/achieved digital information technology maturity timeline) $= 3.580475$

N = 55

Degrees of freedom = 54

t Stat = 1.567267

t Critical two-tail (.05) = 2.0

The critical values associated with df=54 is 2.0. Since t Stat = 1.567267 and 1.567267 < 2.0 we accept H_0.

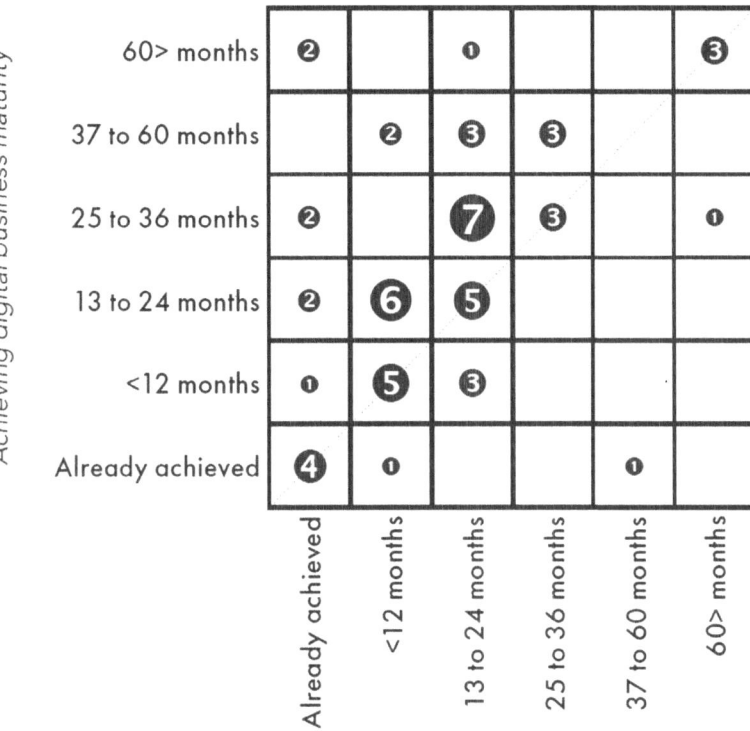

Achieving digital information technology maturity

Fig. 5. Overview of the time required for organizations to achieve digital business and digital information technology maturity (N = 55 – two incomplete responses)

7 Discussion

Organization need to prioritise on where investments and management effort is required to improve the Digital Maturity. There are two themes which require specific attention: partnership and leadership.

Partnerships. Initiating a digital strategy and implementing digital transformations change value chains and require intensive collaboration with partners. To change their organisation into high-performance digital organisations, collaboration with start-ups, scale-ups, tech giants, and universities is necessary. There is no simple recipe, but engaging with start-ups and universities fuels innovation, where scale-ups can help your organisation implement and deliver innovation.

Collaborating with start-ups also contributes to changing the organisation and building a digital mindset. During the full integration of an innovation in the services and product portfolio, the organisation needs tech giants, such as Amazon, Google, IBM and Microsoft, and their products, to deliver at full scale. We also see a lot of organisations struggling to attract talent. An influx of fresh graduates will build the capabilities and contribute to changing the culture. This is where collaboration with universities will play an important role.

In regard to engaging with start-ups and scale-ups, organisations need to decide on exclusivity and potential participation followed by an acquisition to maximise the added value of their ecosystem. Organisations typically agree on a high degree of exclusivity prior to engaging with start-ups to protect their commercial interest and enable developing innovations jointly. The size of most start-ups also prevents them from engaging with multiple partners in parallel. As organisations expect economies of scale and delivery rigour from scale-ups, a more limited degree of exclusivity is required for scale-ups.

Typically, this exclusivity includes named competitors combined with specific geographical restrictions. With respect to participation and acquisitions of start-ups, organisations run the risk that this will kill the culture and innovative spirit and result in attrition. This is less of a risk for scale-ups. However, businesses should only participate or acquire, if the capabilities and knowledge embedded in the start-up or scale-up potentially will be at the heart of your future value propositions and will give you a competitive advantage.

Otherwise, implement partnership relations and engage at arm's length. Apply the partnership approach as well for engaging with tech giants. However, 'supplier relationships' might be a better label due to the market power of these tech giants. University and business school collaboration also requires attention. Larger organisations might consider appointing campus recruiters to enlist fresh graduates. Furthermore, sponsoring conferences and study associations, and providing guest lecturers can be effective partnering mechanisms. Consider in-company programmes provided by business schools or universities, to build not only digital capabilities but also teams. Integration of in-company programmes in management development programmes is highly recommended, as this facilitates assimilation of business and information technology staff. Make serving information technology leadership roles mandatory for business leaders. Similarly, information technology leaders need to fulfil business leadership roles to further their careers. For high-performance digital organisations it is important to understand that digital success can only be achieved by collaborating with start-ups, scale-ups, tech giants and universities.

Leadership. High-performance digital organisations are led by a board of management that lives and breathes digital. The board of management appoints and supports digital leaders and orchestrates and facilitates organisational changes required. The digital leaders execute the digital vision of the board of management by implementing their digital strategy. This goes without saying for born digital organisations. For organisations which are digitally enabled, i.e. using digital to enhance their products and services and optimise processes, and for traditional organisations that are embarking on a digital transformation and that are competing with born digital organisations, this is not a given. Organisations with a less digitally minded board of management will struggle to be successful. Digital leaders and business management need to put forward their digital strategy and have to guide the board of management. This bottom-up approach impacts the effectiveness of digital leaders and the speed of digital adoption of organisations. These organisations must consider a board of management shake-up.

It is well known that successful digital leaders are business and tech savvy, great communicators, and change agents. This requires a thorough understanding of business processes, products and services, and the current market and future markets, as well as an understanding of technology, including architecture and data strategy, security and compliance, and the ability to access the potential of new technologies, including artificial intelligence and machine learning.

Successful digital leaders unceasingly invest in their relationships with the board of management, regardless of the digital maturity of the board of management. Digital leaders explain their digital strategy and pitch their digital proposition at a board level. In order to be successful, a thorough preparation is required. Digital leaders together with senior business managers need to invest in co-creating digital strategies and propositions. This includes market analyses, marketing strategies, and defining the technology requirements that enable the propositions. After all the hard work with business management and the information technology department and their partners, digital leaders have to make their strategy and initiatives presentable to the board of management. This is an intensive and time-consuming effort, but worth every hour. The board of management will challenge digital leaders on the ability to execute. Despite their belief in the need for digital transformation, the experience of board members in information technology is not altogether positive. In addition, their understanding of information technology is sometimes problematic. Digital leaders need to take this context into account. They need to explain, in non-technical terms, how they simplified the information technology landscape and transformed the organisation into the agile organisation. Furthermore, a deep dive into required capabilities is necessary to understand the profile of a digital leader better. Of course, the capabilities of the core leadership, such as designing and implementing a strategy, motivational relationships and communications, are the foundation. To digital leaders, change management capabilities are important. The change is not limited to processes and the organisational structure but is extended to redefining product and service offerings. This includes breaking down traditional silos, challenging everything that is in place at any level, and introducing agility. Let us explore embedding digital leadership into organisations next. In parallel, adjusting processes and turning around the organisation by onboarding digital natives and reclassification of the current workforce is a challenge. On top of this, digital leaders need to build partnerships, creating and maintaining ecosystems instead of contracting information technology services.

Chief digital officers are responsible for defining the digital strategy and implementing digital transformations. Organisations appoint a chief digital officer to create focus on digital, which is important to get things started. The chief digital officer has a change agent profile, has business sense, and is information technology savvy. Finding the right candidate is not easy. Most of the organisations in the survey have both a chief digital officer and a chief information officer. In these organisations, the chief information officers are responsible for providing information technology services and contributing to digitisation in close cooperation with the chief digital officer and business representatives. The focus of chief information officers is shifting from operations towards added value for the company. Regardless of the organisational structure, including responsibilities of the chief digital officer and the chief information manager, it is important to act. Mobilising the business and collaborating with information technology, combined with truly embracing the digital strategy, are essential for digital success. Identification of use cases is important: start small and without any constraints. Promote experimentation! A less orthodox suggestion: invite the children of your employees to unlock innovation and to unlock the potential of your employees by creating 'competition'. Challenge employees (parents) to outperform their children. The potential and success of use cases need to be monitored closely. Proofs of concept and pilot projects that do not meet expectations must be killed earlier rather than later: fail fast and accept failure! Digital leaders must also diversify their portfolio of use cases, including a mix of 'easy initiatives' (low-hanging fruit to prove business value and generate funding for other digital initiatives), 'difficult initiatives' (to prove the added value to criticasters), and 'true impact initiatives' (major contribution to the top line – to be relevant). Managing the portfolio of use cases as a funnel is a prerequisite, and generating sufficient influx is crucial. Furthermore, successful digital leaders identify business leaders and digital enthusiasts to mature their organisation. This includes recruiting, hackathons, and training, e.g. data analytics boot camps for business executives and online digital training for senior management. It will embed digital in the DNA of an organisation.

8   Conclusions

Most organizations of the survey participants have more than twelve months ahead prior to arriving at a combined Digital Business Maturity and Digital Information Technology Maturity. Assessing their Digital Maturity and implementing measures to improve their Digital Maturity requires a structure approach, board level endorsement, senior management attention and budget.

9   Research Limitations and Future Research Direction

This research has been conducted in the Netherlands and included only a limited number of respondents - predominantly Chief Information Officers and their direct reports. Expanding the survey to other countries and business representatives will improve the representativeness of the data. Also collecting data in the years to come will help to understand the best practices for maturing Digital Transformation better – annual survey. These surveys can be supplemented by case studies to understand better the underlying management decisions and issues organizations are facing.

Acknowledgements. The author would like to thank Rob Beijleveld, Christoph Heller and Frances Koster from ICT Media (www.ictmedia.nl) for inviting the members of the ICT Media community to participate in the survey and for facilitating the execution of the survey. This research project facilitated by Informatica (www.informatica.com).

As earlier version of this research in progress has been publish as a whitepaper (https://itexec utive.nl/whitepaper/hoe-word-je-een-high-performance-digital-organisatie/).

References

1. Gartner analysts explore digital transformation: the term and what it means by sector, 21 January 2019. https://www.information-age.com/gartner-digital-transformation-123478351/
2. Matt, C., Hess, T., Benlian, A.: Digital transformation strategies. Bus. Inf. Syst. Eng. **57**(5), 339–343 (2015)
3. Sebastian, I.M., Ross, J.W., Beath, C., Mocker, M., Moloney, K.G., Fonstad, N.O.: How big old companies navigate digital transformation. MIS Q. Executive **16**(3), 197–213 (2017)
4. Hess, T., Matt, C., Benlian, A., Wiesböck, F.: Options for formulating a digital transformation strategy. MIS Q. Executive **15**(2), 123–139 (2016)
5. Kane, G.C., Palmer, D., Phillips, A.N., Kiron, D., Buckley, N.: Strategy, not technology, drives digital transformation. MIT Sloan Manag. Rev. Deloitte Univ.Press **14**, 1–25 (2015)
6. Ross, J.W., Sebastian, I., Beath, C., Mocker, M., Moloney, K., Fonstad, N.: Designing and executing digital strategies: completed research paper. In: Thirty Seventh International Conference on Information Systems, Dublin, Ireland. Hochschule Reutlingen (2016). https://core. ac.uk/download/pdf/80748005.pdf
7. Singh, A., Hess, T.: How chief digital officers promote the digital transformation of their companies. MIS Q. Executive **16**(1), 1–17 (2017)
8. Andriole, S.J.: Five myths about digital transformation. MIT Sloan Manag. Rev. **58**(3), 22 (2017)
9. Hansen, A.M., Kraemmergaard, P., Mathiassen, L.: Rapid adaptation in digital transformation: a participatory process for engaging IS and business leaders. MIS Q. Executive **10**(4), 175–185 (2011)
10. Fitzgerald, M., Kruschwitz, N., Bonnet, D., Welch, M.: Embracing digital technology: a new strategic imperative. MIT Sloan Manag. Rev. **55**(2), 1–16 (2014)
11. Weill, P., Apel, T., Woerner, S.L., Banner, J.S.: It pays to have a digitally savvy board. MIT Sloan Manag. Rev. **60**(3), 41–45 (2019)
12. Bērziša, S., et al.: Capability driven development: an approach to designing digital enterprises. Bus. Inf. Syst. Eng. **57**(1), 15–25 (2015)
13. Shaughnessy, H.: Creating digital transformation: strategies and steps. Strategy Leadersh. **46**(2), 19–25 (2018)
14. Auvinen, T., Sajasalo, P., Sintonen, T., Pekkala, K., Takala, T., Luoma-aho, V.: Evolution of strategy narration and leadership work in the digital era. Leadership **15**(2), 205–225 (2019)
15. Helkkula, A., Kowalkowski, C., Tronvoll, B.: Archetypes of service innovation: implications for value cocreation. J. Serv. Res. **21**(3), 284–301 (2018)
16. Hinings, B., Gegenhuber, T., Greenwood, R.: Digital innovation and transformation: an institutional perspective. Inf. Organ. **28**(1), 52–61 (2018)
17. Benitez, J., Llorens, J., Braojos, J.: How information technology influences opportunity exploration and exploitation firm's capabilities. Inf. Manag. **55**(4), 508–523 (2018)
18. Davenport, T.H., Ronanki, R.: Artificial intelligence for the real world. Harv. Bus. Rev. **96**(1), 108–116 (2018)
19. Mohri, M., Rostamizadeh, A., Talwalkar, A.: Foundations of Machine Learning. The MIT Press, Cambridge (2018)
20. Kahre, C., Hoffmann, D., Ahlemann, F.: Beyond business-IT alignment-digital business strategies as a paradigmatic shift: a review and research agenda. In: Proceedings of the 50th Hawaii International Conference on System Sciences, 4 January 2017, Hawaii, US (2017). http://hdl.handle.net/10125/41736
21. Kesler, G., Kates, A.: Don't chase alignment. People Strategy **40**(2), 9–10 (2017)
22. Hogenhuis, B.N., van den Hende, E.A., Hultink, E.J.: When should large firms collaborate with young ventures? Understanding young firms' strengths can help firms make the right decisions around asymmetric collaborations. Res. Technol. Manag. **59**(1), 39–47 (2016)

23. Usman, M., Vanhaverbeke, W.: How start-ups successfully organize and manage open innovation with large companies. Eur. J. Innov. Manag. **20**(1), 171–186 (2017)
24. Fraser, S., Mancl, D.: Innovation through collaboration: company-university partnership strategies. In: Proceedings of the 4th International Workshop on Software Engineering Research and Industrial Practice, May, Buenos Aires, Argentina, pp. 17–23. IEEE Press (2017)
25. Moore, M., Tambini, D. (eds.): Digital Dominance: the Power of Google, Amazon, Facebook, and Apple. Oxford University Press, Oxford (2018)
26. Dunleavy, P., Margetts, H.: Design principles for essentially digital governance. In: 111th Annual Meeting of the American Political Science Association, San Francisco, 3–6 September 2015 (2015). http://eprints.lse.ac.uk/64125/
27. Welchman, L.: Managing Chaos: Digital Governance by Design. Rosenfeld Media, New York (2015)
28. Bossert, O.: A two-speed architecture for the digital enterprise. In: El-Sheikh, E., Zimmermann, A., Jain, Lakhmi C. (eds.) Emerging Trends in the Evolution of Service-Oriented and Enterprise Architectures. ISRL, vol. 111, pp. 139–150. Springer, Cham (2016). https://doi.org/10.1007/978-3-319-40564-3_8
29. Bondar, S., Hsu, J.C., Pfouga, A., Stjepandić, J.: Agile digital transformation of system-of-systems architecture models using Zachman framework. J. Ind. Inf. Integr. **7**, 33–43 (2017)
30. Bughin, J., Catlin, T., Hirt, M., Willmott, P.: Why digital strategies fail. McKinsey Q., 25 January 2018. https://www.mckinsey.com/business-functions/mckinsey-digital/our-insights/why-digital-strategies-fail
31. Gill, M., VanBoskirk, S.: The digital maturity model 4.0. Benchmarks: Digital Transformation Playbook, 22 January 2016. https://forrester.nitro-digital.com/pdf/Forrester-s%20Digital%20Maturity%20Model%204.0.pdf
32. Kozar, A., Vasiljević, D., Radivojević, M.: Transformation of digital business by applying benchmarking. Int. J. IT Eng. **5**(8), 6–16 (2017)
33. Gurbaxani, V., Dunkle, D.: Gearing up for successful digital transformation. MIS Q. Executive **18**(3), 6 (2019)
34. Weill, P., Woerner, S.L.: Optimizing your digital business model. MIT Sloan Manag. Rev. **54**(3), 71–78 (2013)
35. Westerman, G., Bonnet, D., McAfee, A.: The nine elements of digital transformation. MIT Sloan Manag. Rev. **55**(3), 1–6 (2014)
36. Kane, G.C., Palmer, D., Phillips, A.N., Kiron, D.: Is your business ready for a digital future? MIT Sloan Manag. Rev. **56**(4), 37–44 (2015)
37. Bharadwaj, A., El Sawy, O.A., Pavlou, P.A., Venkatraman, N.: Digital business strategy: toward a next generation of insights. MIS Q. **37**, 471–482 (2013)
38. Ross, J.W., Beath, C.M., Sebastian, I.M.: How to develop a great digital strategy. MIT Sloan Manag. Rev. **58**(2), 7–9 (2017)
39. Mithas, S., Rust, R.T.: How information technology strategy and investments influence firm performance: conjecture and empirical evidence. MIS Q. **40**(1), 223–245 (2016)
40. Luftman, J., Lyytinen, K., Zvi, T.B.: Enhancing the measurement of information technology (IT) business alignment and its influence on company performance. J. Inf. Technol. **32**(1), 26–46 (2017)
41. Tassabehji, R., Hackney, R., Popovič, A.: Emergent digital era governance: enacting the role of the 'institutional entrepreneur' in transformational change. Govern. Inf. Q. **33**(2), 223–236 (2016)
42. DeLone, W., Migliorati, D., Vaia, G.: Digital IT Governance. In: Bongiorno, G., Rizzo, D., Vaia, G. (eds.) CIOs and the Digital Transformation, pp. 205–230. Springer, Cham (2018). https://doi.org/10.1007/978-3-319-31026-8_11

43. Zimmermann, A., Schmidt, R., Jugel, D., Möhring, M.: Evolving enterprise architectures for digital transformations. In: Digital Enterprise Computing, Lecture Notes in Informatics (LNI), Gesellschaft für Informatik, Bonn, pp. 183–194 (2015)
44. Nambisan, S., Lyytinen, K., Majchrzak, A., Song, M.: Digital innovation management: reinventing innovation management research in a digital world. MIS Q. **41**(1), 223–238 (2017)
45. Karpovsky, A.: Information Systems Strategy and the Role of Chief Information Officers: Strategizing and Aligning Practices. Bentley University, Waltham (2015)
46. Gerth, A.B., Peppard, J.: The dynamics of CIO derailment: how CIOs come undone and how to avoid it. Bus. Horiz. **59**(1), 61–70 (2016)
47. Dallemule, L., Davenport, T.H.: What's your data strategy. Harv. Bus. Rev. **95**(3), 112–121 (2017)
48. Vilminko-Heikkinen, R., Pekkola, S.: Changes in roles, responsibilities and ownership in organizing master data management. Int. J. Inf. Manage. **47**, 76–87 (2019)
49. Pink, S., Lanzeni, D., Horst, H.: Data anxieties: finding trust in everyday digital mess. Big Data Soc. **5**(1), 2053951718756685 (2018)
50. Abraham, C., Sims, R.R., Daultrey, S., Buff, A., Fealey, A.: How digital trust drives culture change. MIT Sloan Manag. Rev. **60**(3), 1–8 (2019)
51. Li, Z., Avgeriou, P., Liang, P.: A systematic mapping study on technical debt and its management. J. Syst. Softw. **101**, 193–220 (2015)
52. Alves, N.S., Mendes, T.S., de Mendonça, M.G., Spínola, R.O., Shull, F., Seaman, C.: Identification and management of technical debt: a systematic mapping study. Inf. Softw. Technol. **70**, 100–121 (2016)
53. Rolland, K.H., Mathiassen, L., Rai, A.: Managing digital platforms in user organizations: the interactions between digital options and digital debt. Inf. Syst. Res. **29**(2), 419–443 (2018)
54. Daub, M., Wiesinger, A.: Acquiring the capabilities you need to go digital. McKinsey Global Institute, 1 March 2015. https://www.mckinsey.com/business-functions/mckinsey-dig ital/our-insights/acquiring-the-capabilities-you-need-to-go-digital
55. Edelman, B.: How to launch your digital platform. Harv. Bus. Rev. April 2015. https://hbr. org/2015/04/how-to-launch-your-digital-platform
56. Dai, X.: The digital revolution and governance. Routledge, New York (2018)
57. Tumbas, S., Berente, N., vom Brocke, J.: Three types of chief digital officers and the reasons organizations adopt the role. MIS Q. Executive **16**(2), 121–134 (2017)
58. Haffke, I., Kalgovas, B.J., Benlian, A.: The role of the CIO and the CDO in an organization's digital transformation. In: Thirty Seventh International Conference on Information Systems, Dublin, Ireland (2016). https://aisel.aisnet.org/cgi/viewcontent.cgi?article=1079& context=icis
59. Doonan, M.: So you've just hired a killer chief digital officer–now what? Strategic HR Rev. **17**(1), 17–22 (2018)
60. Tumbas, S., Berente, N., Brocke, J.V.: Digital innovation and institutional entrepreneurship: chief digital officer perspectives of their emerging role. J. Inf. Technol. **33**(3), 188–202 (2018)
61. Fitzgerald, M.: How to hire data-driven leaders. MIT Sloan Manag. Rev. **56**(3), 56301 (2015)
62. David, F.: Tables of the ordinates and probability integral of the distribution of the correlation coefficient in small samples. Cambridge University Press, New York (1938)
63. Cohen, J., Cohen, P., West, S., Aiken, L.: Applied Multiple Regression/Correlation Analysis for the Behavioral Sciences. Routledge, London (2013)
64. Hayes, A.: Introduction to mediation, moderation, and conditional process analysis: A regression-based approach. Guilford Press, New York (2013)
65. Hedges, L., Olkin, I.: Statistical Methods for Meta-Analysis. Academic press, Cambridge (2014)

Smart Contracts for Global Sourcing Arrangements

Jos van Hillegersberg[1(✉)] and Jonas Hedman[2]

[1] Faculty of Behavioral, Management and Social Sciences, Industrial Engineering and Business Information Systems, University of Twente, P.O. Box 217, 7500 AE Enschede, The Netherlands
`j.vanhillegersberg@utwente.nl`
[2] Department of Digitalization, Copenhagen Business School, Howitzvej 60, 2000 Frederiksberg, Denmark
`jhe.digi@cbs.dk`

Abstract. While global sourcing arrangements are highly complex and usually represent large value to the partners, little is known of the use of e-contracts or smart contracts and contract management systems to enhance the contract management process. In this paper we assess the potential of emerging technologies for global sourcing. We review current sourcing contract issues and evaluate three technologies that have been applied to enhance contracting processes. These are (1) semantic standardisation, (2) cognitive technologies and (3) smart contracts and blockchain. We discuss that each of these seem to have their merit for contract management and potentially can contribute to contract management in more complex and dynamic sourcing arrangements. The combination and configuration in which these three technologies will provide value to sourcing should be on the agenda for future research in sourcing contract management.

Keywords: Global outsourcing · Contracts · E-Contracting · Smart contracts · Semantic standards · Cognitive technology

1 Introduction

Sourcing is difficult. Unfortunately, one thing that many sourcing arrangements have in common is a lose-lose scenario. A recent story on Dell's and FedEx's eight-year contract situation illustrates this. In 2005, Dell and FedEx wrote a 100 pages contract with numerous "Supplier shall" paragraphs to manage all possible issues in Dell's hardware return-and-repair process. During the following decade, both parties complied with obligations outlined in the contract. It was even re-negotiated at three occasions. Dell was unhappy with the lack of proactivity from FedEx - no innovation. FedEx was unhappy with the detailed processes description that had to be met - very expensive. At the end of the contract - none of the parties were happy, but none of the parties afforded to cancel or not to continue the relationship [1]. However, this is not a unique story in the history of sourcing arrangements and the contracts governing the relationship.

Contracts have existed since ancient times of trade and barter. Our current conceptualization of contracts can be traced back to the mid-1700s and the industrial revolution.

© Springer Nature Switzerland AG 2020
I. Oshri et al. (Eds.): Global Sourcing 2019, LNBIP 410, pp. 82–92, 2020.
https://doi.org/10.1007/978-3-030-66834-1_5

In particular, the growing British economy and the adaptability and flexibility of the English common law led to the development of modern contract law. Mainland Europe, with its more rigid civil law, was slower in developing a legal framework governing the role contracts. Not until the 20th century and with the growth of global trade and sourcing agreements there was a need for international contract law. Today, we have a number of global conventions, such as the Hague-Visby Rules and the UN Convention on Contracts for the International Sale of Goods, that regulate trade and contracts.

So, what is a contract? Ryan defines a contract as "a legally binding agreement which recognises and governs the rights and duties of the parties to the agreement" that addresses the exchange of goods, services, money, or promises of any of those [2]. With time contracts and its interpretation has evolved. Most recently, a new type of contracts have emerged - so-called e-contracts [3]. The development of e-contracts has followed the emergence of digital signatures and electronic identification [4]. E-contracts, enables that the promise of goods, services, or money can be controlled and monitored by digital technologies and potentially automated [3]. Furthermore, the International Association for Contract and Commercial Management (IACCM) concludes in a recent report that the future of contracts will focus more on relationships instead of costs. Therefore, we expect that contract management will evolve to include a degree of "intelligence" and become "smarter" while becoming more relationship oriented.

A lot of the research on smart contracts related to cryptocurrencies [5–7], but have broadened its scope and include topics such as internet of things (IoT) [8], banking ledger [9], and global shipping [10]. However, there is still not much research on the use of information technology in sourcing contracts. One reason could be the complexity in sourcing agreements, where a contract could last for many years, spanning continents, involving multiple actors, etc. Therefore, our aim is to explore the role of information technology in sourcing contract management.

The remainder of this paper is structured accordingly: In the following section, we review contracts types in sourcing arrangements. In the third section, we broaden our review to issues and challenges in sourcing contract management. Thereafter, we look into the information technology developments for contract management systems including the recent emergence of smart contracts. In the fifth section we provide a synthesis and our assessment of the use of these technologies for sourcing contracts. We conclude the paper by combining and discussing our findings.

2   Contracts in Sourcing Arrangements

Outsourcing arrangements are agreed upon and governed by contracts. Contracts can vary from short and straight-forward to voluminous and highly complex, cf. Dell and FedEx. There are some main different types of contracts. The most common are Firm Fixed Price Contracts and Cost Reimbursement Contracts. In the first type price not subject to any adjustment on the basis of the contractor's incurred costs - this is the simplest form of contracts and imposes a minimum administrative burden. The second type gives the supplier payment of allowable incurred costs, to the extent prescribed in the contract. This opens up for some interpretation and negotiation. The different types of contracts are determined by factors like the regulatory framework, complexity of the outsourcing services specified, total value, duration of the contract, the number of partners involved, and incentive or penalty clauses included. The variety in contracts follows the logic of Roman-based law: usus (right to use a good), fructus (right to what a good produces), and abusus (right to sell a good). Thus, clearly, the contract governing a multi-year multi-million sourcing deal is likely to differ greatly from the contract specification of a relatively simple and largely standardizes micro-service. Still sourcing contracts have much in common as well.

Sourcing Contract Templates, such as the sourcing contract template compiled by the Dutch Platform Outsourcing, give an overview of elements that should be present in a balanced and mature contract. This template was created by a committee of both vendor and client representatives and aimed at medium size to larger organizations and medium to complex services sourced [11]. The full table of contents can be viewed in the appendix. While some of the typical contract elements are relatively static, others require continuous monitoring and management. Think of contract changes, contract performance monitoring and auditing, and the enactment of penalties and bonus/malus schemes based on compliance and service level agreements.

The role of contracts changes throughout the four phases of global sourcing arrangements:

- Pre-sourcing collaboration: A global sourcing arrangement begins when an initiator start exploring the possibility to source services or resources externally via a tender process. In this phase the scope of the collaboration is defined by assigning roles to each company involved, inviting potential companies, and defining the business requirements. During this phase a draft contract or contract frame could be present, but often this phase is largely informal supported by trust and a sense of common purpose.
- Sourcing arrangement creation and consolidation. After a sourcing arrangement is established, procedures are formalization and rules and obligations are described in a contract. This also includes specific pricing agreements, incentive/penalty clauses and duration and renewal conditions. At the end of this phase, the selected services and/or resources should be implemented and made ready to be used.
- Sourcing arrangement delivery. In this phase, the sourced services or resources are executed. The contract should be managed and monitored. That is, actual execution and delivery performance should be monitored against the agreements defined in the contract. Contract rules should be executed when execution events trigger these. Incentives/penalties should be paid or charged as defined in the contract. Before the end date, the contract should be evaluated and renewed, or termination should be initiated.
- Partnership termination or succession In this phase a re-assertion of the contract is organized by the initiator and sourcing partners. Eventually this leads to termination of the contract, straight forward renewal or renewal after adaptation.

3 Challenges in Sourcing Contract Management

Sourcing and contract management is not easy. A case study on IT offshoring at Shell Global IT functions, clearly illustrates the central role a contract plays in a sourcing relationship [12]. Based on interviews with internal and external experts the study reveals that a contract is instrumental in governance of a sourcing relationship. It is input to joint processes between customer and vendor including performance management (is service delivery in line with the contract), financial management (is cost allocation and pricing in line with the contract), and escalation and relationship management (are measures taken in case of anomalies in line with the contract). Clearly the contract is also central in the contract management process. The Shell case also shows that interactions between the many roles in a sourcing relationship are better manageable if well-defined contracts are in place. Think of interactions between purchaser (client) and contract manager (vendor), service manager (client) and delivery manager (vendor), and innovation manager (client) and competence manager (vendor). Moreover, risk management and compliance benefit from well specified contracts. This included risks of confidentiality and compliance to legislation.

The main results of the Shell case are confirmed in a survey by McKinsey [13] that who reviewed 200 live sourcing contracts of over 50 companies, analysing three main dimensions: general terms and conditions, commercial terms and conditions, and governance structure. The review showed several frequent issues that hindered both supplier and customer. Some remarkable results of the McKinsey study, related to Sourcing Contract Management, are; (1) Purchasers and providers faced unclear definition of quality of service and limited tracking and control of business and financial targets (60%). (2) Few incentives for joint innovation (90%). (3) Limited collaboration (90%). (4) Key performance indicators had not been defined (75%), (5) No value-based negotiation on price and no mutual incentives and gain-sharing initiatives (67%).

Companies are often involved in multiple sourcing arrangements. Each of these arrangements may include multiple partners and a mix of services and resources (multi-vendor sourcing). "However, the lack of expressivity in current SLA specifications and the inadequacy of tools for managing SLA and contract compositions is relevant." [14]. Outsourcing contracts span hundreds of pages of legal contractual language that describes the delivered services and their performance. As the terms and conditions use a variety of metrics usually specified in natural language, it becomes increasingly difficult to monitor the performance of the contract [15].

Empirical research into IT outsourcing contracts has revealed that a large variety exists in their structure. Moreover, perhaps counter-intuitive, their length and complexity tends to grow as contract partners gain experience [16]. The contracts are unlikely to be synchronized, i.e. a variety of contracts in different phases of their life cycle need to be managed. In many cases contract management cannot keep up with the increasing dynamics and complexity of the arrangements. This leads to insufficient monitoring and execution of contracts, no insight in compliance, incorrect payments, ignoring the rules specified and violation of renewal or termination conditions. Most contracts are still defined in natural language and no support for automatic negotiation of smart contracts is provided [17]. Contract management of sourcing arrangement can thus become a time consuming and complex endeavor.

Many of these issues require organizational measures and practices to improve the sourcing relationship contracting, Still, there also seems to be ample opportunity for emerging technology for contract management to address the issues described above, reduce the risks in sourcing of services and increase the value. While the research into e-Contracting has made considerable progress over the last decades, there is no comprehensive proposal that covers the full e-contracting life cycle [18].

4 IT for Sourcing Contract Management Systems

4.1 Contract Management Systems

Contract Management Systems are emerging that support the phases of sourcing arrangements and managing the lifecycle of contracts. Clearly, the possibilities of contract management systems are much more powerful if the contracts that are managed are e-contracts or smart contracts and not simply digital scans of printed documents. Recent, Contract Management Systems software is stand-alone program or series of related software programs for storing and managing agreements with sourcing partners. Its overall purpose is to streamline administrative tasks and reduce overhead by providing a single, unified interface to manage new contracts, capture data related to the contract and document authoring, contract creation and negotiation. The contract management system can then follow the contract as it goes through the review and approval process, providing documentation for digital signatures and execution of the contract, including post-execution tracking and commitments management. Most contract management systems are designed from the perspective of the buyer and have thereby a cost focus. This view is criticized by [1] since a contract fundamentally deal with at least two parties - buyer and seller. However, the contract management systems providers do not view or see a contract management system as a platform business or as a two-sided market.

Various standards, architecture and tools have been supported to facilitate the contract management process. These include automated support for identifying service providers and for negotiation and offer building. Business architectures have been proposed to build upon e-contract SLA standards. A study by [18] describes the design of such an environment that supports contract management processes such as price offering and billing, compliance, arbitration and mediation, reporting, and termination and archiving and eventually also support for negotiation and merging of subcontractors terms and conditions.

On the technology side, there is a historical progression from paper to digital format with varying degrees of possibilities of re-negotiation. In its simplest form a digital contract is just a tick off box at the end of a page or an app. For instance, when a company signs up for a Dropbox account to store or share different files. The other extreme is a contract management system that supports all activities related to pre-sourcing collaboration, sourcing arrangement creation and consolidation, sourcing arrangement delivery, and partnership termination. Clearly, the role of information technology varies between these extremes of digitalizes sourcing contracts from keeping track of approval to contract life-cycle management.

4.2   Semantic Standards for Contract Management

E-contract is any type of contract formed in the interaction between two or more parties using electronic means. The parties may be human or digital agents (computer software). This includes even contracts between two digital agents that are programmed to recognize the existence of a contract. See for instance the Uniform Computer Information Transactions Act that provides rules regarding the formation, governance, and basic terms of an e-contract. E-commerce is the legacy of most research and conceptualizations of e-contracts.

Based on nine contracting templates, a study by IBM research developed a Generic SLA Semantic Model for the Execution Management of e-Business Outsourcing Contracts [19]. They also use actual service agreements and based on these, develop a semantic model of a service contract that includes data common data elements (see Table 1). As the area of e-Business hosting is relatively well-understood, the study manages to standardise common service level agreements and measurement data, and based on these, define refund/reward specifications that can be automatically executed. The researchers also report they have successfully developed a contract management system based on the semantic model and a service specification language that would reduce the financial risk of service-level violations [20].

Table 1.   Typical elements in an E-business service contract source: [19]

Description of service
Functional requirements of the service system
Start date and duration of service
Pricing and payment terms
Terms and conditions for service installation, revisions, and termination
Planned service maintenance windows
Customer support procedures and response time
Problem escalation procedures
Acceptance testing criteria, i.e., quality requirements that must be met before the service can be deployed for production use. These criteria could be stated in terms of, for example, benchmark-based transaction throughput performance, business-oriented synthetic transaction processing performance, fail-over latency, service usability, service system configurations (e.g. computer main memory size), etc.

More recently, and with the advent of cloud computing, studies have addressed contracting of cloud services. Advances have been made in viewing services as dynamic compositions and striving for machine readable SLA's based on standardised quality attributes and contract elements. The design of a tool named DAMASCO (DAta MAnager for Service COmposition) that offers SLA evaluation and assessment capabilities to IT professionals during the design phase is an example of such a study [14]. The authors propose an extension to the Web Service Agreement (WS-Agreement) standard proposed by the Open Grid Forum (OGF) to define agreements and their contexts between providers and consumers, as well as a set of service attributes (e.g., name; context; guarantee terms; constraints), to obtain a flexible template for IT service contracts. A contract is composable of sub-contracts and includes standard specifications of items such as cost, duration, service quality and penalty.

4.3 Cognitive Technology for Sourcing Contract Management

An alternative to striving for more formal specification of SLAs is using text-mining techniques to elicit SLAs stated in the contract in natural language and evaluate their performance using data from service performance logs. A study by [15] is an example of such a study, proposing Fitcon - a contract mining system that detects service level agreements from contracts, tracks the delivery performance against them and predicts the health of long-term contracts. The study develops a framework to automatically extract SLAs and SLA metrics from contract documents, using IBM's Watson Document Conversion Service (DCS). Next SLAs and their performance are mapped to internal standards. Terms and conditions are extracted using a Natural Language Toolkit that works on top of DCS. The approach was tested on actual client contracts and evaluated with subject matter experts, demonstrating promising results.

Thus, the availability of a widely agreed, standardized model that would enable to apply templates to every type of contracts and SLAs, and to categorize contract terms to be used in different services domains is still a significant need [14].

4.4 Smart Contracts and Blockchain Applications for Sourcing Contract Management

More recently the secure storage of contracts in distributed ledger technology (DLT) or blockchain has been proposed to allow for open access by partners involved in the arrangement. Moreover, a DLT architecture can store mutually agreed upon transactions in a safe and decentral manner. For instance, a decentralized and blockchain based platform for temporary employment contracts is proposed in [21]. Their platform design address ensures temporary employees with the fair and legal remuneration (including taxes) of work performances and respect for the rights for all actors involved in a temporary and offers the employer support for processing contracts with a fully automated and fast procedure. The full transparency and immutability that blockchain offers would enable compliance checking of the rights of both of the worker and of the employer. Their proposed decentralized infrastructure makes use of the Smart Contract feature included in new generation block chain architectures such as Ethereum. The Smart Contract is stored in the blockchain and opens the possibility to store and execute contractual agreements without dependence on a regulator. The design by [21] proposed a work ledger, that is used to register work offers to which workers can apply. Agreements and work hours are also stored in the ledger. Smart contracts are used to check certification of workers, allow governments to check compliance to legislation, manage the relationship and transfer value automatically. The study describes an application of the concept to agriculture but does not include an implementation nor a field test. While many details still need to be addressed, the idea could also apply to international contracting of service workers in outsourcing arrangement without an intermediary platform or a sourcing vendor. Smart contracting could thus be used to reduce the coordination costs involved in resource-based sourcing contracts.

A related development is the verifiable storage of degrees, credentials and certificates of professionals using blockchain and smart contracts. Especially in time/resource-based contracts, verification of the qualifications of professionals could enhance trust in the sourcing relationship. A conceptual architecture and prototype to this end is developed in [22]. They use the Ethereum blockchain and Smart contracts written in Solidity to manage the issuing of certificates to learners. Certification authorities validate or revoke these, and smart contracts verify that only accredited certification authorities can manage certification rights. Similar proof of concepts have been implemented by specific universities such as University of Nicocia, MIT, and University of Twente [23]. Using blockchain and smart contracts have also been piloted by companies such as SAP for their professional courses. Combined with educational domain standards (e.g. openbadges.org) such infrastructures may evolve into trustable global infrastructures that allows companies to verify qualifications and make the verification steps part of their contract.

A study by [17] applies the idea of Smart contracts to managing dynamics in cloud services. They propose a formal contracting language that should allow a contract to be updated automatically to include new requirements such as increased service capacity needs. This language is used to manage automatic adaptation, consistency check, and verification and change management of contracts. In addition, the authors propose a mechanism for autonomous negotiation based on the joint utility of client and cloud provider. The study is innovative in that it does not strive to achieve an exact match between client requirements and provider offerings. They focus on modelling the dynamic aspects of SLAs, i.e. under what conditions can SLAs change such as a pricing increment for enhanced response times of services. The smart contract proposal here focuses more on the automatic reconfiguration of the contract rather than on a blockchain architecture.

A smart contract application proposed by [24] even goes a step further. They implement a distributed peer-to-peer cloud storage platform DStore using smart contracts for the storage lease and automating the transfers. This offers a secure and effortless storage cloud that also facilitates financial settlement based on actual usage. Their proposal eliminates the role of third parties thus offering efficiency gains, especially when the demand for storage space is dynamic.

5   Assessment of Technologies for Sourcing Contracts

Based on the properties of the three technologies discussed, we provide an assessment of the potential of each of them to address contracting requirements (Table 2).

In Table 2, We indicate a clear and promising match between requirements and the features of the technology with a (+), and leave cells empty were we do not see a clear application of the technology. Where more research is needed to identify the match, we place a "?". The assessment presented in Table 2 illustrates that no single technology can address all requirements for Smart Contracts in isolation. The three emerging technologies should be combined and further developed to meet the demands of complex and evolving sourcing arrangements.

Table 2. Our assessment of the potential of reviewed technologies to address contracting issues

Contracting phase	Requirements for Contract Management Technologies based on current issues	Semantic Standards	CognTech	Block chain Smart Contr
Contract Definition and updating	Can value based negotiation be supported?	+	+	+
	Can contracts and subcontracts be linked and aggregated?	+		?
	Is service quality well defined, e.g. as precisely defined SLAs?	+		
	Can KPI's be defined?	+		
	Can terms and conditions be precisely specified?	+		?
	Can incentives for joint innovation be defined?	?		?
	Can renewal/terminal conditions be specified?	?		?
	Can multiple roles access the contract and update/change the contract according to their rights?			+
Contract Execution and Monitoring	Are collaborative processes in defining and updating the contract supported?			+
	Monitoring if service delivery in line with the contract?	+		+
	Monitoring if cost allocation and pricing in line with the contract?	+		+
	Are business and financial targets tracked?	+		+
	Can mutual incentives and gain-sharing initiatives be implemented?		+	
	Are measures taken in case of anomalies in line with the contract?	+		+
Contract Compliance and Health	Can the health of the contract be assessed?		+	
	Can business and financial targets be predicted?		+	
	Can Confidentiality be managed?			+

The next challenge is to evaluate to what extent these technologies, possibly combined, can relieve the sourcing contract issues and improve contract management practices and performance. We are currently working on theorizing on how a particular type of IT artefact - namely Contract Management Systems - can deploy a combination of semantic, cognitive and smart contracting technologies.

6 Conclusions and Future Research

We started out by revisiting the role of contracts in sourcing relationships. the literature on this area is vast, so we centred our introduction around the type of contracts currently in use during the phases in the life cycle of a contract. Clearly, sourcing contracts are a core element of a sourcing relationship and are of eminent importance. Next, we reviewed issues with sourcing contracts reported on in the literature. Remarkably, while both clients and vendors in sourcing relationships often have very mature knowledge of IT and process automation, the sourcing contracts in place and the contract management process are usually not deploying and technology beyond traditional document management.

At the same time, various information technologies have emerged to support contract management. We evaluated the potential use of these technologies and systems in improving contracting for global sourcing arrangements. In this paper we illustrated this by reviewing three technologies: (1) Semantic standards, (2) Cognitive technology (3) Smart Contracting and Blockchain. These technologies have all received increasing attention over the past few years.

However, while they have been applied to (micro) IT-outsourcing, they have not been discussed and compared in the context of complex and long-running sourcing contracts. Pilots are mainly reported on in computer science-oriented conferences and journals and usually make use publicly available sourcing contracts or relatively standardized e-business or cloud sourcing arrangements. In Sect. 4, we provide an initial assessment of the match of the three technologies survey on smart contract requirements. We believe further work on this question is needed to advance the use of technology in sourcing contract management.

References

1. Frydlinger, D., Hart, O.D.: Overcoming contractual incompleteness: the role of guiding principles. National Bureau of Economic Research, Working Paper 26245, September 2019. https://doi.org/10.3386/w26245
2. Ryan, D.F.: Contract Law. Round Hall Ltd, Dublin (2006)
3. Krishna, P.R., Karlapalem, K.: Electronic Contracts. IEEE Internet Comput. **12**(4), 60–68 (2008). https://doi.org/10.1109/MIC.2008.77
4. Eaton, B., Hedman, J., Medaglia, R.: Three different ways to skin a cat: financialization in the emergence of national e-ID solutions. J. Inf. Technol. **33**(1), 70–83 (2018). https://doi.org/10.1057/s41265-017-0036-8
5. Bartoletti, M., Pompianu, L.: An empirical analysis of smart contracts: platforms, applications, and design patterns. In: Brenner, M., et al. (eds.) FC 2017. LNCS, vol. 10323, pp. 494–509. Springer, Cham (2017). https://doi.org/10.1007/978-3-319-70278-0_31
6. Luu, L., Chu, D.-H., Olickel, H., Saxena, P., Hobor, A.: Making smart contracts smarter. In: Proceedings of the 2016 ACM SIGSAC Conference on Computer and Communications Security, New York, NY, USA, pp. 254–269 (2016). https://doi.org/10.1145/2976749.2978309
7. Velner, Y., Teutsch, J., Luu, L.: Smart contracts make bitcoin mining pools vulnerable. In: Brenner, M., et al. (eds.) FC 2017. LNCS, vol. 10323, pp. 298–316. Springer, Cham (2017). https://doi.org/10.1007/978-3-319-70278-0_19
8. Christidis, K., Devetsikiotis, M.: Blockchains and smart contracts for the internet of things. IEEE Access **4**, 2292–2303 (2016). https://doi.org/10.1109/ACCESS.2016.2566339
9. Peters, G.W., Panayi, E.: Understanding modern banking ledgers through blockchain technologies: future of transaction processing and smart contracts on the internet of money. In: Tasca, P., Aste, T., Pelizzon, L., Perony, N. (eds.) Banking Beyond Banks and Money. NEW, pp. 239–278. Springer, Cham (2016). https://doi.org/10.1007/978-3-319-42448-4_13
10. Jensen, T.D., Hedman, J., Henningson, S.: How TradeLens Delivers Business Value with Blockchain Technology, 2019, vol. Forthcoming (2019)

11. Platform Outsourcing Netherlands, "Template Sourcing Agreements v1.0." Dutch Outsourcing Association (2011). www.platformoutsourcing.nl, https://sourcingnederland.nl/
12. de Jong, F., van Hillegersberg, J., van Eck, P., van der Kolk, F., Jorissen, R.: Governance of offshore it outsourcing at shell global functions IT-BAM development and application of a governance framework to improve outsourcing relationships. In: Oshri, I., Kotlarsky, J. (eds.) Global Sourcing 2010. LNBIP, vol. 55, pp. 119–150. Springer, Heidelberg (2010). https://doi.org/10.1007/978-3-642-15417-1_8
13. McKinsey, "Five ways to unlock win–win value from IT-services sourcing relationships. McKinsey (2017). https://www.mckinsey.com/business-functions/mckinsey-digital/our-insights/five-ways-to-unlock-win-win-value-from-it-services-sourcing-relationships. Accessed 09 Oct 2019
14. Longo, A., Zappatore, M., Bochicchio, A.M.: Service level aware - contract management. In: 2015 IEEE International Conference on Services Computing, June 2015, pp. 499–506. https://doi.org/10.1109/scc.2015.74
15. Madaan, N., et al.: A system for predicting health of an E-Contract. In: 2018 IEEE International Conference on Services Computing (SCC), July 2018, pp. 57–64. https://doi.org/10.1109/scc.2018.00015
16. Chen, Y., Bharadwaj, A.: An empirical analysis of contract structures in IT outsourcing. Inf. Syst. Res. **20**(4), 484–506 (2009). https://doi.org/10.1287/isre.1070.0166
17. Scoca, V., Uriarte, R.B., Nicola, R.D.: Smart contract negotiation in cloud computing. In: 2017 IEEE 10th International Conference on Cloud Computing (CLOUD), June 2017, pp. 592–599. https://doi.org/10.1109/cloud.2017.81
18. Gómez, S.G., Rueda, J.L., Chimeno, A.E.: Management of the business SLAs for services eContracting. In: Wieder, P., Butler, J., Theilmann, W., Yahyapour, R. (eds.) Service Level Agreements for Cloud Computing, pp. 209–224. Springer, New York (2011). https://doi.org/10.1007/978-1-4614-1614-2_13
19. Ward, C., Buco, M.J., Chang, R.N., Luan, L.Z.: A generic SLA semantic model for the execution management of e-Business outsourcing contracts. In: Bauknecht, K., Tjoa, A.M., Quirchmayr, G. (eds.) EC-Web 2002. LNCS, vol. 2455, pp. 363–376. Springer, Heidelberg (2002). https://doi.org/10.1007/3-540-45705-4_38
20. Buco, M., Chang, R., Luan, L., Ward, C., Wolf, J., Yu, P.: Managing eBusiness on demand SLA contracts in business terms using the cross-SLA execution manager SAM. In: The Sixth International Symposium on Autonomous Decentralized Systems. ISADS 2003, April 2003, pp. 157–164 (2003). https://doi.org/10.1109/isads.2003.1193944
21. Pinna, A., Ibba, S.: A blockchain-based decentralized system for proper handling of temporary employment contracts. In: Arai, K., Kapoor, S., Bhatia, R. (eds.) SAI 2018. AISC, vol. 857, pp. 1231–1243. Springer, Cham (2019). https://doi.org/10.1007/978-3-030-01177-2_88
22. Gräther, W., Kolvenbach, S., Ruland, R., Schütte, J., Torres, C., Wendland, F.: Blockchain for Education: Lifelong Learning Passport (2018). https://doi.org/10.18420/blockchain2018_07
23. Brinkkemper, F.L.: Decentralized credential publication and verification : a method for issuing and verifying academic degrees with smart contracts, 28 June 2018. https://essay.utwente.nl/75199/. Accessed 14 Oct 2019
24. Xue, J., Xu, C., Zhang, Y., Bai, L.: DStore: a distributed cloud storage system based on smart contracts and blockchain. In: Vaidya, J., Li, J. (eds.) ICA3PP 2018. LNCS, vol. 11336, pp. 385–401. Springer, Cham (2018). https://doi.org/10.1007/978-3-030-05057-3_30

Outsourcing and Offshoring to Individuals

Paul Alpar(✉), Lars Osterbrink, and Eva Klein

University at Marburg, 35037 Marburg, Germany
`alpar@staff.uni-marburg.de`

Abstract. We examine jobs on a popular freelancing platform that are marked or described as potentially ongoing jobs. We consider them to have characteristics of outsourcing tasks, but they are geared towards individuals rather than companies. Our empirical research shows that such jobs are offered in programming like in traditional IT outsourcing but also in many Internet-related jobs like content writing and writing in social media, search engine advertising, or e-mail marketing. Most employers are located in the U.S. or other English-speaking countries. This makes English language skills very valuable. The data indicate that jobs are often outsourced to countries with lower wage levels. However, employers often try to outsource them to the country where they are located, or at least to a country in a similar time-zone. In such cases, they are obviously willing to pay more for the work in order to have better communication possibilities. Outsourcing to individuals creates opportunities for these individuals. However, given their relatively weak position towards outsourcing companies they risk more and probably earn less than employees in these companies or at outsourcing suppliers.

Keywords: Outsourcing · Offshoring · Gig economy · Freelancer · Upwork

1 Introduction

We define outsourcing for information system services following [1] as an "intermediate to long-term" arrangement between an outsourcing firm and one or more independent vendors who are contracted to provide the firm repeatedly with various information system services throughout the life of the contract. In the original definition, the timeframe "intermediate to long-term" has been specified as five to ten years, but this has been reduced meanwhile to a shorter period because ten years, for example, turned out to be too long in the context of information technology. This definition is rooted in the theoretical explanation of outsourcing by transaction cost economics (TCE) [2] with cost saving as the primary goal. Over the last decades, additional reasons for outsourcing have emerged such as acquiring resources not available in the company or business transformation [3], but cost cutting remains an important incentive for outsourcing [4]. Consequently, other theoretical explanations are used for the new contexts, e.g., the resource-based view (RBV) of the firm or organizational theory [3], but the above definition still applies and TCE can often be used to interpret such cases, too.

Sometimes the "other" company is located in a distant country (often on another continent) and the arrangement is referred to as offshoring. This other company may be

© Springer Nature Switzerland AG 2020
I. Oshri et al. (Eds.): Global Sourcing 2019, LNBIP 410, pp. 93–109, 2020.
https://doi.org/10.1007/978-3-030-66834-1_6

partly or wholly owned by the company that outsources work, which is then referred to as captive sourcing. What is common in all these variations of outsourcing is the fact that the unit that executes the work is organized as a company. In recent years, more ongoing work is being outsourced to individuals. This work is smaller in size than activities usually outsourced to other companies, but it can be quite significant in sum.

One of the practical reasons for the rise in contracting outsiders (often referred to as freelancers) is the availability of platforms like Upwork.com, Freelancer.com, or Fiverr.com that make contracting with outsiders a simple process. In addition, many workers from all over the world are eager to take tasks offered by employers on these platforms who are themselves often located in another part of the world. A World Bank report used the term "online outsourcing" to describe this type of online contracting [5]. A survey [6] reported that 3.7 million more Americans freelanced in 2018 than four years before. It was predicted that this trend will continue, especially since young people are more prone to advantages of freelancing, which seems to be true for both employers and freelancers. In the context of outsourcing, it is not known yet exactly how prevalent this phenomenon is and what its consequences may be. As people and companies become more experienced and familiar with freelancing, outsourcing of even important activities of a company to freelancers might be a reasonable action. In future, outsourcing to freelancers may be the only viable option for some companies because of talent shortages, particularly in the IT sector [7].

A suitable theoretical explanation for the rise in freelancing can be the modular organization of the firm [3, 8]. Here, it relates to the modularization of supply. A modular organization of activities replaces a hierarchical organization by a flexible network of loosely coupled activities (modules). The company needs to develop its capability to coordinate such a supply network, so it can quickly and appropriately react to changes in its environment. These goals can be achieved to some extent by outsourcing of activities. [9], for example, illustrate the concept with modular legal services for law firms. In our context, the outsourcing activities seem to be increasingly delivered by individuals for several reasons. Individuals can offer their services at lower cost because they usually do not have overhead costs (e.g., office rent, management and secretarial services). They are more flexible because they can better adjust to demand since they are self-employed. Due to platforms like Upwork, hiring them incurs lower transaction costs than in the past. There are also less legal constraints, which gives firms more freedom to act. The platforms have also extended the size of the available workforce. In one important area, programming, the flexible organization is also enabled by more standardization. There are more tools and libraries available, which are not only contributed by very motivated individuals (like in the beginnings of Linux) but also by tech giants who do not make money with software but want to create ecosystems with their free-to-use or open source software (e.g., Google with the operating system Android). This way, skilled individuals can write and maintain powerful modules without teams. It can be summarized that the modular organization has been taken one step further by outsourcing some activities to individuals rather than companies. Alternative work arrangements as a consequence of modular organization were already considered years ago, though only agency workers were considered at that time [8]. Of course, the mentioned advantages of outsourcing to freelancers can also have disadvantages, both for outsourcing firms and freelancers, as explained below.

Some research on contracting individuals [10] analyzed whether the platforms support labor arbitrage, but its authors considered all work offered on the platforms to be "outsourcing". Following this logic, any transaction with a third party, even an employee buying a sandwich from a food truck, could be considered outsourcing. The majority of tasks offered on freelancing platforms are small one-time market transactions. For example, [11] analyzed the platform Rent A Coder (now Freelancer.com) where 95% of winning bids (assigned contract values) were below $500. However, job postings on Upwork suggest that employers do not only recruit freelancers for well-defined and limited projects but also for ongoing activities and indefinite relationships. Such ongoing job postings can be in technical areas like web development or IT consultancy but also in creative areas like writing blog posts or graphic design. Further, profile histories of both employers and freelancers provide evidence that some work relationships last over more than seven years and are still in progress. This is longer than the duration of many company-to-company outsourcing contracts written in the last years. Since there is no explicitly defined category of outsourcing tasks on the freelancing platforms, we use different criteria to identify tasks that can be considered outsourcing jobs before analyzing them in more detail.

We examine the phenomenon empirically. This is done by analyzing data from Upwork, one of the biggest platforms for freelance work [5, 12]. Upwork reported for 2018 a gross service volume of $1.76bn (28% increase compared to 2017) and a revenue of $253.4m (25% increase compared to 2017) [13]. This work is mainly exploratory. First, we research to what extent and scope one of the biggest freelancing platforms offers ongoing jobs to determine the facts. Second, cost savings is one of the most dominant reasons for outsourcing [4] and, as explained above, outsourcing to individuals may help to save costs. Thus, we investigate the costs for outsourcing to individuals and compare them with costs of employed workers. Third, we examine whether other decision criteria beyond costs play an important role. If not, most jobs would go to the less developed countries with (much) lower wages. [5] suggest that online outsourcing may be a great opportunity, especially for developing countries, to get access to profitable jobs on the global market. We explore specifically:

1. What is the current extent and scope of outsourcing to individuals?
2. Does outsourcing to individuals save labor costs?
3. Are there other criteria beyond costs in the outsourcing decision to individuals?

First, we discuss outsourcing and offshoring and the meaning of freelancing and the role of freelancing platforms. Then, we consider the theoretical advantages and disadvantages of outsourcing to individuals instead of to companies. This is followed by an empirical investigation. In this section, we report how we collected data and the results. Then, we interpret the findings, name the limitations, and give some conclusions.

2 Theoretical Background

2.1 Outsourcing and Offshoring

The global market size of outsourced services (both domestically and offshore) almost doubled from 45.6bn U.S. dollars in 2000 to $85.6bn in 2018 [14]. $62bn of those $85.6bn was outsourcing of information technology and the remaining $23.6bn was business process outsourcing [15]. Preferred outsourcing locations changed through the years and decades for different reasons. A survey by [16] rated the location suitability of countries for outsourcing across four dimensions: financial attractiveness, people skills and availability, business environment, and digital resonance. According to this survey, the current top five countries for outsourcing and offshoring are all Asian countries, namely India, China, Malaysia, Indonesia, and Vietnam (in this order). However, in recent years, also western countries, namely the U.S., United Kingdom, and Germany, achieved a high ranking due to high people skills and availability and a good business environment [16]. This indicates that reasons for and risks in outsourcing are complex. [4] summarized reasons and risks for outsourcing. Reasons are, for example, focusing on strategic issues, increasing flexibility, improving quality, omit routine tasks, getting access to technology, and reducing staff/technology costs. Risks are, among others, insufficient quality of the provider's staff, excessive dependence on the provider, security issues, an ambiguous cost-value ratio, and potential opposition of the regular employees [4].

2.2 Online Freelancer and Freelancing Platforms

Freelancing as a term for a work relationship is not clearly defined [17]. It has some similarities and some dissimilarities with other types or definitions of work relationships. Freelancers are a part of workers who are not salaried [18] and they are often self-employed. In general, they are independent from employers and, therefore, also called "independent contractors" [19]. They are highly autonomous and self-organized, which is different from, e.g., temporary workers who also have short-term contracts with different employers but are mostly organized and controlled by agencies [20]. However, also freelancers partly rely on agencies as intermediaries to contact or gain access to employers, but they give up less control in doing so [21]. Further, people do not have to be a full-time freelancer, a combination of different work forms is possible. For example, regular employees can also do part-time freelancing [17]. In the past, full-time freelancers often worked in the media industry (e.g., journalists) where they were called "Boundaryless Worker" [22]. After the rise of the IT industry, freelancers also had the opportunity to work as independent software developers [23]. Nowadays, freelancing exists in a wide array of different industries. The difficulty of tasks assigned to freelancers also varies a lot as opposed to, e.g., "independent professionals" who by definition possess high skills in some area [24].

Not only agencies but also online platforms can function as intermediaries, whose business model is to connect employers with freelancers [25]. In addition to providing a place to meet for employers and freelancers, online platforms can also provide services like algorithm-based freelancer recommendations and individual consultation. The aim is to decrease transaction costs and provide incentives to use the platform for both employers and freelancers [26]. The business model of such platforms is usually based on getting a share of a freelancer's and employer's revenue and/or monthly payments from employers for services. In 2015, only 0.5% of all U.S. workers indicated using an online intermediary (while 15.8% were in "alternative work arrangements" like freelancing or temporary work), but this number increases rapidly [19].

There is a great number of platforms mediating between employers and freelancers with different types of specializations. Some platforms are not sector-specific (e.g., Upwork.com, Fiverr.com), while others are specialized, e.g., 99designs.com for design services, Writeraccess.com for authors, or Topcoder.com for programming. Famous examples for platforms mediating physical local activities are Uber.com for transports or Taskrabbit.com for household chores. Furthermore, some platforms do not operate world-wide but only in one or a few countries like Freelance.de in Germany.

2.3 Outsourcing to Individual Online Freelancers

The World Bank differentiated two sectors for work platforms, namely microtask crowdsourcing and online freelancing [5]. Microtask crowdsourcing includes mainly small tasks with low skill requirements like tagging pictures or searching for information on the Internet. Popular platforms for microtask crowdsourcing are, for example, Amazon Mechanical Turk (MTurk.com) and Crowdflower.com. Online freelancing entails primarily lengthier and more complex tasks like web development or accounting. Well-known platforms for online freelancing are Upwork.com, Freelancer.com, and Fiverr.com. There is a substantial overlap, meaning that work on freelancing platforms can sometimes be relatively easy and short like writing a review or transcribing an audio file [5].

Outsourcing of an ongoing job can have several theoretical advantages for outsourcing employers and individual freelancers. The employer does not need to commit to big outsourcing projects, which can be a big risk in outsourcing to firms [4]. It is much easier to terminate individual outsourcing contracts than a big one. For example, [5] reported that an online startup in India uses online freelancing to test people with small low-risk projects before assigning them larger projects or even hiring them when the work quality is high. The freelancer can work for more than one employer at the same time, which reduces his or her dependence on one employer. Often, the needed specialists are not available on the local market, even if a company would want to hire them [7]. But they may be available for work from abroad. By approaching them individually, it should be easier to find the right skills at the right time and for less money (no payment for overhead costs of a partner organization). It is not necessary to write contracts for long periods. The definition of complex contracts is usually not needed because jobs assigned to individuals are usually smaller and less complex than big outsourcing contracts with other firms, e.g., there is less necessity to define penalties for bad contract fulfillment or early contract abortions [4]. This does not imply that contracts with freelancers never fail. However, potential damage and costs are relatively low compared to larger outsourcing contracts with other firms. Entering an ongoing relationship is beneficial compared to several short fixed-time jobs because it creates trust and reduces information asymmetry between the involved parties.

However, coordination of work must be accomplished internally or by another paid third party if many different freelancers work on a related project. This increases the cost of outsourcing. Furthermore, when outsourcing to a large professional firm, there are usually benefits due to economies of scale [4], which is less prevalent for individuals. It is usually riskier to rely on an individual than on an established company because, e.g., in case of illness of an individual, a company has more flexibility to address the issue. In case of high damages to the outsourcer caused by the work of an individual, no individual freelancer will be able to take financial responsibility for it (unless the freelancer has enough insurance for such a case).

In sum, companies need to weigh potential advantages and disadvantages, carefully select jobs for outsourcing, and then select appropriate freelancers (incl. their location, as will be discussed below).

3   Empirical Investigation

3.1   Data Collection

We investigate job postings from Upwork.com as mentioned above to answer the posed questions. The freelancing platforms Elance.com and ODesk.com merged in 2015 to form Upwork. Upwork uses the term "Client" for work providers and "Freelancer" for those who seek work. The offered work is called "Job" and clients may also have a higher-level "Project", for which they can hire multiple freelancers for multiple jobs. We chose Upwork because it is one of the biggest online freelancing platforms and it is not sector-specific. Further, job postings are freely accessible and well-structured. Figure 1 depicts the main part of an exemplary job posting on Upwork.

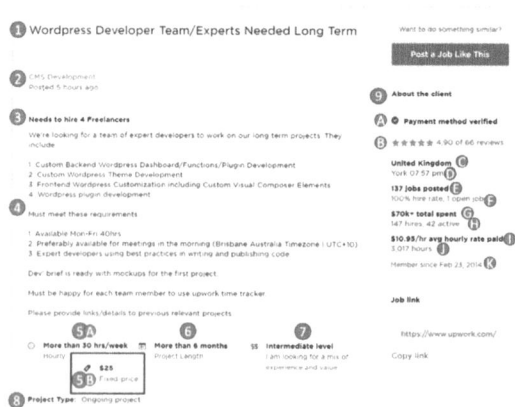

Fig. 1. Job posting on Upwork (main part)

As Fig. 1 illustrates, a job posting can be very detailed on Upwork. A job posting consists of a job title (1), a pre-defined specific job category (2), the number of freelancers needed (3), a free text description of the job (4), whether payment is hourly based (5A) or fixed (5B), the expected project length (6), the desired level of freelancer experience (7), whether it is an ongoing or one-time project (8), and information about the client (9). Furthermore, job postings can entail questions for applying freelancers, needed skills and expertise, preferred qualifications, and activities on the specific job posting. We describe some of the variables in more detail as they become relevant for the results and discussion section. Note that not all specifications are mandatory when creating a job posting, which creates differences between job postings regarding the extent of given information.

Our aim is to analyze ongoing jobs. Upwork offers some filters to simplify the search for job postings, but it is not possible to filter for "ongoing projects", which would have been the obvious way to filter. However, Upwork allows filtering for keywords in the job description and even some "one-time projects" indicate in the job description that a long-term work relationship is possible if work results are satisfactory. Thus, we used keywords in the job description to identify job postings for ongoing jobs. We read several hundreds of unfiltered job postings to identify recurring keywords describing an ongoing job. Most job postings used the keywords "long-term" or "ongoing" (with different spellings, e.g., with or without a hyphen) to describe an ongoing job, but also keywords like "continuous", "longtime", and "further work" were being used. We applied all these keywords to filter for job postings with ongoing jobs.

The collection of the data has been conducted from 1st to 3rd July 2019, using the web scraping tool "Web Scraper" (Version 0.4.1, webscraper.io). It took three days to collect all relevant job postings because Upwork restricts excessive website queries by using CAPTCHAs every once in a while. All the variables from each job posting are publicly available for the time being (upwork.com/freelance-jobs, February, 2020), but a free registration is needed to use more sophisticated job search functions.

Some preprocessing was necessary to correctly identify and specify variables, which was done with KNIME Analytics (Version 4.0.0, knime.com). See description in the Appendices for more details.

3.2 Results

After preprocessing, 13,236 job postings for (potentially) ongoing work relationships remain in our dataset. Most of the retrieved job postings are defined as ongoing projects as one would expect. However, some one-time jobs were also retrieved (see Fig. 2) and

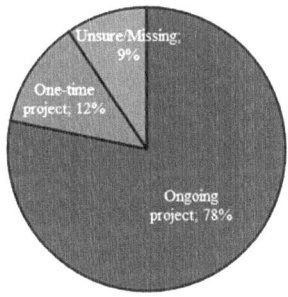

Fig. 2. Frequencies of project types

retained because they indicate in their description that ongoing work relationships are possible if the work on the given project is successful.

Furthermore, 76% of ongoing job postings come from clients with at least some actual hires, while 63% of ongoing job postings are from clients with at least six actual hires. This suggests that ongoing jobs are not just posted, but clients actually hire freelancers for such work.

1. What is the current extent and scope of outsourcing to individuals? Around the time of data collection (July 2019), the total number of job postings on Upwork fluctuated around 100,000. Thus, ongoing job postings appear to have a share of ~13% of all job postings and are not just rare single cases. The numbers of job postings translate to a multiple of job openings because a post may include a search for more than one freelancer.

Although we only scraped details of ongoing job postings, we retrieved the relative frequencies of broad job categories for all available job postings at the time of our data collection. Figure 3 depicts the relative frequencies for ongoing job postings compared to all job postings.

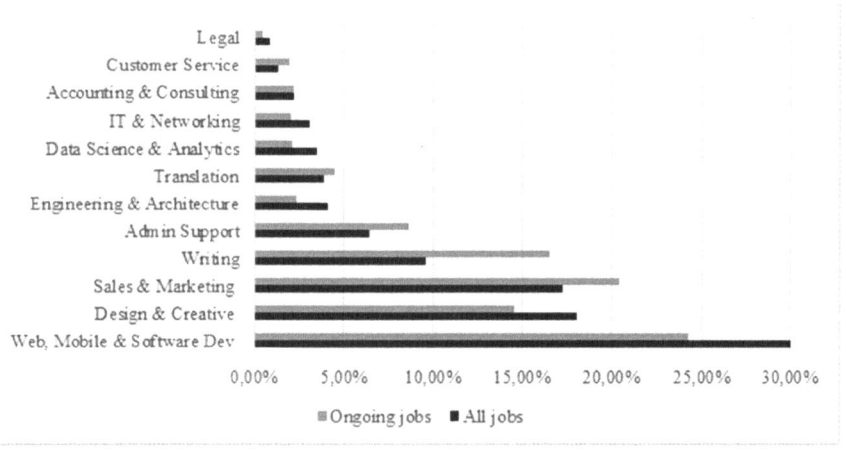

Fig. 3. Relative frequencies of broad job categories (ongoing and all job postings)

Analyses of broad categories revealed that Sales & Marketing mostly includes various forms of electronic marketing (SEA, SEO, e-Mail) and Admin Support often means work with some software or system (like Amazon, Zendesk, or Microsoft). However, job descriptions show that the allocation of posts to broad categories is ambiguous. A SEO job may be allocated to Sales & Marketing or Admin Support. As Fig. 3 shows, Web, Mobile & Software Dev, Sales & Marketing, Writing, and Design & Creative are the most common broad job categories for both ongoing and all job postings. Web, Mobile & Software Dev is less frequent in ongoing job postings compared to all job postings (24% vs 30%), while Writing appears to be more frequent in ongoing job postings (17% vs 10%).

Furthermore, ongoing jobs appear to be relatively long-term oriented, as Fig. 4 illustrates the relative frequencies of estimated project length. The estimated length of a project is often not specified (38%), but, if there is an estimate, 59% of all ongoing job postings are estimated to take longer than six months (longest available option on Upwork).

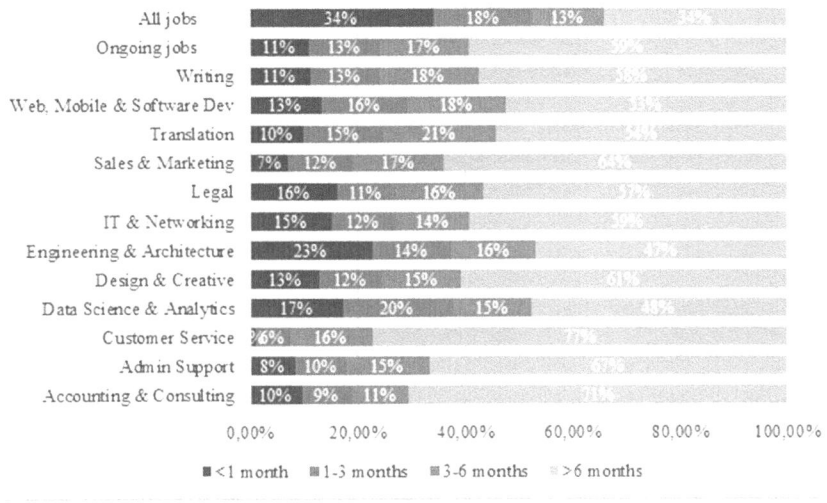

Fig. 4. Project length for each broad job category (38% missing for ongoing jobs)

Project length confirms for most categories that most ongoing jobs are meant for more than 6 months. We further analyzed the ongoing job postings by depicting estimated project hours for each broad job category in Fig. 5. Upwork offers only two categories in this case.

The estimated project hours per week are often missing or unsure ("hours to be determined") and only 34% of non-missing values indicate a need for more than 30 h of work per week. *Admin Support*, *Design & Creative*, and *Writing* tend to need less than 30 h per week, while *Web, Mobile & Software Dev* contains many projects that require more than 30 h per week. In sum, the extent and scope of outsourcing to individuals is substantial.

2. Does outsourcing to individuals save labor costs? Rough estimates about wages can be made by looking at the preferred experience level for freelancers. These levels can be translated to hourly rates following Upwork's definitions. Upwork defines as follows: entry level indicates an hourly rate below $13.50 ("I am looking for freelancers with the lowest rates"), intermediate level indicates $13.50 to $40 per hour ("I am looking for a mix of experience and value"), and expert level indicates an hourly rate above $40 ("I am willing to pay higher rates for the most experienced freelancers"). This is clearly communicated when creating a job posting. Figure 6 illustrates the preferred experience level for all jobs, for all ongoing jobs, and for ongoing jobs by broad job category.

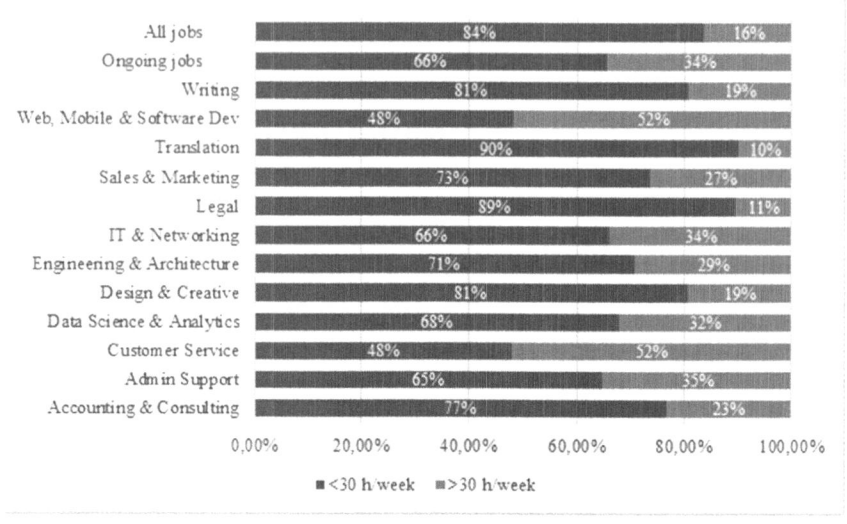

Fig. 5. Project hours for each broad job category (59% missing for ongoing jobs)

Furthermore, the U.S. hourly labor wage 75th percentile is given for comparison [27]. Reading example: 25% of U.S. workers in the "Writing"-category have an hourly labor wage of $41.49 or higher.

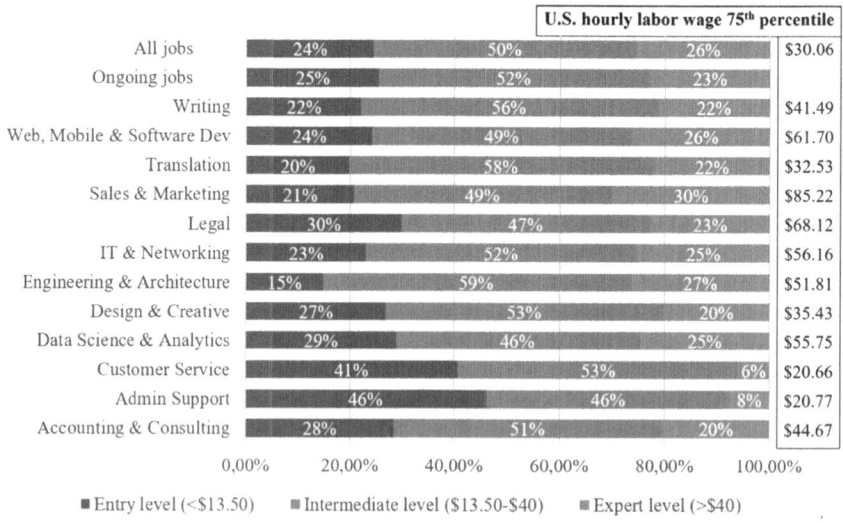

Fig. 6. Preferred experience (wage level) for freelancers compared to U.S. hourly labor wage

The distribution of preferred experience level (~hourly wage) for ongoing jobs is similar to the corresponding distribution of all jobs (see rows one and two). However, clients with jobs in Admin Support and Customer Service have almost no preference for expert level experience but are often satisfied with entry level skills. In Sales & Marketing, Engineering & Architecture, and IT-related jobs more experts are needed than on average. Most clients search for freelancers with an intermediate level of experience as can be seen in Fig. 6. Based on the given information, we cannot exactly say how costly outsourcing to individuals is. However, for a rough estimation, we can compare the freelancer wage level with the hourly labor wage of U.S. employees for each category, as given in Fig. 6. Similar to freelance work, the U.S. hourly labor wage is lowest for Customer Service and Admin Support and highest for Sales & Marketing. In relation to U.S. employees, Upwork freelancers appear to cause lower labor costs in most job categories, especially in Web, Mobile & Software Dev, Sales & Marketing, Legal, IT & Networking, and Data Science & Analytics. For clients, the difference is even larger because of additional costs like paid leave, supplemental pay, insurance, retirement and savings, and other legally required benefits, which make U.S. employees on average ~45% more expensive [28]. In comparison, clients on Upwork only have to pay a 3% fee and optionally up to $499 per month (upwork.com/i/pricing/). The exact matchings of specific job categories and more information about U.S. hourly labor wages can be found in Table 1 in the Appendices.

In sum, labor costs and especially effective costs for employers appear to be much lower for freelancers.

3. Are there other criteria beyond costs in the outsourcing decision to individuals?

Upwork stated in its annual report that most of the revenue generated by freelancers goes to the U.S. (25%), India (16%), and the Philippines (10%) [13]. The other half was generated by freelancers in other countries. Further, the revenue generated from clients mostly came from the U.S. (73%) [13]. This corresponds to findings from [5] and [29], showing that most freelancing jobs originate from Western countries but are often outsourced to non-Western countries, suggesting that cost-saving is a major factor for outsourcing firms. However, a substantial amount of jobs remains in Western and developed countries (see above and Fig. 8). We examine language requirements and location preferences as potential reasons for such behavior.

Interestingly, most job postings do not define a preferred English proficiency in the designated field (68% missing), although most clients come from an English-speaking country (see Fig. 8). This could mean that the world has become flat in the sense that distance and language do not matter much and everybody can compete for all jobs [30]. However, the language requirement is often specified in the job description as our natural language analysis revealed (about 1320 cases). Reasons to place it there are that often more than one language proficiency is needed (e.g., for translation jobs or when customers in many countries should be supported) or that the exact requirement can be better described in the project description (e.g., "Perfect English with excellent grammar"). Further, at least basic English proficiency is implicitly given because English is the only officially supported language on Upwork and almost all job postings and all of our scraped ongoing job postings are written in English. Therefore, it does not really need to be specified if basic proficiency is enough. It is also possible that clients do not care to specify it because they want to peruse all applications and check whether the freelancers possess an official language certificate, which can be uploaded in the profile (e.g., IELTS). There are also job postings requiring proficiency in other languages like German, Russian, or Japanese, which explains a portion of missing values for English proficiency. If a preferred English proficiency is defined, ~79% of job postings prefer a fluent or native/bilingual level, as can be seen in Fig. 7. It also confirms our observation that basic knowledge is seldom specified.

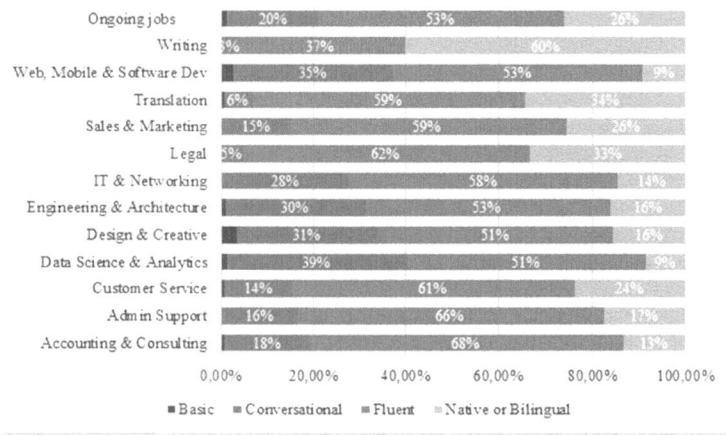

Fig. 7. English proficiency for each broad job category (68% missing for ongoing jobs)

Upwork operates worldwide. While all job postings originate from a clearly defined country, only 17% define explicitly at least one preferred freelancer location, which can be a country but also a continent, as shown in Fig. 8. As described above, these specifications are sometimes found in the job description or clients decide after receiving applications. The broad categories were further grouped in IT (Data Science & Analytics, IT & Networking, Web, Mobile & Software Dev, Engineering & Architecture), Professional (Accounting & Consulting, Legal, Translation), Creative (Design & Creative, Writing), and Service (Admin Support, Customer Service, Sales & Marketing). Reading example: 392 job postings from the U.S. listed Philippines as (one of the) preferred locations of a freelancer.

Figure 8 illustrates that most job postings originate from developed countries and primarily from the U.S. Almost two-thirds (62.4%) of all job postings originate from the shown four countries. However, the share of job postings with at least one preferred location is much higher for job postings from the U.S. (45%) and United Kingdom (35%) compared to Australia (10%) and Canada (15%). U.S. clients often prefer low-cost countries for their ongoing jobs (Philippines, India, and Ukraine). In the case of Philippines, these are mostly jobs in the service area. Many creative and IT jobs remain in the U.S. or Canada. In the case of Americas as the desired destination, this can be a mixture of goals, low cost, and same time zone. The choice of Europe for IT jobs is probably the expectation of high quality. The choice of Ukraine probably reflects the availability of IT people and the desire for high quality and low costs. There is also some

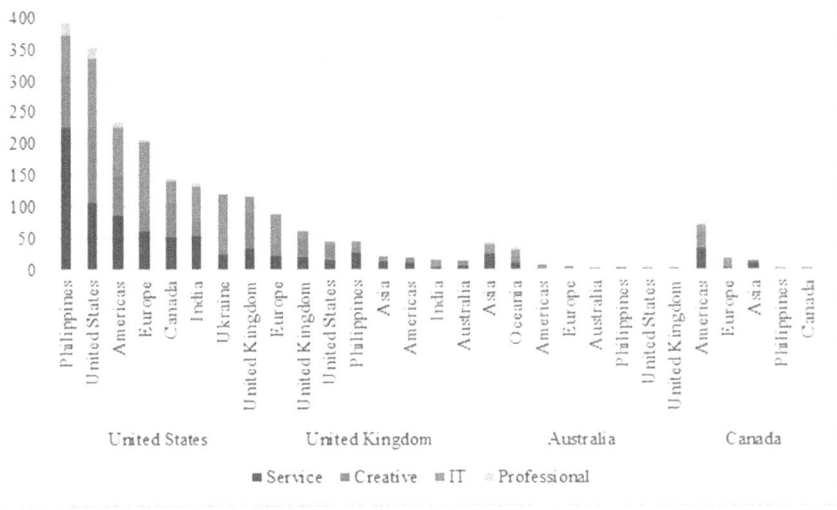

Fig. 8. The top four countries posting jobs and their most frequent preferred freelancer locations

working time overlap with Europe and Ukraine. In the case of United Kingdom, the desire for same country or same time zone is even stronger. Australia has such a small population and is so far from most other countries that it must be open to other countries and continents. However, even there, one can recognize a desire for proximity (Asia and Oceania). Finally, Canada, also with a small population, shows preference for same time zone (Americas).

In sum, low-cost workers from abroad are a major part, but it is not always the goal of outsourcing firms to use these workers just to save costs. Language and time zone can still be important decision criteria and, therefore, obstacles preventing the world from becoming completely flat.

4   Discussion

Outsourcing to individuals is wide-spread in Internet-based non-programming areas like electronic marketing and writing of content or posts in social media. In IT jobs, clients outsource to less developed countries where there is enough talent (which is usually also cheaper than in developed economies). It must be assumed that this is the case when jobs are or can be isolated from other software development at the client. In cases where this is not possible, clients seem to put an emphasis on outsourcing to the same time zone (even if the costs are higher than in less developed countries). With the increasing use of agile development methods this makes sense because there is an increased need for communication when exact and exhaustive specifications become rare. This is also often true for design and creative jobs. In all these cases, labor arbitrage is of limited value. The world is not becoming flat as [30] argued.

However, freelancers in developed countries who take outsourcing jobs have contracts that are usually shorter and easier to terminate than regular employee contracts.

Also, they do not receive any benefits. The contracts are less complex and less clear in legal terms, which makes them more vulnerable than in regular employment. In sum, many freelancers in developed countries probably earn less and bear more risk than their employed counterparts. This is the price for more flexibility (whether it is desired or not) [19]. Companies that outsource to individuals, be it their own will or necessity, must have good skills in splitting and planning jobs and coordination of independent freelancers. Companies taking outsourcing jobs face now competition from individuals who until a few years ago were not able to compete for such outsourcing jobs [5]. This puts pressure on their prices, at least for small outsourcing jobs.

Concerning limitations of this article, it is possible that clients used other keywords to describe ongoing activities, which we did not include or that some of our included job postings are in fact not really ongoing oriented. However, we manually read several hundreds of unfiltered job postings and the included job postings, which all confirmed our choices for the search of ongoing jobs. A substantial bias is unlikely. Furthermore, our analysis is based on one large platform and one point in time. Results may vary between platforms and different times. Finally, rules, laws, and regulations concerning online outsourcing are unclear and ambiguous in many countries at the moment [5]. For example, the "Arbeitnehmerüberlassungsgesetz" (AÜG) in Germany (tries to) prohibit extensive use of temporary workers (including online freelancers) to prevent pseudo self-employment. Thus, companies need to pay close attention to their (sometimes changing) national laws before they decide to outsource to individuals.

5 Conclusion

The presented research is exploratory but tries to establish facts that can serve as a rationale for further theory-based or practice-oriented research. It has been established that the biggest world-wide platform for freelancer work is being used for outsourcing to individuals, esp. for Web, Mobile & Software Development, service tasks, Writing, and Design & Creative jobs. The preferences for location of freelancers make it obvious that saving costs is not the only goal of outsourcers. Based on the facts, an interesting research goal may be to develop methods for effective coordination of work of several independent freelancers.

Appendices

The scraped data from Upwork needed considerable preprocessing to make it usable for analysis. For example, the reviews statistics for the client (9B in Fig. 1) were scraped like "4.90 of 66 reviews" in one column. We divided that column into two columns called "ReviewsScore" and "ReviewsCount" and deleted the words "of" and "reviews" to switch the data format from string to number. Further, we sorted out invalid job postings. First, we identified and deleted duplicates that occurred because of our time lag in the scraping process or because of job postings using more than one of the keywords. Second, we identified, reviewed, and deleted job postings having a negation of one of our keywords, e.g., "This is not an ongoing task" by using a regular expression:

/.*([Nn]o|[Nn]ot)(\S|\s|\s[Aa]|\s|\s[Aa]n\s)([Ll]ong.[Tt]erm|[Ll]ongterm|[Oo]n.[Gg]
oing| [Oo]ngoing|[Cc]ontinuous|[Ll]onger.term|[Ff]urther.[Ww]ork|[Ll]ong.[Tt]ime).*/

Less than 20 job postings had such a negation and all of them were deleted from the dataset after reviewing them. Lastly, we added an additional variable for the broad job category of a job posting because the given job category is quite specific (e.g., "CMS Development", 2 in Fig. 1). Although the broad job category is not given in the job posting, every specific job category is predefined and clearly attributed to a broad job category by Upwork. We retrieved the attributions with the creation tool for job posting within Upwork.

Table 1. Matching of Upwork and U.S. Bureau of Labor Statistics job categories

Upwork	2018 U.S. National Hourly Wages (in $) [27]					
Category	Category	Mean	PCT10	PCT25	Median	PCT75	PCT90
All jobs	All occupations	24.98	9.95	12.37	18.58	30.06	47.31
Writing	Writers and editors	34.58	16.18	22.23	30.53	41.49	56.55
Web, mobile and software dev	Software developers and programmers	50.23	27.20	36.07	48.04	61.70	76.78
Translation	Interpreters and translators	26.55	13.09	17.53	24.00	32.53	43.56
Sales & marketing	Marketing and sales managers	68.75	30.28	42.87	61.59	85.22	>=100
Legal	Legal occupations	52.25	18.04	25.47	38.85	68.12	>=100
IT & networking	Database and systems administrators and network architects	45.09	25.15	32.29	42.79	56.16	70.09
Engineering & architecture	Architecture and engineering occupations	42.01	21.33	28.72	38.55	51.81	66.98
Design & creative	Arts, design, entertainment, sports, and media occupations	28.74	10.99	15.39	23.70	35.43	50.36
Data science & analytics	Computer and information analysts	45.67	26.28	33.36	43.31	55.75	70.01

(*continued*)

Table 1. (*continued*)

Upwork	2018 U.S. National Hourly Wages (in $) [27]						
Category	Category	Mean	PCT10	PCT25	Median	PCT75	PCT90
Customer service	Customer service representatives	17.53	10.65	12.85	16.23	20.66	26.59
Admin support	Other office and administrative support workers	17.28	10.14	12.40	16.16	20.77	26.22
Accounting & consulting	Accountants and auditors	37.89	20.99	26.48	33.89	44.67	59.06

References

1. Alpar, P., Saharia, A.N.: Outsourcing information system functions: an organization economics perspective. J. Organ. Comput. (1995). https://doi.org/10.1080/10919399509540251
2. Williamson, O.E.: Economic Organization. Wheatsheaf Books, Brighton (1986)
3. Hätönen, J., Eriksson, T.: 30+ years of research and practice of outsourcing: exploring the past and anticipating the future. J. Int. Manag. (2009). https://doi.org/10.1016/j.intman.2008.07.002
4. González, R., Gascó, J., Llopis, J.: Information systems outsourcing reasons and risks: review and evolution. J. Glob. Inf. Technol. Manag. (2016). https://doi.org/10.1080/1097198X.2016.1246932
5. Kuek, S.C., Paradi-Guilford, C., Fayomi, T., Imaizumi, S., Ipeirotis, P.: The global opportunity in online outsourcing (2015). http://documents.worldbank.org/curated/en/138371468000900555/The-global-opportunity-in-online-outsourcing. Accessed 9 Jan 2020
6. Freelancer Union and Upwork: Freelancing in America 2018 (5th Annual Report) (2018). https://www.upwork.com/i/freelancing-in-america/2018/. Accessed 9 Jan 2020
7. Harvey Nash, KPMG: CIO survey. A changing perspective (2019). https://www.hnkpmgciosurvey.com/. Accessed 9 Jan 2020
8. Schilling, M.A., Steensma, H.K.: The use of modular organizational forms: an industry-level analysis. Acad. Manag. J. (2001). https://doi.org/10.2307/3069394
9. Giannakis, M., Doran, D., Mee, D., Papadopoulos, T., Dubey, R.: The design and delivery of modular legal services: Implications for supply chain strategy. Int. J. Prod. Res. (2018). https://doi.org/10.1080/00207543.2018.1449976
10. Beerepoot, N., Lambregts, B.: Competition in online job marketplaces: towards a global labour market for outsourcing services? Glob. Netw. (2015). https://doi.org/10.1111/glob.12051
11. Gefen, D., Carmel, E.: Is the world really flat? A look at offshoring at an online programming marketplace. MIS Q. (2008). https://doi.org/10.2307/25148844
12. Gheorghe, M.: State of freelancing in IT and future trends. Int. J. Soc. Behav. Educ. Econ. Bus. Ind. Eng. (2015). https://doi.org/10.5281/zenodo.1338254
13. Upwork: Upwork Annual Report (2019). https://investors.upwork.com/static-files/556b56e7-5646-4e7a-bc8e-a98ea5a8f55f. Accessed 9 Jan 2020
14. Statista: Global market size of outsourced services from 2000 to 2018 (in billion U.S. dollars) (2019). https://www.statista.com/statistics/189788/global-outsourcing-market-size/. Accessed 9 Jan 2020

15. Statista: Global outsourcing industry revenue from 2010 to 2018, by service type (in billion U.S. dollars) (2019). https://www.statista.com/statistics/189800/global-outsourcing-industry-revenue-by-service-type/. Accessed 9 Jan 2020
16. A. T. Kearney: Digital resonance: the new factor impacting location attractiveness (2019). https://www.atkearney.com/digital-transformation/gsli/2019-full-report. Accessed 9 Jan 2020
17. Kitching, J., Smallbone, D.: Are freelancers a neglected form of small business? J. Small Bus. Enterp. Dev. (2012). https://doi.org/10.1108/14626001211196415
18. Kalleberg, A.L.: Nonstandard employment relations: part-time, temporary and contract work. Ann. Rev. Sociol. (2000). https://doi.org/10.1146/annurev.soc.26.1.341
19. Katz, L.F., Krueger, A.B.: The rise and nature of alternative work arrangements in the United States, 1995–2015. ILR Rev. (2019). https://doi.org/10.1177/0019793918820008
20. Connelly, C.E., Gallagher, D.G.: Emerging trends in contingent work research. J. Manag. (2004). https://doi.org/10.1016/j.jm.2004.06.008
21. Kalleberg, A.L., Dunn, M.: Good jobs, bad jobs in the gig economy. Perspect. Work **20**, 10–14 (2016)
22. Popiel, P.: "Boundaryless" in the creative economy: assessing freelancing on Upwork. Crit. Stud. Media Commun. (2017). https://doi.org/10.1080/15295036.2017.1282618
23. Slaughter, S., Ang, S.: Employment outsourcing in information systems. Commun. ACM (1996). https://doi.org/10.1145/233977.233994
24. Leighton, P., Brown, D.: Future working: the rise of Europes independent professionals. European Forum of Independent Professionals (EFIP) (2013). http://www.crse.co.uk/research/future-working-rise-europe%E2%80%99s-independent-professionals. Accessed 9 Jan 2020
25. Kuhn, K.M., Maleki, A.: Micro-entrepreneurs, dependent contractors, and instaserfs: understanding online labor platform workforces. Acad. Manag. Perspect. (2017). https://doi.org/10.5465/amp.2015.0111
26. Acquier, A., Daudigeos, T., Pinkse, J.: Promises and paradoxes of the sharing economy: an organizing framework. Technol. Forecast. Soc. Chang. (2017). https://doi.org/10.1016/j.techfore.2017.07.006
27. Bureau of Labor Statistics: May 2018 national occupational employment and wage estimates United States (2019). https://www.bls.gov/oes/current/oes_nat.htm#15-0000. Accessed 9 Jan 2020
28. Bureau of Labor Statistics: Employer costs for employee compensation-June 2019 (2019). https://www.bls.gov/news.release/archives/ecec_09172019.pdf. Accessed 9 Jan 2020
29. Lehdonvirta, V., Kässi, O., Hjorth, I., Barnard, H., Graham, M.: The global platform economy: a new offshoring institution enabling emerging-economy microproviders. J. Manag. (2019). https://doi.org/10.1177/0149206318786781
30. Friedman, T.L.: The World is Flat. Brief History of the Twenty-First Century, 3rd edn. Picador, New York (2007)

Understanding the Impact of Isomorphic Influences on Business Services Outsourcing Decisions: An Institutional Theory Approach

Research in Progress

Muath Abdulrahman[✉], Ciara Heavin, and Gaye Kiely

University College Cork, Cork, Ireland
`116220814@umail.ucc.ie, {c.heavin,gaye.kiely}@ucc.ie`

Abstract. Outsourcing decisions are complex, and a variety of factors must be considered. These include: (i) the drivers for outsourcing (reducing costs, accessing resources, focusing on core business); (ii) what the company will outsource (part ownership, management of IT); (iii) the procedures to be used (specific steps and tools needed to arrive at a decision); (iv) how the firm will outsource (implementation phase); and (v) the outsourcing outcomes (measured by realisation of expectations, satisfaction, and performance).

Outsourcing drivers can be technical, strategic, or economic. Given the range and complexity of the factors involved, there is a risk that outsourcing decisions may not be aligned with organisational goals. It is therefore necessary for companies to recognise that the factors affecting outsourcing decisions may include social, cultural, structural, or political dimensions. Research indicates that hidden factors are frequently overlooked, undervalued, or misinterpreted. The goal of this study is to augment current understanding of the social, cultural, and structural factors influencing outsourcing decisions. Institutional isomorphism theory has been used to explore these other factors but has had limited application in the business services context. This research investigates the factors embodied in institutional isomorphic influences and how they affect business services outsourcing decisions. Our model is based on DiMaggio and Powell's [14] causation model and on Dibbern et al.'s [13] adaptation of Simon's [61] four stage model of decision-making. Our aim is to increase the explanatory power of isomorphic theory to interpret the business services outsourcing decisions of organisations.

Keywords: Outsourcing · IT outsourcing · Business services outsourcing · Isomorphism institutional theory · Decision making · Managerial decision making

1 Introduction

Outsourcing has become a vital practice for companies that seek to be and to remain competitive in the globalised economy [12, 72]. The well-known outsourcing agreement in 1989 between Kodak and three vendors—IBM, DEC and Businessland—marked the

© Springer Nature Switzerland AG 2020
I. Oshri et al. (Eds.): Global Sourcing 2019, LNBIP 410, pp. 110–123, 2020.
https://doi.org/10.1007/978-3-030-66834-1_7

establishment of services outsourcing. Since then, business service outsourcing (BSO) has continued to grow [13]. Global estimates of market size for both information technology outsourcing (ITO) and business process outsourcing (BPO) were worth $952 billion in 2013 [32]. Recent Gartner figures indicate that the ITO industry alone 'has since surpassed $288 billion USD in 2013, with an expected compound annual growth rate of up to 5.5% from 2013 to 2017' ([26], p. 3). Notwithstanding this growth, existing research indicates that the success rate of these outsourcing contracts remains moderate [21, 36, 71]. Several studies indicate that outsourced projects either fail outright or fail to meet expectations by more than 40% [22, 45]. One of the major reasons for the increased likelihood of failure is the complexity of the outsourcing activities and processes [8, 37, 46].

Whilst the dominant and key driver in outsourcing services is cost reduction, drivers include strategic and social needs, such as accessing qualified staff and improving service levels [26]. A variety of factors are involved in the outsourcing decisions, whether they are directly related to the major motivation to outsource or related to other activities impacted by the outsourcing decision. Factors that may feature in a decision to outsource include: (i) the vendor's perspective, (ii) the client firm's characteristics, (iii) the country's characteristics, (iv) the relationship with the client and (v) whether the decision involves multi-sourcing, offshore sourcing or crowdsourcing [30–33]. These factors will differ in importance and priority in relation to the stages of the outsourcing decision process.

Recognising the complexity of the factors involved in business outsourcing decisions, existing research suggests that some of the factors associated with outsourcing decision-making are often overlooked, undervalued, or misinterpreted [46, 69]. This can contribute to a lack of success in outsourcing and its misalignment with organisational strategic goals [45, 46].

Coming from a theoretical perspective, existing studies identify factors in the outsourcing decision process as being either economic, relationship based, or strategic. The lenses applied by the various theories highlight different factors. These theories include: (i) transaction cost theory [74], (ii) agency theory [24], (iii) game theory [17, 62], (iv) interorganisational relationships (IOR) theory [58] and (v) the marketing channels literature [13, 57].

A number of theories consider the influences that affect the outsourcing process, and many studies have investigated factors that relate to the economic, relational, technical and strategic perspectives [4]. In contrast, this research investigates external factors, such as the social, cultural, and structural aspects. These aspects are embodied in the institutional isomorphic influences and affect all stages of the outsourcing decision-making process.

This study will investigate the basic stages of the decision-making process in outsourcing. To do this, we consider the outsourcing process as described by [13], who in turn, were inspired by the decision-making model of Harbert Simon [61]. The research will then investigate the external factors affecting the decision-making process.

The study considers general business service outsourcing (BSO) as a combination of information technology outsourcing (ITO) and business process outsourcing (BPO) [32]. In this paper, unlike most other recent studies, the focus will be on the non-economic and non-technical factors that affect each stage of decision-making. In particular, the focus will be on the social, cultural and structural factors affecting BSO decision-making. Most previous studies have examined only one of the three factors indicated by DiMaggio and Powell [14]. In contrast, this research considers all three factors together. In this way, we expect to discover new patterns between these factors, and to understand better the extent of their impact on the decision-making process.

The remainder of this article is structured as follows: Section two reviews the literature related to outsourcing decision-making and related theories. The proposed model is described in the third section. The fourth section discusses the proposed methodology. The final section outlines the expected contributions.

2 Theoretical Foundations

This study explores two bodies of existing literature. First, we consider BSO activities, with a particular focus on the organisational BSO decision-making process. Second, we review the literature that addresses institutional theory as applied specifically to the BSO domain and as related generally to the information technology/information systems (IT/IS) context. This literature is used to identify gaps in current knowledge and to justify the research questions posed.

2.1 Decision Making in Outsourcing

When an organisation considers BSO as a strategic approach, it is usually oscillating between options to 'buy' or 'make' [74], whether it is for assessment or to make a decision [40, 69]. It may also consider the decision consequences in terms of 'success' or 'failure' [30]. Although these assumptions are not wrong, scholars have considered this to be the simplest conceptualisation [30, 40]. In reality, outsourcing decisions involve many activities that make sourcing options more complex [8, 32]. Such a decision can swing between several types of 'buy' options, including, but not limited to, outsourcing to a domestic provider or to an offshore provider, multi-sourcing to several providers, or even outsourcing to a rural-based provider [38, 55, 65]. These options may entail sourcing a provider with a social mission to train and employ people from marginalized populations, which is an example of what it is known as 'outsourcing to an impact source' [6].

During recent decades, an abundance of theoretical frameworks and qualitative and quantitative studies on IT/IS outsourcing and on business process outsourcing have been produced. However, researchers have dealt with the complexity of outsourcing by examining outsourcing decisions and outcomes individually [30]. For example, in addition to the central motivations of service quality and cost deliberation, existing research has investigated other motivations such as access to global markets, focus on core capabilities and improvement and their impacts on outsourcing decisions [56, 65]. Considering the decision from the outsourcing outcomes perspective, researchers have studied related factors such as transaction attributes, relational governance and provider firm capabilities [30, 32, 41, 51].

Although a number of studies have dealt with the various types of BSO decision and their outcomes individually, there is a need to consider the sourcing decision-making process from a broader perspective to help managers to minimise the risk and to improve the whole sourcing process. Examining the outsourcing process as a whole may generate new insights, findings or congruent patterns that are difficult to identify when considering the individual elements of outsourcing decisions and outcomes. The literature on outsourcing includes some articles that deal in depth with building models for outsourcing activities, whether empirically (e.g. [8, 34, 58]) or conceptually (e.g. [13]).

Following their examination of stakeholder relationships in IT/IS outsourcing, Lacity and Willcocks (2000) identified six phases in outsourcing activities: (i) scoping, (ii) evaluation, (iii) negotiation, (iv) transition, (v) middle, and (vi) mature phases. These phases 'can be mapped into the more general Ring and Van de Ven model of interorganizational relationships' ([69], p. 16). However, unlike the outsourcing models mentioned, this study distinguishes between the decision-making process and its outcomes and focuses on the decision-making process in BSO from the institutional perspective. In this way, the factors associated with decision-making will be studied in depth before the decision comes into effect, which will reduce the level of the risk. It therefore adopts Dibbern et al.'s [13] conceptual framework as this separates the decision-making process from the outcomes of the outsourcing activity.

2.2 Institutional Theory in Outsourcing Research

For more than three decades, studies have adopted institutional theory in disciplines such as social science [46, 76] and political science [52]. This approach has also been applied, but to a lesser degree [49, 70] in IT/IS as a lens for examining related phenomena such as IT innovation, IS development and implementation and IT adoption and use [9, 10, 39, 66]. However, institutional theory has yet to be leveraged in the context of outsourcing [30–33]. It is important that institutional theory should be extended to the field of outsourcing as it can help to uncover external factors that may significantly affect decisions. This theory enables us to include factors such as how government requirements [23] have a coercive influence, and what types, forms and degree of influence they have on the various stages of the outsourcing decision-making process.

Institutional theory was developed in response to the need to understand why, in different socio-economic and political contexts, organisational structures and practices may react differently to similar internal and external influences [49, 63]. These influences may be issued by political and legal systems, capital markets and various governance mechanisms, as well as by other organisations and professional and cultural standards [60, 63]. Logical myths and norms recognized by Mayer and Rowan [47] dialectic lead to isomorphism (structural similarities), where formal structures of organisations need to align with society to acquire legitimacy [68]. In a different direction, DiMaggio and Powell [14] introduced concepts of coercive, normative and mimetic institutional influences by shifting the focus from a society to the organisational level.

As the objective of this chapter is to take stock of how institutional theory affects decision-making in business services outsourcing, DiMaggio and Powell's [14] three isomorphic influences will receive further attention as part of the causation model presented in the next section.

2.3 A Gap in the Literature and Justification of the Research Questions Theory in Outsourcing Research

Existing outsourcing studies based on the institutional approach have mostly focused on single factors and have not considered multiple factors [30]. However, while the mimetic influences have been extensively examined in the outsourcing body of knowledge, the normative and coercive influences have received less attention [30, 32]. Hence, there is a need for studies that identify the factors contributing to the isomorphic influences and their impact on outsourcing activities. For example, several factors may contribute to the mimetic influence such as government regulations (e.g. [2]) and local culture (e.g. [44]).

Our first research question therefore asks: (i) what are the factors that contribute to the isomorphic influences in the outsourcing context, as described by DiMaggio and Powell [14]?

Westphal and Sohal [72] investigated a range of outsourcing decision-making models available in the academic literature and found a relationship between the decision-making context and the adoption of a particular type of decision-making process. The investigation concluded that the adoption of different process types leads to different results [72]. However, there is a lack of empirical research into the outsourcing decision process, and the decision makers therefore 'adhere to more rational and formalized decision-making processes resulting in better decision outcomes' ([72], p. 1). While part of this research is designed to increase our understanding of the complexity of the decision-making process and the factors that drive managers when making BSO decisions, our second question seeks to explore (ii) how the isomorphic influences interact in the stages of the BSO decision-making process.

3 Conceptual Framework and Research Model

The conceptual framework presented in Fig. 1 illustrates the relationships between the institutional theory factors, the BSO decision-making process and BSO implementation.

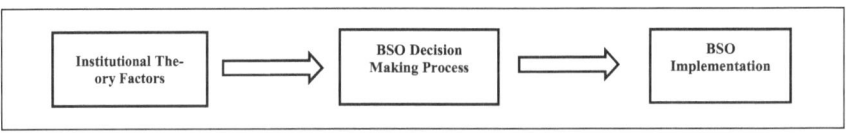

Fig. 1. Conceptual framework

Institutional theory factors refer to the external and internal societal, inter-organisational and individual factors that influence the behaviour and structure of organisations within their social ecosystems [9, 14, 47, 59, 76]. The effects may vary and may be direct or indirect in nature [9]. Whether the factors are external or internal, the institutional theory factors are equally important when investigating institutional environments and considering how they both continue and change over time [76]. The three major institutional theory factors are: (i) rationalised myths [47], (ii) isomorphism [14] and (iii) institutional logics [67]. Some authors consider these factors to be key when investigating the IT/IS context as a social phenomenon [25, 59].

The conclusion of institutional theory leads to the fact that institutions in a certain context transform the behavior of organisations to become isomorphic by adopting similar structures and practices [47, 76]. DiMaggio and Powell [14] expand on this view by identifying three different influences that lead to this isomorphism. These three influences are: (i) a coercive influence that stems from political influence and the problem of legitimacy, (ii) a mimetic influence that results from standardised responses to uncertainty and (iii) a normative influence that is associated with professionalisation [14]. By using the isomorphic influencers revealed, researchers have been enabled to understand the similarities between certain social and organisational behaviours [25, 29].

3.1 Coercive Influence

Coercive influence refers to the pressures on firms that result from power relationships, politics and the problem of legitimacy, causing them to adopt similar structures and practices. This type of influence may be informal or formal in nature [33, 42], and it puts pressure on companies both directly and indirectly [39]. This type of influence will 'result from power relationships and politics; prototypically these are demands of the state or other large actors to adopt specific structures or practices, or else face sanctions' ([5], p. 80). Informal coercive influence may also arise 'from cultural expectations in the society within which the organisations function' ([14], p. 150). Formal coercive influence includes government rules and regulations, various initiatives programs, and national security [2, 10, 23]. However, these requirements are not only demanded by authorities and by major customers and suppliers [1, 66] but can also arise as a result of 'resource dependence, such as demands to adopt specific accounting practices to be eligible for state grants or requirements of ISO certification to become a supplier' ([5], p. 80). The direct influences consist of unified action packages from government agencies and are supported by specific systems and modules [29, 39]. The indirect influences arise from government-based agencies or local governments and industry associations that recognise local companies as 'model' in their service provision, which increases their reputation and access to business opportunities [39].

3.2 Mimetic Influence

Mimetic Influence arises primarily from uncertainty [47, 59]. Under conditions of uncertainty, organisations tend to imitate the practices of their successful peers or competitors to protect the legitimacy of their decisions [14]. For example, when the decision process for a particular service is highly ambiguous, such as the use of consultants, focus on hiring employees from other companies in the same field. Also, its forms in-clude companies' tendency to follow the behavior of others, such as participation in industry associations and outsourcing firms, using consultants, participating in industry associations and outsourcing, the firms will tend to follow the behaviour of others [35, 41, 54]. This mimicking practice can be either a radical approach [20] or a gradual approach [11]. Mimetic influences are important in outsourcing as they cover difficult, high-risk and expensive practices such as selecting between competing but similar technologies or services [68].

3.3 Normative Influence

Normative influence refers to a key isomorphic factor that occurs primarily as a result of professionalisation in organisations resulting from the similar education of employees and training in similar professional values [5, 18, 48]. Normative influence can be defined as 'the collective struggle of members of an occupation to define the conditions and methods of their work, to control the production of the future member professionals, and to establish a cognitive base and legitimization for their occupational autonomy' ([14], p. 152). Normative influences are usually expressed through a network of professional affiliations [29]. According to Liang et al. ([39], p. 68) the chain of 'a group of closely related suppliers and customers is a more important route through which normative influences permeate in the context of this study'. When organisations share similar positions and allocate people who are almost identical in professional background (e.g. similar networks and formal education), the individuals will possess a 'similar orientation and disposition that overrides the variations in traditions and control mechanisms otherwise shaping distinctive organizational behavior' ([39], p. 68). The following section discusses the decision-making process in business service outsourcing.

3.4 BSO Decision Making Process Phase of the Why, What and Which Stages

Using Simon's [61] four stage model of decision-making, Dibbern et al. [13] developed a two-phase model of outsourcing that includes five stages, which are parallel to Simon's intelligence, design, choice, and implementation stages. Dibbern et al.'s [13] five stages are divided into two main phases: the decision process phase, involving the 'Why', 'What' and 'Which', and the implementation phase, consisting of the 'How' and the outcomes [13]. This is presented in Fig. 2. To elaborate a little, the decision stages can be explained as follows: (1) Why is the organisation considering outsourcing? (e.g. the drivers and antecedents); (2) What is to be outsourced? (e.g. functions or organisations) and (3) Which choices are made? (e.g. using a decision model or guidelines). The implementation stage involves: (4) How is the outsourcing carried out? (e.g., selection of vendors, transition of knowledge) and (5) The outcomes of outsourcing (e.g., the experience, lessons learned) [13].

The first stage in the BSO decision making process phase is 'Why?'. This phase investigates the determinants of outsourcing, including the conditions that may lead to the decision to outsource, the advantages and disadvantages and the associated risks and rewards from outsourcing. Some studies, such as that by Loh and Venkatraman [43], have attempted to identify the drivers of IS outsourcing from a diffusion of innovation perspective. For this research, the objective is to explore institutional isomorphic influences on the determinants of BSO outsourcing. The second stage is the 'What'. This question helps 'with two parameters of the dependent variable–outsourcing–that must be defined carefully: (1) the level of analysis and (2) the degree of outsourcing' ([13], p. 47). Having decided why and what to outsource, the next question is 'which choice to make' [13]. In making the choice to outsource, organisations adopt procedures that

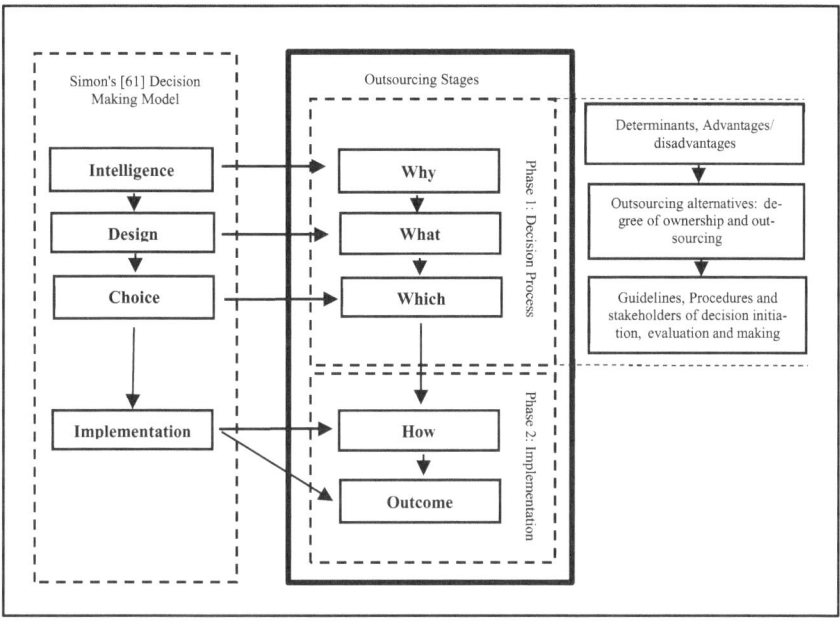

Fig. 2. Stage model of outsourcing [13]

involve 'a step-by-step process for arriving at an outsourcing decision; guidelines to help them assess the various selection criteria and their choice; and the actual selection of the final decision' ([13], p. 51). The 'Which' decision process has generally received less attention in the body of knowledge as no conceptual frameworks have been applied to this stage [13]. Therefore, it may be helpful to consider the various stakeholder roles in the decision-making process at this stage [13].

This research provides an opportunity to use key constructs from the two theories to focus specifically on the decision process by exploring the impact that isomorphic influences play in the decision-making process. As shown in Fig. 3, the research uses DiMaggio and Powell's [14] causation model and Dibbern et al.'s [13], which is adapted from Simon's [61] four stage model of decision-making.

4   Proposed Methodology

The aim of this research is to investigate and analyse the institutional isomorphic factors involved in outsourcing decision-making processes that enable managers to make their BSO decisions. As mentioned in Sect. 2, existing studies on isomorphism institutional theory have tended to study the isomorphism constructs separately [31–33], or they have tested them together but in different contexts, and these have all been quantitative studies (e.g. [39]). To investigate meaningfully the isomorphic factors salient to the decision process, this research will pursue a qualitative approach using multiple case studies [15, 75]. Data will be collected through semi-structured interviews. This will allow us to

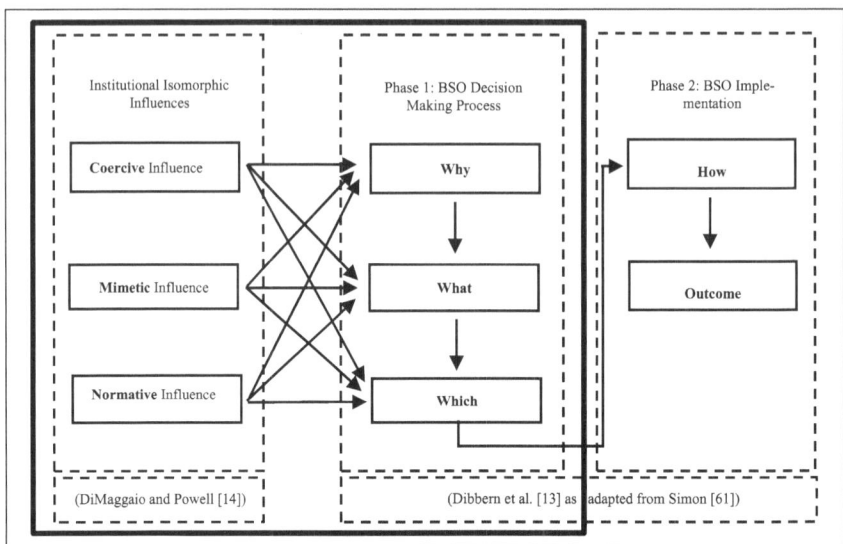

Fig. 3. Research model

explore new ideas, capture new phenomena and identify the rich contextualised detail of complex concepts such as managerial decision-making in BSO [4, 7].

The intention of our study is to show that a large number of factors contribute to the isomorphism occurring during the decision-making process, across a wide range of multinational organisations. Our aim in conducting three case studies in different organisations is to provide a holistic and comprehensive understanding of a complex phenomenon in a real-world business situation [3]. These three case studies will involve organisations that have recently adopted outsourcing decisions for their IT services as these services are especially critical among functional area executives [8, 39].

In comparison to quantitative research, a qualitative study aims to comprehensively understand complex and dynamic phenomena rather than achieve generalization, and therefore its sample size is normally smaller [19]. Therefore, the interviews will be undertaken with a minimum of six to eight individuals per case study organisation. As outsourcing is considered to be a strategic activity [27, 53], interviewees will include managers in the top and middle management levels of the organisations [28].

For data analysis, we will adopt the four processes of Miles and Huberman [50] and, as the first phase of coding, we will analyse the data thematically. To obtain a comprehensive data analysis, a technique recommended by Strauss and Corbin [64] will be implemented. This recommends that three coding procedures (open coding, axial coding and selective coding) should be used in the process of analysing qualitative data.

These approaches will allow us not only to understand clearly and deeply the social reality, but also to record it across a complex and subtle set of interpretive categories [16].

5   Expected Contribution

This study is motivated by gaps identified in prior work [31–33, 57]. Previous studies have discussed many factors affecting BSO decisions that are technical, economic, and strategic in nature [32, 39, 57]. This study aims to augment existing research by empirically identifying social, cultural and structural influences, thereby providing a more complete understanding of the factors affecting BSO decisions.

This research will make a number of contributions to both research and practice. First, it will investigate the factors embodied in the three high-level institution influences (the mimetic, the coercive, and the normative). IT/IS literature has identified some of these factors. For example, factors such as government requirements in coercive influence [23], the use of consultants in mimetic influence [42] and trading partners in normative influence [1]. However, we seek to investigate these influences further in an attempt to discover additional factors influencing the business services outsourcing context.

Second, this research will provide a more complete understanding of the influences on the BSO decision-making process. Existing studies on the institutional approach to outsourcing have mostly focused on single factors, as outlined by DiMaggio and Powell [14], and fail to consider multiple factors [30]. By considering the factors together, we expect to observe new patterns between these influences and to understand better the extent to which they affect the decision process.

Third, by using DiMaggio and Powell's [14] causation model and Dibbern et al.'s [13] model adapted from Simon's [61] four stage model of decision-making, our aim is to increase the explanatory power of IS theories for a better understanding of how organisations evaluate and implement BSO.

Fourth, there is an effective relationship between the decision-making context and the type of decision process, which will lead to different results [72]. This research will provide an understanding of how the isomorphic influences interact at the various stages of the BSO decision-making process. In this way, we will present new insights into how to improve the individual's decision-making performance.

This research provides an opportunity to leverage key constructs from two theories to understand management decision-making in business service outsourcing. By employing multiple theories, we aim to enrich this research domain by investigating real-life cases to gain a better understanding of the factors influencing BSO decisions and the factors that determine successful outcomes.

References

1. Aubert, B., Léger, P.-M., Larocque, D.: Differentiating weak ties and strong ties among external sources of influences for enterprise resource planning (ERP) adoption. Enterp. Inf. Syst. **6**(2), 215–235 (2012)
2. Ball, K., Daniel, E., Dibb, S., Meadows, M., Spiller, K.: Transferring the 'war on terror' to the private sector: a practice perspective on organisational tensions. In: Strategic Management Society Conference (2010)
3. Bernard, H.R., Bernard, H.R.: Social Research Methods: Qualitative and Quantitative Approaches. Sage, Thousand Oaks (2013)

4. Bhattacherjee, A.: Social Science Research: Principles, Methods, and Practices. Sage, Thousand Oaks (2012)
5. Boxenbaum, E., Jonsson, S.: Isomorphism, diffusion and decoupling: concept evolution and theoretical challenges. Sage Handb. Organ. Institutionalism **2**, 79–104 (2017)
6. Carmel, E., Lacity, M.C., Doty, A.: The impact of impact sourcing: framing a research agenda. In: Nicholson, B., Babin, R., Lacity, M.C. (eds.) Socially Responsible Outsourcing. TWG, pp. 16–47. Palgrave Macmillan UK, London (2016). https://doi.org/10.1007/978-1-137-557 29-2_2
7. Cassell, C., Symon, G.: Essential Guide to Qualitative Methods in Organizational Research. Sage, Thousand Oaks (2004)
8. Cullen, S., Seddon, P., Willcocks, L.P.: Managing outsourcing: the life cycle imperative. MIS Q. Executive **4**(1), 4 (2008)
9. Currie, W.: Contextualising the IT artefact: towards a wider research agenda for IS using institutional theory. Inf. Technol. People **22**(1), 63–77 (2009)
10. Currie, W.L., Guah, M.W.: Conflicting institutional logics: a national programme for IT in the organisational field of healthcare. J. Inf. Technol. **22**(3), 235–247 (2007)
11. Davenport, T.H., Stoddard, D.B.: Reengineering: business change of mythic proportions?. MIS Q. 121–127 (1994)
12. Delen, G., Peters, R., Verhoef, C., Van Vlijmen, S.: Lessons from Dutch IT-outsourcing success and failure. Sci. Comput. Program. **130**, 37–68 (2016)
13. Dibbern, J., Goles, T., Hirschheim, R., Jayatilaka, B.: Information systems outsourcing: a survey and analysis of the literature. SIGMIS Database **35**(4), 6–102 (2004)
14. DiMaggio, P., Powell, W.W.: The iron cage revisited: collective rationality and institutional isomorphism in organizational fields. Am. Sociol. Rev. **48**(2), 147–160 (1983)
15. Eisenhardt, K.M.: Building theories from case study research. Acad. Manag. Rev. **14**(4), 532–550 (1989)
16. Feagin, J.R., Orum, A.M., Sjoberg, G.: A Case for the Case Study. UNC Press Books, Chapel Hill (1991)
17. Fudenberg, D., Tirole, J.: Noncooperative game theory for industrial organization: an introduction and overview. Handb. Ind. Organ. **1**, 259–327 (1989)
18. Galaskiewicz, J., Burt, R.S.: Interorganization contagion in corporate philanthropy. Adm. Sci. Q. 88–105 (1991)
19. Gentles, S.J., Charles, C., Ploeg, J., McKibbon, K.: Sampling in qualitative research: insights from an overview of the methods literature. Qual. Rep. **20**(11), 1772–1789 (2015)
20. Hammer, M., Champy, J.: Reengineering the Corporation: A Manifesto for Business Revolution 2001. Nicholas Brealey, London (1993)
21. Hopwood, M.N.: Effective Strategies for Managing the Outsourcing of Information Technology (2018)
22. Huber, T.L., Fischer, T.A., Kirsch, L., Dibbern, J.: Explaining emergence and consequences of specific formal controls in IS outsourcing–a process-view. In: 47th Hawaii International Conference on System Sciences, pp. 4276–4285. IEEE Press (2014)
23. Hutter, B.M.: The role of non-state actors in regulation. Centre for Analysis of Risk and Regulation. London School of Economics (2006)
24. Jensen, M.C., Meckling, W.H.: Theory of the firm: managerial behavior, agency costs and ownership structure. J. Financ. Econ. **3**(4), 305–360 (1976)
25. Jensen, T.B., Kjærgaard, A., Svejvig, P.: Using institutional theory with sensemaking theory: a case study of information system implementation in healthcare. J. Inf. Technol. **24**(4), 343–353 (2009)
26. Jeong, J., Kurnia, S., Samson, D., Cullen, S.: Enhancing the Application and Measurement of Relationship Quality in Future IT Outsourcing Studies (2018)

27. Kern, T., Kreijger, J., Willcocks, L.: Exploring ASP as sourcing strategy: theoretical perspectives, propositions for practice. J. Strateg. Inf. Syst. **11**(2), 153–177 (2002)
28. Knoke, D.: Networks of elite structure and decision making. In: Advances in Social Network Analysis: Research in the Social and Behavioral Sciences, p. 274 (1994)
29. Krell, K., Matook, S., Rohde, F.: The impact of legitimacy-based motives on IS adoption success: an institutional theory perspective. Inf. Manage. **53**(6), 683–697 (2016)
30. Lacity, M., Yan, A., Khan, S.: Review of 23 years of empirical research on information technology outsourcing decisions and outcomes. In: Proceedings of the 50th Hawaii International Conference on System Sciences (2017)
31. Lacity, M.C., Khan, S., Yan, A., Willcocks, L.P.: A review of the IT outsourcing empirical literature and future research directions. J. Inf. Technol. **25**(4), 395–433 (2010)
32. Lacity, M.C., Khan, S.A., Yan, A.: Review of the empirical business services sourcing literature: an update and future directions. J. Inf. Technol. **31**(3), 269–328 (2016)
33. Lacity, M.C., Solomon, S., Yan, A., Willcocks, L.P.: Business process outsourcing studies: a critical review and research directions. J. Inf. Technol. **26**(4), 221–258 (2011)
34. Lacity, M.C., Willcocks, L.P.: Relationships in IT outsourcing: a stakeholder perspective. In: Framing the Domains of IT Management: Projecting the Future through the Past, pp. 355–384 (2000)
35. Lai, K.-H., Wong, C.W., Cheng, T.E.: Institutional isomorphism and the adoption of information technology for supply chain management. Comput. Ind. **57**(1), 93–98 (2006)
36. Lai, Y.-H.: The factors affecting partnership quality of hospital information systems outsourcing of PACS. In: Fujita, H., Ali, M., Selamat, A., Sasaki, J., Kurematsu, M. (eds.) IEA/AIE 2016. LNCS (LNAI), vol. 9799, pp. 484–492. Springer, Cham (2016). https://doi.org/10. 1007/978-3-319-42007-3_42
37. Lee, J.-N., Kim, Y.-G.: Effect of partnership quality on IS outsourcing success: conceptual framework and empirical validation. J. Manage. Inf. Syst. **15**(4), 29–61 (1999)
38. Levina, N., Su, N.: Global multisourcing strategy: the emergence of a supplier portfolio in services offshoring. Decis. Sci. **39**(3), 541–570 (2008)
39. Liang, H., Saraf, N., Hu, Q., Xue, Y.: Assimilation of enterprise systems: the effect of institutional pressures and the mediating role of top management. MIS Q. 59–87 (2007)
40. Liang, H., Wang, J.-J., Xue, Y., Cui, X.: Outsourcing research from 1992 to 2013: a literature review based on main path analysis. Inf. Manage. **53**(2), 227–251 (2016)
41. Lioliou, E., Zimmermann, A., Willcocks, L., Gao, L.: Formal and relational governance in it outsourcing: substitution, complementarity and the role of the psychological contract. Inf. Syst. J. **24**(6), 503–535 (2014)
42. Liu, H., Ke, W., Wei, K.K., Gu, J., Chen, H.: The role of institutional pressures and organizational culture in the firm's intention to adopt internet-enabled supply chain management systems. J. Oper. Manage. **28**(5), 372–384 (2010)
43. Loh, L., Venkatraman, N.: Diffusion of information technology outsourcing: influence sources and the Kodak effect. Inf. Syst. Res. **3**(4), 334–358 (1992)
44. Madon, S., Reinhard, N., Roode, D., Walsham, G.: Digital inclusion projects in developing countries: processes of institutionalization. Inf. Technol. Dev. **15**(2), 95–107 (2009)
45. Marchewka, J.T., Oruganti, S.: A combined model of IT outsourcing partnerships and success. Commun. IIMA **13**(2), 6 (2013)
46. McKenna, D., Walker, D.H.: A study of out-sourcing versus in-sourcing tasks within a project value chain. Int. J. Manag. Projects Bus. **1**(2), 216–232 (2008)
47. Meyer, J.W., Rowan, B.: Institutionalized organizations: formal structure as myth and ceremony. Am. J. Soc. **83**(2), 340–363 (1977)
48. Mezias, S.J.: An institutional model of organizational practice: financial reporting at the fortune 200. Adm. Sci. Q. 431–457 (1990)

49. Mignerat, M., Rivard, S.: Positioning the institutional perspective in information systems research. In: Willcocks, L.P., Sauer, C., Lacity, M.C. (eds.) Formulating Research Methods for Information Systems, pp. 79–126. Palgrave Macmillan UK, London (2015). https://doi.org/10.1057/9781137509888_4

50. Miles, M.B., Huberman, A.M.: Qualitative Data Analysis: An Expanded Sourcebook. Sage, Thousand Oaks (1994)

51. Narayanan, S., Narasimhan, R.: Governance choice, sourcing relationship characteristics, and relationship performance. Dec. Sci. **45**(4), 717–751 (2014)

52. Olsen, J.P., March, J.G.: Rediscovering Institutions: The Organizational Basis of Politics. Free Press, New York (1989)

53. Omizzolo Lazzarotto, B.: Analysis of management practices in performance-based outsourcing contracts. Bus. Process Manage. J. **20**(2), 178–194 (2014)

54. Pearson, A.M., Keller, H.: Explaining web technology diffusion: an institutional theory perspective. Commun. Assoc. Inf. Syst. **25**(1), 44 (2009)

55. Poston, R.S., Simon, J.C., Jain, R.: Client communication practices in managing relationships with offshore vendors of software testing services. CAIS **27**, 9 (2010)

56. Premuroso, R., Skantz, T., Bhattacharya, S.: Disclosure of Outsourcing in the Annual Report: Causes & market returns effects. Int. J. Account. Inf. Syst. **13**(4), 382–402 (2012)

57. Rajaeian, M.M., Cater-Steel, A., Lane, M.: A systematic literature review and critical assessment of model-driven decision support for IT outsourcing. Dec. Support Syst. **102**, 42–56 (2017)

58. Ring, P.S., Van de Ven, A.H.: Developmental processes of cooperative interorganizational relationships. Acad. Manage. Rev. **19**(1), 90–118 (1994)

59. Scott, W.R.: Institutions and Organizations: Ideas and Interests. Sage, Thousand Oaks (2008)

60. Sharma, S., Daniel, E.M.: Isomorphic factors in the adoption of ERP by Indian medium-sized firms. J. Enterp. Inf. Manage. **29**(6), 798–821 (2016)

61. Spence, M.: Product selection, fixed costs, and monopolistic competition. Rev. Econ. Stud. **43**(2), 217–235 (1976)

62. Staw, B.M., Epstein, L.D.: What bandwagons bring: effects of popular management techniques on corporate performance, reputation, and CEO pay. Adm. Sci. Q. **45**(3), 523–556 (2000)

63. Strauss, A., Corbin, J.: Basics of Qualitative Research. Sage Publications, Thousand Oaks (1990)

64. Su, N., Levina, N.: Global multisourcing strategy: integrating learning from manufacturing into IT service outsourcing. IEEE Trans. Eng. Manage. **58**(4), 717–729 (2011)

65. Teo, H.-H., Wei, K.K., Benbasat, I.: Predicting intention to adopt interorganizational linkages: an institutional perspective. MIS Q. 19–49 (2003)

66. Thornton, P.H., Ocasio, W.: Institutional logics. Sage Handb. Organ. Institutionalism **840**, 99–128 (2008)

67. Tingling, P., Parent, M.: Mimetic isomorphism and technology evaluation: does imitation transcend judgment? J. Assoc. Inf. Syst. **3**(1), 5 (2002)

68. Veltri, N.F., Saunders, C.: Antecedents of information systems backsourcing. In: Information Systems Outsourcing. Springer, pp. 83–102 (2006). http://doi.org/10.1007/978-3-540-348 77-1_4

69. Weerakkody, V., Dwivedi, Y.K., Irani, Z.: The diffusion and use of institutional theory: a cross-disciplinary longitudinal literature survey. J. Inf. Technol. **24**(4), 354–368 (2009)

70. Westphal, P., Sohal, A.S.: Taxonomy of outsourcing decision models. Prod. Plann. Control **4**(4–5), 347–358 (2013)

71. Westphal, P., Sohal, A.: Outsourcing decision-making: does the process matter? Prod. Plann. Control **27**(11), 894–908 (2016)

72. Williams, C., Durst, S.: Exploring the transition phase in offshore outsourcing: decision making amidst knowledge at risk. J. Bus. Res. (2018)
73. Williamson, O.E.: Markets and Hierarchies, Analysis and Antitrust Implications: A Study in the Economics of Internal Organization. Free Press, New York (1975)
74. Yin, R.K.: Case Study Research and Applications: Design and Methods. Sage Publications, Thousand Oaks (2017)
75. Zucker, L.G.: The role of institutionalization in cultural persistence. Am. Sociol. Rev. 726–743 (1977)

Towards Business Services 4.0 - Digital Transformation of Business Services at a Global Technology Company

Robert Marciniak$^{(\boxtimes)}$ iD, Peter Moricz iD, and Mate Baksa iD

Institute of Management, Corvinus University of Budapest, Budapest, Hungary
{robert.marciniak,peter.moricz,mate.baksa}@uni-corvinus.hu

Abstract. The digital transformation brought new opportunities as well as challenges to the business services sector. New digital technologies like cognitive automation, blockchain, or process mining could facilitate all significant business aims service centres. These could contribute not only to the efficiency metrics of operation but to the effectiveness of the business as well. The different levels of digital transformation presented in this paper all contribute to these benefits, and the future holds new opportunities with the further advancement of cognitive solutions. These technologies have already proven their capabilities, but their implementation is always difficult and should be custom-made. Quantitative and qualitative research was conducted to discover business practices related to the digitalisation of the business services sector in a Central and Eastern European country. This paper provides insight into a major Hungarian-based business services centre with three unique cases of digital technology implementation projects. Through these cases, the paper reveals the process of selection and introduction as well as outcomes of digitalisation projects in the examined company. The paper ensures an overview of new technologies that could be used in the sector to build a framework called Business Services 4.0.

Keywords: Business services centre · Digital transformation · Service automation and robotisation · Cognitive systems · Digitalisation

JEL codes: L86 · M14 · M15 · M19 · M19

1 Introduction

Today, the primary driving force behind the digital transformation process is the emergence and incorporation of new digital (sometimes called as game-changing or disruptive) technologies into organizational operations. Over the past decades, most of the big companies built their sourcing strategies, optimized the location portfolio, streamlined the operation of back-office function in cooperation with outsourcing, and shared services partners.

It is worth examining each stage of digital transformation, such as digitisation, digitalisation, automation, and business transformation. By incorporating automation, virtualization, advanced analytics, and other digital technologies, companies could enhance

© Springer Nature Switzerland AG 2020
I. Oshri et al. (Eds.): Global Sourcing 2019, LNBIP 410, pp. 124–144, 2020.
https://doi.org/10.1007/978-3-030-66834-1_8

efficiency that is the primary motive for their existence. New technologies related to these terms could be ground-breaking for business services centres as well. The easiest utilization of digital solutions is to scan the business processes and automate manual tasks entirely or partially to improve operational metrics and return-of-investments. As technologies support better, data-based decision making, it impacts effectiveness as well. Another benefit of technological development is that expectations towards employee expertise and skills change. It could be the need to hire and train employees to ensure the specialized skills required. However, adopting technologies could alter the operating model as well. Digital technologies provide the opportunity to deliver a more customized and broad service portfolio, maintaining a streamlined operation. It also enables companies to rethink the sourcing strategy and governance model if the significance of labour arbitrage is decreasing with deploying technologies. New technologies could also launch new services and products as business outcomes.

According to the literature, companies face many challenges should they wish to exploit the full potential of new technologies. A high ratio of business services centres are not prepared for a full-scale shift [1]. However, what is the reality of transformational projects in the business services centres? Where are these organizations in this transformational journey? What are the standard technologies and how are they used in these centres? This paper is looking for the answers.

2 Literature Review

2.1 Terms Related to Digital Transformation

The recent digital technologies boomed digital transformation projects in all industries. The developments like cloud computing, internet of things (IoT), artificial intelligence (AI), or blockchain technologies concern mostly social media, mobile, and big data but they impact customer behaviour in every area. Often, the consumed services are more advanced in our private life, therefore there is a significant pressure on professional employers to improve their digital solutions in the whole work environment. All of these expectations increase the industrial competition, which starts a virtuous circle in the digital transformation [2]. These elements (technologies, customer behaviour and competition) are the external drivers of the digital transformation [3]. Other scholars identified five purposes of digital transformation as increasing efficiency, improving customers experiences and engagement, improving decision making, improving innovation, and transforming the business into digital [4].

Verhoef and Bijmolt [2] argue that the use of digital technologies is changing systems, structures, activities, and processes. These digital developments also change business models by implementing a new business logic using digital technologies to create and capture value. Hess et al. [16] define the digital transformation as the sum of organizational changes that reform the business models, products, processes, and structures of organizations by the use of digital technologies. According to Matt et al. [5], each digital transformation project addresses four main aspects that build a digital transformation framework (DTF). The technology usage aspect (1) refers to the ability to discover and use new digital technology solutions. Changes in value creation (2) and structural changes (3) affect the operation of the company: the former refer to the transformation of the way value is created, and the latter to the development of organizational structures, processes and capabilities. Finally, financial aspect (4) refers to the profitability of the core business and the possibility of financing the digital transformation project.

Some researchers discuss that digital journey of companies has three phases as digitisation, digitalisation and digital transformation [5, 6]. Other scholars state digital transformation as an umbrella term of digitisation, digitalisation, and automation [3, 7]. It is not easy to distinguish the two. In fact, there is some confusion around them in the literature [8]. The first concept means a conversion of analogue, paper-based data and information into digital one (e.g., scanning a paper), to be edited, transmitted, stored, or used in any way more quickly and cheaply. It primarily focuses on efficiency and operational excellence. According to literature [9, 10], not only data but also processes can be digitised in this way, but the process level is more related to the digitalisation according to most literature.

Digitalisation can be interpreted more broadly. It primarily means the adaptation of digital technologies at the process or organizational level that ends in a digital solution. The goal is not only to digitise the existing process but also to improve the consumer and user experience with the help of digital solutions. The digital process does not focus only on efficiency but effectiveness as well. It explores how to add value for stakeholders through digitalisation. Srai and Lorentz [11] argues that digitisation means the material process of converting analogue data, but digitalisation refers to the technology of digitalising information (Table 1).

Table 1. Terms related to digital transformation

	Digitisation	Digitalisation	Automation	Robotisation	Digital Transformation
Action	Conversion	Adaption	Replacement	Imitation	Value Creation
Focus, scope	Data and Information (/Process)	Process	Activity, Process	Activity, Process	Business area, Organisation
Aim	Efficiency	Efficiency, Effectiveness	Efficiency	Efficiency	Effectiveness
Support	Computers	IT Systems	Physical machines and/or Computer	Physical machines and/or Computer	IT Systems, Computers, Physical machines
Process stage of Digital Transformation	Business digitisation	Business Digitalisation, Digital optimisation	Digital optimisation	Digital optimisation	Business transformation

Scholars also highlight a significant term, automation, that is related to digital transformation [7]. Automation (or automatization) refers to the use of machines and computers to do work that was previously done by people. In many cases, automation results in a complete replacement of human presence; in other cases, it is only a reduction in human involvement. However, automation always requires human labour (as physical and software robots are designed, built, set up, maintained, repaired, etc. by individuals). Although automation existed before digitisation (it could be entirely mechanical as well), in general, the digitisation of activity is not a prerequisite for automation, but today a new wave of automation is realized primarily with the help of physical and software robots where digitisation is also required in all cases [12]. Automation can affect an activity, but it can be extended to an entire process, so it can even replace organizational units or organisations as well. Automation aims to optimise the operation and reduce costs [13].

Within automation solutions, some researches differentiate robotisation as well. Automation and robotisation are similar terms in that they both refer to the replacement of human labour [14, 15]. Robotisation is a subset of automation and it means those advanced solutions when autonomous robots carry out the work. During automation, companies may change the physical or virtual environment of tasks or workflows, which in some cases, is accompanied by a complete transformation. During robotisation, agents (called robots or software bots) operating in a physical or virtual space take over the complete task of human employees without any or significant changes. These agents are independent and resemble the human workforce in relevant characteristics and qualities (e.g., their extension, appearance, capabilities, or licenses). In general, the similarity of robots to human appearance is not determinative, but in some cases, for example, in services that need interactions with humans, the development of robots with human appearance (i.e., androids) may be necessary. In other words, while the essential feature of automation is that the course of processes does not require human intervention, the essence of robotisation is to replace the human workforce with artificial agents that mimic the human functioning. In some cases, robots could substitute only some parts of human work, and the human agents assist the operation of end-to-end process.

Digital transformation as the most advanced stage of the digital journey refers to the process of change when the abovementioned activities take place in an organized, conscious, and extended way, which requires a fundamental change in management, organizational culture, and employee thinking in order to create value for stakeholders with new digital solutions [9, 16, 17]. It could be interpreted as a digital value proposition. Digital transformation can be interpreted at much higher organizational level, at the level of some business area or the entire organization. Digital transformation, like all transformations, involves a significant change in organizational skills and identity that brings valuable results to the organization along with some relevant goals that they would not be able to achieve without it.

2.2   Cognitive Systems and Levels of Software Automation

In the virtual environment, automation is performed by software robots (bots) that could be categorised by their capabilities. The basic level of automation means short software programs (scripts) and is typically able to perform a fixed sequence of activities based on well-structured databases. The tasks suitable for basic automation are typically high-volume and often repetitive. Such an activity, which is typical of almost all business organizations and is mostly automated, is the preparation of employee payrolls or, in the case of larger business organizations, the entry of analytical accounting items in the general ledger within the ERP system.

The next level of software automation that is now the most popular solution in the business services environment is the robotic process automation (RPA) [18]. In the case of RPA, automation is performed by a bot that mimics human workers using software such as ERP systems and can already work with semi-structured databases as well [19]. Its operation is not limited to a specific IT application but is able to bridge several different software environments and databases, thereby integrating many fragmented steps of a whole business process. The process becomes robotic as the software bot performs the task through the user interfaces of IT systems like a human by mimicking the human activity step-by-step, but much faster and more accurately [15, 20].

The most recent advancement of automation solutions uses cognitive systems or artificial intelligence (AI) technologies. They refer to the use of technologies like machine learning (ML) or deep learning (DL), natural language processing (NLP), text analytics and sentiment analytics, or/and computer vision to perform tasks requiring human intelligence [21]. Cognitive systems exceed digitisation, digitalisation and automation in their ability to learn from past decisions and outcomes as well as in continuous self-improvement ability. They can make human-like intelligent decisions. The level of automation that deploys cognitive systems is called cognitive or intelligent automation. It is able to automate non-standard processes using unstructured databases based on artificial intelligence. Cognitive automation uses continuous learning and development with the help of scenarios and data to handle increasingly complex processes and make decisions. Through cognitive process automation, intelligent written or oral communication can be maintained with external and internal customers, based on which the software identifies the essence of the request, problem, and then associates and initiates the appropriate solution process.

Sometimes, literature distinguishes between cognitive automation (CA) and intelligent process automation (IPA), other times, scholars deem them as equals [22]. If there is a difference between them, then CA is more advanced than IPA. Intelligent process automation refers to a preconfigured software instance that combines business rules, experience-based context determination logic. The deep learning and cognitive technology extend rule-based automation with decision-making capability [23]. It mimics the activities of the human workforce and learns to do them even better. It can overpass the error by applying past patterns stored in its memory [24]. While cognitive automation performs corrective actions driven by the knowledge of the underlying analytics tool itself, it also iterates its automation approaches and algorithms. The algorithm of CA should (1) integrate knowledge from various structured and unstructured databases, past experiences and current state, (2) interact with users by natural language or visualisation and (3) generate novel hypotheses and capabilities and test their effectiveness [22].

2.3 Business Services 4.0

Digital transformation is strongly connected with the term industry 4.0 (I4.0) that appeared as an industry development strategy but is recently used generally as a technological framework for novel technologies that can renew any part of the economy. As the technologies of I4.0 spread in the whole economy and society, other sectors and business areas coined their similar technological models (like Controlling 4.0, Procurement 4.0, Fintech, Insuretech, Proptech, etc.). Services 4.0 generally refers to a significant development in the service industry as a result of the leverage of digital technologies. It embraces technologies like big data and analytics, cloud computing, edge computing, RPA, bionic computing, cognitive computing, virtualisation, augmented reality, smart devices and IoT [25]. These developments enable the service industry to exploit new opportunities for increasing operational efficiency and customer experiences (CX). According to scholars, the service industry is lagging behind in manufacturing in utilising of lean principles [25, 26]. These technologies allow services companies to catch up and offer proactive and customised services through multiple channels. The advancement of services is not only an investment into the future but a necessity because of high customer expectation to deliver simple, intuitive, proactive, and personalised services in real-time [25].

The digital transformation affects business services centres on several levels. On the one hand, in the field of data digitisation, on the other hand, at the level of process digitalisation and automation, and by shaping the service portfolio as well, as it can provide a new business model for service centres. The top drivers of business service centres are cost-cutting, specialisation with grouping tasks, ensuring expertise of the critical mass and improvement of quality and speed. Digital technologies like RPA or cloud computing could radically increase the efficiency of operation and improve quality. Business services centres are focusing on digitalising their processes in order to free up the human workforce from transactional processes. If manual processes could be replaced with automation solutions and creating more complex, more value-adding and attractive jobs, it could also enhance employee satisfaction and motivation (especially for talents) with a decreasing turnover ratio.

Although business services centres have high digital maturity as a result of using such digital solutions such as cloud computing, SaaS, ERP, workflow systems, OCR and ICR technologies, e-invoicing, real-time reporting, and collaborative platforms but cognitive solutions (like Big Data and Advanced Analytics or NLP) could add further opportunities for the centres to transform not only the operational processes but the whole organizational strategy and structure. Business services 4.0 refers to a framework that includes service improvement technologies for this sector. The service centres adopting business services 4.0 technologies transform themselves from supporting organizations into high value-add, intelligent service providers.

3 Research Method

In order to reach a thorough understanding of digital transformation in business services centres, a case study research was conducted [27] to assess the three unique technology implementation projects at the Hungarian subsidiaries of TECH. (The name of the company was changed in this paper at their request). TECH is a major US-based global technology and innovation firm that ranks among Fortune 500 and has several BSCs in Hungary, of which this research examined two at different locations (the capital and a Tier-2 city). For similarity reason, they will be called as TECH BSC in this study. The analysis of these three projects made it possible to illustrate the most significant drivers and expectations of digital transformation. TECH was exceptionally well suited for finding answers to these questions as they develop and use state-of-the-art technology solutions that are dominant in their fields. To ensure that TECH BSC would support the conduction of this research, the first contact was established with its CEO. She was the one who helped to build contacts with the responsible project leads, technology experts, and business line managers who were substantial stakeholders of these projects. Table 2 provides an overview of the interviewed individuals from all three projects examined.

Table 2. Technology implementation projects and interviewed individuals included in this study

Projects	Company and corporate functions	Interviewees
Travel and expense	TECH BSC, Location #1 Human resources	• Managing director • Chief information officer • HR services lead • HR transformation lead
Invoice processing	TECH BSC, Location #1 Accounts payable	• Managing director • Chief information officer • Indirect tax automation lead • Accounts payable automation lead
IT event management	TECH BSC, Location #2 IT operations	• Site executive • Head of automation • Service quality analytics expert

3.1 Data Collection

For triangulation purposes [27], both qualitative and quantitative data were collected. Besides semi-structured individual interviews, group interviews were carried out to provide an opportunity for key stakeholders to reflect and comment on each other's statements [28]. Qualitative interviews were complemented by a survey on the use of technology solutions administered to interviewees beforehand. Data collection was initiated in Fall and Winter of 2018 after the formal approval of the managing director of TECH BSC was assured. Based on the recommendations of the managing director and research design considerations, interview candidates were selected and invited. Altogether, six individual interviews (60 min on average), and two group interviews (115 min on average) were conducted. Every interview was executed following pre-established internal guidelines based on qualitative research handbooks [29, 30] and followed the recommendations of Myers and Newman [28] on qualitative research in information systems inquiry. All interviews were conducted at the first or the second location of TECH BSC. Interviews were tape-recorded and transcribed afterwards. Transcriptions were later annotated by additional comments and observations made by the interviewers during the conduction of interviews.

3.2 Data Analysis

Interview transcriptions were re-read several times, and external codes [29] were applied to mark common themes and aspects of each purposefully selected technology implementation project. As the interview transcriptions were laden with company-specific and technology-based jargon, the researchers' interpretations were checked by the managing director and other staff members of TECH BSC to mitigate the risk of language ambiguity. The four common topics identified in technology projects were as follows: (1) drivers and planning, (2) implementation, (3) responsibilities, and (4) outcomes, effects, and learning points. Recurring themes and relationships between them were depicted and visually analysed. The results of the survey on technology usage were compared with interview transcripts. Finally, a theoretical coding of the interview transcripts was created to synthesize and connect empirical findings with established models in the literature.

4 Business Services Sector in Hungary

4.1 Hungarian Business Services Sector

Business Services Sector (BSS) has a decades-long tradition in Hungary. The first Business Services Centres (BSC) settled immediately after the regime change, in the early 1990s, when global firms moved labour-intensive activities from their core countries to Central and Eastern Europe (CEE), taking advantage of low labour costs coupled with high skills and available free labour. At that time, the parent companies of BSCs chose Hungary competing mainly with India and other offshore outsourcing countries, and accordingly, they created service centres primarily with low value-added, transactional work.

With the intensification of privatizations and free-market competition, these centres have worked partly domestically, but in many cases even abroad. The boom of this sector was brought about by the entry to the European Union. The country became popular already during the pre-accession legal harmonization, although labour arbitrage was still the determining location choice factor. Today, however, the market will be dominated not by outsourcing providers but by shared services centres (SSC) providing internal services for their own company. Typically, besides low value-added activities higher value-added activities were also transferred to the Hungarian centres.

Competition in the Hungarian Business Services Sector is low to medium, as SSCs are rarely terminated by parent companies, yet sometimes activities are relocated geographically, or outsourced to an external provider. Cost pressures are constant in these companies because cost reduction justifies existence of the centres. This pressure requires constant process optimization and technological development from the BSCs.

Hungary is a dependent market economy, and the operation of the industry also consists primarily of subsidiaries of international companies, which principally export services, so they are highly dependent on foreign customers. Domestic economic policy has been paying more attention to the sector since 2010, encouraging foreign direct investments (FDI) through direct and indirect means, and supporting higher value-added activities. The Hungarian government also supports the BSS through individual government decisions, but mainly greenfield investments and the focus of support is still on creating or retaining labour, thus maintaining the labour-intensive nature of the sector and slowing down technological developments.

Internationally, there is significant competition in business services, regionally dominated by Poland and the Czech Republic, but Romania has also become popular with its cheap and vast labour supply. The industry's current most significant challenge has emerged with the proliferation of automation technologies in office work environments. This can significantly transform both the workforce of the industry and the geographical location of the players.

In 2020, the Hungarian Business Services Market expanded around 150 Business Services Centres and 70,000 employees that mainly dominated by Shared Services Centres of big international companies. 80% of the centres and their employees work in the capital, Budapest [31].

4.2 Digital Transformation in the Hungarian BSCs

The degree of digitalisation in the sector is high, but the level of automation is still relatively low today. However, automation has an enormous growth potential, and almost all domestic companies have embarked on this path. Continuous cost-cutting pressures, labour shortages, and the high turnover ratio are forcing technological advancements for replacing lower value-added jobs. Technology suppliers are available for improvements. Customers also keep suppliers under constant cost pressure and set high-quality expectations.

Mainly, the sector is represented by international companies. Domestic companies typically perform low or medium complex and knowledge-intensive work. The sector has a strong IT orientation and a culture of continuous improvement. There is a general openness to development and improvement so that the services of the centres are of higher quality. Strategy of the domestic centre is cascaded from higher levels, and intense top-down pressure, and coordination coupled with intensive knowledge sharing was observable.

In this environment, smaller pilot initiatives are possible. Almost all companies participating in digital transformation have Centres of Excellence (CoE), which are often the starting point for international knowledge sharing. On the customer side of business service centres, there is also typically a digital strategy and action plan and an advanced innovation environment, but these are often less explicit in domestic service providers.

4.3 The Digitalisation of the Business Services Industry

While the most exciting part of digital transformation is to better understand and serve customer needs, at the same time, organisations can gain enormous opportunities by digitising their internal business processes. Business service centres organise their operations on a process basis and typically provide services to other business units of the parent company or other external customers. For this reason, the potential for digitisation and automation is exceptionally high in these organisations.

The ubiquitous IT work environment, along with well-defined, deterministic, and repetitive service activities, enable the rapid deployment of automation technologies in business services organisations. While companies in the manufacturing industry had been using automation since the early 20th century, and the robotisation of production started decades ago, robotics in business services is a relatively new phenomenon. One reason is that unlike the manufacturing industry, business processes might only be automated or robotised if the processes run in an entirely digital environment.

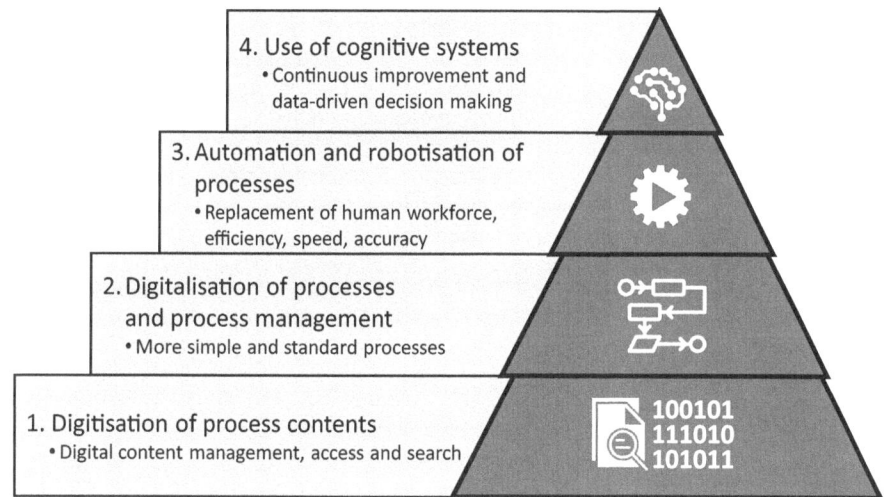

Fig. 1. Technological levels of digitalisation in the business services sector

The first step is the digitisation of process contents that means a transformation from physical (i.e., hand-written or printed) documents to digital materials. Technologies that support this are core business applications (ERP, CRM, SCM, document management), optical character recognition (OCR), and cloud computing. This step opens the way to the digitalisation of processes through the application of various technologies (e.g., ticketing and workflow systems, process analytics, and self-service solutions) to exploit possible gains from digital management and operation of processes [32] (Fig. 1).

Once processes are designed and operated digitally, they can be automated or robotised. Automation permits the reduction of human interaction required for process completion. Robotisation explicitly refers to the application of technologies that can substitute the human workforce. Macros, scripts, software robots (RPA, robotic process automation), and chatbots can perform specific tasks and functions otherwise carried out by humans.

The final step of the digital transformation of processes is the use of machine learning, cognitive systems, and different kinds of artificial intelligence. These systems (including natural language processing, computer vision, process mining, and predictive analytics) exceed the previous levels in their ability to learn from past decisions and outcomes as well as being able to improve themselves continuously. In this way, cognitive systems can make decisions that are more likely to be accepted by managers and can create predictions based on past cases.

These technologies are not equally widespread in the business services sector. While early adopters already apply machine learning or cognitive chatbots to their daily work, the late majority still rely on technologies like the core business applications or OCR. (See Table 3.) Even so, innovators may as well have backlogs at mature technologies like ERP or workflows.

Table 3. Diffusion of digital transformation technologies at the business services industry

Innovators	Early adopters	Early majority	Late majority	Laggards
Machine learning Cognitive RPA and chatbot Process and system simulation (digital twin) Blockchain Artificial intelligence Cybersecurity Augmented reality	Intelligent character recognition Natural language processing Computer vision Predictive analytics/big data Process mining	Self-service workflows Robotic process automation Chatbot Process analytics and dashboards IoT	Cloud computing Ticketing and workflow systems Automation tools (macros, scripting, routing) Server virtualisation	Core business applications (e.g., ERP, CRM, document management) Optical character recognition (OCR) Smart/mobile devices

5   Case Study Findings

5.1 Background Information

TECH is a US-based global technology and innovation company. It offers a wide range of technology and consulting services globally, including cognitive technologies, business applications, technology, and cloud computing platforms, IT infrastructure, and finance. With its solution, TECH is a key player in the cognitive technology market, and its developments can be considered pioneer in the fields of natural language processing, big data analysis, machine learning, and blockchain.

TECH has been present in Hungary with subsidiaries for more than 80 years. It previously operated several domestic production bases of which one remains still active. TECH BSC operates several business services centres in Hungary, of which our case study deals with two locations The centre at "Location #1" was established in the mid-2000s. Now, it is the 5th most significant centre of the TECH company worldwide, with more than 1,500 employees. The centre provides services in HR, sales, purchasing, accounting, and finance. This unit supplies mainly internal customers, i.e., the TECH company globally. About 20% of the activities are delivered to external clients. The other centre of TECH BSC at "Location #2" also employs more than one thousand employees. IT services account for 90% of its activity. It covers services like operation and maintenance of IT systems, including monitoring and support, data storage and database management services, virtualization and cloud services and IT development, e.g., in the field of artificial intelligence. The centre at "Location #2" serves internal and external customers as well. The external customers are mainly the global clients of the TECH company. In this case, the centre competes with other subsidiaries of the TECH company, e.g., in India or Mexico. At both locations of TECH BSC, a highly skilled workforce delivers services. Beyond the professional expertise, e.g., in accounting, finance, or IT, language skills are of paramount importance. The two locations of TECH BSC are capable of providing business services in 24 languages.

5.2 Automation Projects

As automation and digital transformation projects are running simultaneously, their management requires considerable attention from TECH BSC leaders and senior experts. Project labour savings range from a few hundred to several thousand working hours. Small projects save 200–1,000, medium projects save 1,000–5,000, and large projects save 5,000–20,000 working hours per year. Some projects require as many as ten employees. Sometimes, there might be 50–100 concurrent medium projects at the same client, while other times, 20 overly complex projects might cause far more work to do. The three examples shown in Table 4 illustrate typical projects of the company. The projects were selected purposefully to cover different areas of activities (business functions, internal and external clients) and different ways of initiation and implementation (top-down, bottom-up, etc.).

5.3 Travel and Expense: Implementation of a Cloud-Based Workflow System

Business trips are very common in the mother company of TECH BSC and affect a large numbers of employees. Employees organise their own trips; however, reservations and credit cards are administered by a global financial service provider. Decades ago, the mother company developed an in-house system to manage business trips, covering the approval of travel requests, through the reservation of tickets and accommodation, to the accounting of costs incurred.

This "travel and expense" system used to be a success story: in the 1990s, the mother company did not only use it but sold it to dozens of large corporate customers. More recently, because this software was not in the focus of TECH's strategy and solution portfolio, its features and capabilities became increasingly outdated compared to those of the competitors. External customers gradually changed to cutting edge solutions that made it more and more expensive to sustain this software developed by the mother company.

"It did not provide the expected user experience" – the head of IT at TECH BSC justified the change to the new system. He was also responsible for its global implementation. A transformation project was initiated following the decision of executives at the mother company. Corporate IT analysed the most significant 3–4 systems on the market that support the travel and expense processes. Then the global HR function responsible for business trips selected the best IT solution available. The analysis, shortlisting, and selection of service providers took more than one year. A continuously improved,

Table 4. Summary of selected process automation projects led by TECH BSC

Process transformed	Travel and expense	Invoice processing	IT event management
Organizational function	Human resources	Accounts payables	IT operations
Process customer	All employees of the mother company	Procurement and treasury functions of the mother company	External and internal clients with IT systems maintained by TECH
Motives	User experience was below expectations (the previous system was outdated)	Last (e-mail based) solution did not support automation; high probability of error, labour-intensive, expensive	High potential for automation, external clients' needs
Technologies in use	Workflow (cloud-based), chatbot (cognitive) for supporting purposes	Ticketing, OCR, ICR (cognitive), chatbot for supporting purposes	Scripting, ticketing system, dashboards, predictive analytics, big data, machine learning
Source of technology	Purchased (SaaS)	Own development	A mix of purchase, and central or local development
Project timeframe	3,5 years	Two years	From weeks to months
Source of initiative	Top-down: global HR selected the vendor	Bottom-up: a local solution from their idea	Mixed (central toolset, bottom-up process selection, and solution)
Roll-out	Globally designed implementation in multiple waves	Global implementation from a local initiative	Voluntary local implementation of a global initiative

cloud-based software available from all types of devices and with a use-based license fee was selected as the winner.

All requests, approvals, and subsequent invoices are managed in one workflow system. This system is capable of intelligent invoice processing (from the detection of texts and numbers on scanned invoices to the identification and recording of data in the ERP system); however, the company has not yet purchased this feature.

To support the implementation process, the company created some traditional educational videos and put a helpdesk chatbot in use. The chatbot proved to be an immense success with its ability to understand and answer natural language questions. The knowledge base behind the chatbot interface uses machine learning algorithms to gradually enhance its ability to respond. Users have rated answers to their questions increasingly higher as the knowledge base grew in the background.

The whole project took three and a half years to accomplish. Active cooperation was necessary between the TECH mother company and the service provider. Business analysts and software developers of the software vendor participated in the project together with HR analysts and IT experts from the mother company. As the external system receives data from and provides data to multiple corporate IT systems (e.g., budgets, payroll, and procurement), it took more than ten months to explore and understand each other's systems and their connections. In the meantime, the HR function prepared settings like account database, permissions, or corporate policies regarding accommodation categories and flight classes. Being a software as a service (SaaS) solution, the initial costs of the implementation project primarily consisted of the costs of employees involved. The company also spent money on the improvement of existing systems, but infrastructural costs did not incur. The corporate functions of HR and procurement financed the project together.

It took two years to completely roll out the new system in the organisation of the mother company. In the first wave, they focused on small countries and countries that have a relatively simple tax system. Before a new implementation wave, project managers always consulted local experts responsible for the travel and expense process. They developed detailed communication strategies to address future users. E-mail notifies sent six and three weeks before go-live, posters, information desks in offices, and educational videos were part of these strategies. There was always a transition period of about one month when the old and new systems were running simultaneously. After the transition day, new travel requests could only have been opened in the new system, while they gave enough time for ongoing processes to be closed. Global implementation was completed in 2018 and affected around 700,000 employees worldwide.

5.4 Invoice Processing: A Ticketing System to Handle and Distribute Requests

TECH BSC is one of the business services centres where the mother company centralised the complete administration of incoming invoices (accounts payable). One critical area of the administration procedure is the processing and answering of questions about payments. In the past, it was managed through virtual mailboxes in the corporate mail system: requests sent to these boxes were distributed among employees based on request type or country. This solution required much human workforce, and there was a high probability of error in choosing the correct one from 20 virtual mailboxes. Overall, this solution was unstructured and cumbersome. Virtual mailboxes did not support automation technologies, so these improvements would have been expensive, if at all possible.

It was a bottom-up initiative coming from the internal developer of the routing scripts and the team lead of request handling to develop a ticketing system in place of the virtual mailboxes. In the beginning, TECH BSC launched a low-budget development project financed by the previous year's residual budget. The invoice processing unit also had its developers whom they could use to work on new solutions. The developers created an internet-based system in which they distinguished initially 10, later around 100 different types of request types. To start a new case, the requester should choose a request type and country, as well as upload all required attachments. The ticketing system dispatches the request to the corresponding administrator and tracks the whole process until resolution without any human participation.

At this business unit, they also used advanced digital technologies to process invoices. The majority of incoming invoices are digital, but in case of a smaller number of paper-based invoices, intelligent character recognition (ICR) supports their processing. This technology can learn from previous examples: it stores the layouts of already processed invoices to become increasingly successful in finding the common data fields on new ones.

The core of the ticketing system was developed in one year. Cost savings measured in working hours were so convincing that regional and global managers decided to extend this solution to every account payable department of the mother company. It took another year to set all possible request types in the system. Although the variety of request types make the ticketing system slightly challenging to use, it is now possible to analyse the processes in greater detail. The user interface got a new outlook, and the company started to close the previous virtual mailboxes.

By 2018, all European, Middle-Eastern, and African subsidiaries converted to the new system. Unsurprisingly, there was some initial resistance against leaving the e-mail system every employee was used to. These days, the company is working on the global implementation of this ticketing system, now complemented by further automation solutions in North-America. *"As this system is not based on e-mails anymore, we could start automating the processes,"* says the manager of accounts payables at TECH BSC who coordinates the automation projects from Hungary.

5.5 IT Event Management: Dynamic Automation of Issue Detection and Resolution

IT operations and maintenance are some of the core activities at TECH BSC. More than 500 employees maintain the IT infrastructure of TECH's external clients or operate TECH's servers internally. These employees handle various IT events (errors, incidents, outages, etc.), deviations from the regular operation of systems, environments, and processes. Before automation, the experts of TECH BSC monitored critical indicators, for example, CPU usage statistics, and intervened in case of events, based on the priorities pre-determined by the clients. For instance, lower priority processes can be temporarily stopped by the robot in order to avoid critical failures. The automation of such activities offers significant labour-saving opportunities.

A new approach called dynamic automation started in 2014 at the TECH company. It is based on a software solution from an external vendor. However, the TECH company combined this solution with its internally developed platform that analyses historical records of incidents, provides users with diagnostic tools, and visualises data. A simplified scheme of dynamic automation is shown in Fig. 2. An automated system monitoring platform, based on predefined alarm levels, reports the IT events (incidents) to the event management system. This module filters and prioritises the events, by flagging duplicated events, critical incidents, etc. Tickets for the incidents are created in the ticketing system automatically. The ticketing system, also accessible for the client, logs all the steps taken in order to resolve the issue, connected to the customer, and the steps taken to solve the problem are recorded on them. In some cases, the resolution process can be automated as well. The dynamic automation robot, if access is granted by the client, may log into the client's system and intervene in its operation, based on a predefined scheme. If this intervention is not successful, the robot escalates it (forwards to a human specialist) for manual resolution.

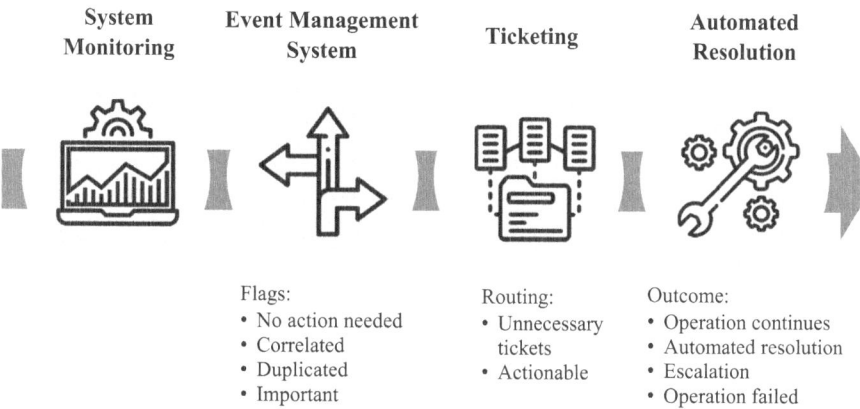

Fig. 2. A simplified scheme of dynamic automation in the field of IT event management

The dynamic automation of IT event management has been enhanced with cognitive solutions recently. As a start, an enormous "data lake" was built based on the past IT events, as several 10 million incidents were recorded from the entire customer base of TECH IT operations. This data lake enables the storage and analysis of past experiences. The cognitive capability of the platform runs the diagnostic tools, tries to recognise patterns in the data, and, with predictive analytics, identifies a potential risk of errors at the specific element in the IT infrastructure, based on its actual status.

Dynamic automation has been expanded to more than 800 customers worldwide at TECH. In Hungary, TECH BSC has been used since 2015. More simple forms of automation had been deployed even earlier. The IT staff had tried to handle repeating events with scripts and macros developed in-house. However, dynamic automation is a more complex tool. Therefore, an independent team of about 18–20 specialists was set up to support automation of event management at TECH BSC. This team develops end-to-end automation solutions and promotes them as a value-added service to the external clients. It is also this team that develops automated solutions based on ad-hoc yet specific client requests. By 2019, more than 130 IT event management tasks were automated. TECH BSC serves nearly 300 European clients and more than one hundred thousand of their servers by the tools of dynamic automation.

The measure of success of automation is the average rate of automatic resolution. By the end of 2018, around 45% of the IT incidents were resolved without human intervention. Already at this rate, the HR savings are enormous. Because of the tens of millions of incidents handled by TECH BSC annually, dynamic automation can be associated with saving the work hours of hundreds of full-time employees (FTEs), both for TECH BSC and its clients. On the other hand, in order to return the investment, automation needs a large enough scale. According to the experience at TECH BSC's

IT event management, about five hundred tickets per week are the order of magnitude at which it is already worth setting up such automation. By 2019, the 130 automation solutions cover almost all large-scale tasks in the field of Windows or Unix server environments. Therefore, the dynamic automation team has started to examine the area of middleware and the database layers, where there is still room for automation in the event handling. There are also plans to automate ad-hoc client requests like a new user request, without human intervention, through automation or robotics.

6   Discussion

TECH BSC showed an example of how digitalisation adds a further layer to the process transformation in business service centres. Centralizing business processes from local subsidiaries generally entails standardisation. Yet, even after decades of process optimisation, challenges in process efficiency and effectiveness remained. Business processes are not entirely paperless. Because of the ongoing developments in the technological environment, processes are supported by several information systems in parallel, instead of being covered by a fully integrated system. Without a seamless integration, errors may occur, and the need for manual intervention increases. Processes, even if centralized, often remain more labour-intensive and expensive. Traditional process transformation projects aimed to reduce complexity and a variety of processes. Because of the enormous number of business processes in global companies, this is a constant challenge. The case study showed further opportunities to advance in transparency and predictability of the business processes. From the clients' perspective, process optimization in the past occasionally retained silos of channels. Some transformation had a rather internal focus, less tailored to customer experience and needs.

One of the areas where digital transformation excels prior to processing transformation initiatives is the area of customer interactions. The travel & expenses project at TECH BSC was driven by the expected digital customer experience. In this example, the interaction between the client and the service provider follows principles observed at global mobility (e.g., Uber, Lime) or financial (e.g., Transferwise, Lemonade) services of the 2010s. This implies personalised and straightforward processes developed through sophisticated analysis of "use cases". The new travel & expenses application at TECH BSC adopts intuitive and proactive user interfaces that eliminate mistakes and therefore enhance customer experience while saving costs at the same time. Standardization across channels enables the clients to use different touchpoints at different stages of the process, without any difficulty. A higher level of self-service was also incorporated in the new travel & expense process. Self-service also appeared in the invoice processing project. Instead of manually routing the incoming e-mails, now requesters serve themselves on an online form. Other projects at TECH BSC also offer interactive tools and remote access that extends the self-service capabilities.

Digital transformation projects increasingly address the area of customer complaints. In the field of IT operations and maintenance, advanced prediction tools help the service providers to intervene before an issue occurs. As TECH BSC benefits from the cutting-edge cognitive solutions of its parent company, automated issue detection and even automated, scripts and routines are increasingly deployed to resolve common issues

Table 5. From 1.0 to 4.0: The potential of the digital transformation at business services

Business Services 1.0–3.0 Challenges	Business Services 4.0 Expectations
• Paper documents still exist • Multiple IT systems across processes with missing links and functions • Highly labour-intensive and expensive, high level of wastes • High complexity and variety of processes • Flaws, service issues, missing transparency, and predictability • Slow and cumbersome interactions, silos of channels • Limited customer experience, unmet customer needs	• Simple, intuitive, proactive, real-time, and personalized interactions • Seamless switch between multiple channels • Self-service, remote access and interactive tools support customers • Swift handling of complaints, or even preventing the complaint by prediction of potential issues or automated issue detection and resolution • Enhanced, real-time, or personalized offerings enabled by advanced technologies and the integration of internal and external (big) data

in IT services. By putting big data technologies in action, the company is able to further advance in issue detection and prediction. The lessons learned from the IT event management's dynamic automation project are that both the service provider and the client benefits from the digital transformation.

Based on the case study, Table 5 summarises how digital transformation projects are driven by traditional process optimization challenges on the one hand and by new expectations based on advanced technologies, on the other hand.

7   Conclusions and Further Research

7.1   Conclusions

The case study highlighted that digital transformation technologies spread from the top to the bottom of the "digitalisation pyramid". Even in a global company with highly developed business service centres and cutting-edge cognitive solutions, there is still room for digitisation and digitalisation, as well as for automation and robotisation. These result in projects that utilise technologies that already existed around the millennium, like optical character recognition, workflow solutions, or ERP systems. However, the case study pinpointed those new technologies that enhance the previous set of corporate IT applications: RPA tools, chatbots, intuitive mobile interfaces, big data, and advanced analytics, and especially cognitive solutions. These technologies not only affect the speed, the accuracy, and the cost of business processes but also enhance the customer experience or even the role of the business process. Based on the insights from the accumulating process data, the emphasis is increasingly put on the added value of the service delivery, i.e., the advisory role of the service provider.

While it would be easy to link the digital transformation projects to cost-cutting pressures, the business service sector follows these trends also because of customer expectations. Whether external or internal, clients of business services demand faster and cheaper services with zero errors and in an intuitive online form. These expectations accelerate the implementation of and experimentation with digital technologies. This is the reason why the size of the business service sector has not started to reduce, despite the severe labour savings thanks to software robots and automation tools. Instead, technological developments are shifting the business service sector towards higher value-added jobs, which demand a highly skilled and educated workforce more than ever before.

The Hungarian business services sector is still dominated by transactional jobs that could be easily automated. Former jobs that were established because of labour arbitrage are burdens that slow down the pace of the changes in the business service sector. The vast majority of the business service centres operate as a data centre and have already implemented a largely digitized operation. Centres like TECH BSC show a viable scenario of how a business service centre can transform itself into a digital service centre that offers automated, robotic service processes supported by self-service, and cognitive solutions. These sets of expectations outline a new level of business services that can be labelled, as a reference to Industry 4.0 in the manufacturing industry, as Business Services 4.0.

7.2 Further Research

The case study in this paper confirms the authors' research findings from other business service centres and the business service sector in general in Hungary [31, 32]. Nevertheless, in a globalised sector like business services, further research is needed to examine the regional differences. Business services centres in other global hotspots like India or Mexico likely face similar customer expectations and digitalisation challenges. Because of the different macroeconomic environments, digital transformation may have region-specific patterns as well.

Business services 4.0 may be a concept that "translates" the Industry 4.0 label to this sector while identifying the novelty and the technologies of the digital transformation of the business services. The authors already participate in researches where other sectors are investigated with a similar perspective. Some evidence that identifies common characteristics and sector-specific patterns of digital transformation (and the label "4.0") already exists. However, as the terminology and the concepts of the digital transformation evolve, the now blurred line between the traditional IT-enabled process optimisation and the digital transformation of processes can be further examined.

It is a common expectation that with the growing digital maturity of customers, business service centres serving companies in different industries will continue to adapt to new digital technologies. This could be facilitated by lower technology prices and the development of the digital literacy of the human workforce. It needs further analysis of how digital transformation forms the services portfolio of these centres. The COVID19 epidemic seemingly supported a more positive attitude towards digitalisation, both in society and the business. On the other hand, the labour shortage, a significant driver of digital transformation in the business services sector, may be mitigated by the growing labour supply because of the economic downturn. Further research should be conducted in order to draw the conclusion of how the COVID-19 pandemic impacts the pace and focus of the digital transformation of the business services sector.

Acknowledgements. This research was supported by project No. EFOP-3.6.2-16-2017-00007, titled Aspects of the development of intelligent, sustainable, and inclusive society: social, technological, innovation networks in employment and the digital economy. The project has been supported by the European Union, co-financed by the European Social Fund and the budget of Hungary.

References

1. Chandok, P., Chheda, H., Edlich, A.: How shared-services organizations can prepare for a digital future, New York (2016)
2. Verhoef, P.C., Bijmolt, T.H.A.: Marketing perspectives on digital business models: a framework and overview of the special issue. Int. J. Res. Mark. **36**(3), 341–349 (2019). https://doi.org/10.1016/j.ijresmar.2019.08.001
3. Verhoef, P.C., et al.: Digital transformation: a multidisciplinary reflection and research agenda. J. Bus. Res. (July 2018) (2019). https://doi.org/10.1016/j.jbusres.2019.09.022
4. Kane, G.C., Palmer, D., Phillips, K.D., Buckley, N.: Strategy, not technology, drives digital transformation. MIT Sloan Manag. Rev. **159**(9), 1–25 (2015)
5. Matt, C., Hess, T., Benlian, A.: Digital transformation strategies. Bus. Inf. Syst. Eng. **57**(5), 339–343 (2015). https://doi.org/10.1007/s12599-015-0401-5
6. Loebbecke, C., Picot, A.: Reflections on societal and business model transformation arising from digitization and big data analytics: a research agenda. J. Strateg. Inf. Syst. **24**(3), 149–157 (2015). https://doi.org/10.1016/j.jsis.2015.08.002
7. Savic, D.: From digitization, through digitalization to digital transformation. Online Searcher **2019**(January/February), 37–39 (2019)
8. Reis, J., Amorim, M., Melão, N., Cohen, Y., Rodrigues, M.: Digitalization: a literature review and research agenda. In: Anisic, Z., Lalic, B., Gracanin, D. (eds.) IJCIEOM 2019. LNMIE, pp. 443–456. Springer, Cham (2020). https://doi.org/10.1007/978-3-030-43616-2_47
9. Westerman, G., Bonnet, D., McAfee, A.: The nine elements of digital transformation. MIT Sloan Manag. Rev. **54**(2), 1–6 (2014)
10. Matzner, M., et al.: Digital transformation in service management. J. Serv. Manag. Res. **2**(2), 3–21 (2018). https://doi.org/10.15358/2511-8676-2018-2-3
11. Srai, J.S., Lorentz, H.: Developing design principles for the digitalisation of purchasing and supply management. J. Purch. Supply Manag. **25**(1), 78–98 (2019). https://doi.org/10.1016/j.pursup.2018.07.001
12. Shehu, N., Abba, N.: The role of automation and robotics in buildings for sustainable development. J. Multidiscip. Eng. Sci. Technol. **6**(2), 9557–9560 (2019)
13. Sebastian, I.M. Ross, J.W., Beath, C.: How big old companies navigate digital transformation: Discovery Service for Saudia Digital Library. MIS Q. Exec. **16**(3), 197–214 (2017)
14. Edlich, A., Watson, A., Whiteman, R.: What does automation mean for G&A and the back office? McKinsey Q. **2017**(2), 97–101 (2017)
15. Syed, R., et al.: Robotic Process automation: contemporary themes and challenges. Comput. Ind. **115**, 103162 (2020). https://doi.org/10.1016/j.compind.2019.103162
16. Hess, T., Matt, C., Benlian, A., Wiesböck, F.: Options for formulating a digital transformation strategy. MIS Q. Exec. **15**(2), 103–119 (2016)
17. Ismail, M.H., Khater, M., Zaki, M.: Digital Business Transformation and Strategy: What Do We Know So Far? (2017)
18. Lhuer, X.: The next acronym you need to know about: RPA (robotic process automation). Digit. McKinsey **17**(December), 1–5 (2016)

19. Lacity, M.C., Willcocks, L.P.: A new approach to automating services. MIT Sloan Manag. Rev. **58**(1), 11 (2016)
20. Asatiani, A., Penttinen, E.: Turning robotic process automation into commercial success - Case OpusCapita. J. Inf. Technol. Teach. Cases **6**(2), 67–74 (2016). https://doi.org/10.1057/jittc.2016.5
21. Watson, H.J.: Preparing for the cognitive generation of decision support. MIS Q. Exec. **16**(3), 153–169 (2017)
22. Suri, V.K., Elia, M.D., Arora, P., van Hillegersberg, J.: Automation of knowledge-based shared services and centers of expertise. In: Kotlarsky, J., Oshri, I., Willcocks, L. (eds.) Global Sourcing 2018. LNBIP, vol. 344, pp. 56–75. Springer, Cham (2019). https://doi.org/10.1007/978-3-030-15850-7_4
23. Lacity, M.C., Willcocks, L.P.: Robotic Process and Cognitive Automation: The Next Phase. SB Publishing, Stratford-upon-Avon (2018)
24. Anagnoste, S.: The road to intelligent automation in the energy sector. Manag. Dyn. Knowl. Econ. **6**(3), 489–502 (2018). https://doi.org/10.25019/mdke/6.3.08
25. Rehse, O., Hoffmann, S., Kosanke, C.: Tapping into the Transformative Power of Service 4.0, Düsseldorf (2016)
26. Borchersen, S.: Service 4.0 – What Is It ? What Impact Will It Have on It Service Management ? Horsholm (2018)
27. Yin, R.K.: Case Study Research: Design and Methods. SAGE Publications, Los Angeles (2009)
28. Myers, M.D., Newman, M.: The qualitative interview in IS research: examining the craft. Inf. Organ. **17**(1), 2–26 (2007). https://doi.org/10.1016/j.infoandorg.2006.11.001
29. Denzin, N.K., Lincoln, Y.S. (eds.): The SAGE Handbook of Qualitative Research. SAGE Publications, Los Angeles (2011)
30. Yin, R.K.: Qualitative Research from Start to Finish. The Guilford Press, New York (2011)
31. Drótos, G., Marciniak, R., Ránki-Kovács, R., Lente, D., Willbrandt, N.: Business Services Hungary 2019 - Report on the Hungarian Business Services Industry, Budapest (2019)
32. Marciniak, R., Moricz, P., Baksa, M.: Intelligent business services operation. In: Proceedings of 10th International Symposium on Intelligent Manufacturing and Service Systems, no. September 2019, pp. 110–120 (2019)

What Do You See in Your Bot? Lessons from KAS Bank

Ilan Oshri[1](✉) and Albert Plugge[2]

[1] University of Auckland Business School, The University of Auckland, Auckland, New Zealand
ilan.oshri@auckland.ac.nz
[2] Faculty of Technology, Policy and Management, Delft University of Technology, Delft, The Netherlands

Abstract. The introduction of robotic process automation (RPA) has created an opportunity for humans to interact with bots. While the promise of RPA has been widely discussed, there are reports suggesting that firms struggle to benefit from RPA. Clearly, interactions between bots and humans do not always yield expected efficiencies and service improvements. However, it is not completely clear what such human-bot interactions entail and how these interactions are perceived by humans. Based on a case study at the Dutch KAS Bank, this paper presents three challenges faced by humans, and consequently the perspectives humans develop about bots and their abilities to perform work. We then provide a set of five practices that are associated with the management of the interactions between humans and bots.

Keywords: Human-bot interaction · RPA · Case study · Challenges and practices

1 Introduction

The last decade has witnessed a tremendous interest in the automation of services through what has been coined as robotic process automation (RPA). RPA refers to the application of software programs that process certain tasks previously performed by humans [1–3]. RPA has been implemented to automate repetitive and rule-based functions typically handled by back-office employees. In selecting a candidate function for automation, firms usually consider certain criteria such as the degree of process complexity, the degree of human interventions and human-bot hand-overs, and the degree of structured data usage [4]. Typical processes that have been automated are cost accounting, payables and receivables, reporting, invoice sharing, and month-end close processes. A recent study by KPMG [5] on intelligent automation (IA), an umbrella term for RPA, machine learning and artificial intelligence, predicts that global spending on such technologies will reach \$US232 billion by 2025. Recent reports have persistently suggested that RPA is likely to deliver significant benefits to firms. For example, it has been suggested that RPA is likely to increase the accuracy of business operations by minimizing human error, execute business processes with extreme precision at very high velocity, improved

© Springer Nature Switzerland AG 2020
I. Oshri et al. (Eds.): Global Sourcing 2019, LNBIP 410, pp. 145–161, 2020.
https://doi.org/10.1007/978-3-030-66834-1_9

capabilities including monitoring and analytics, allow to scale-up processing infrastructure while significantly reducing operational cost [6, 7]. Literature on RPA identifies various practical implementations both from a client and service provider perspective. From a client side, Lacity and Willcocks [4] studied RPA implementations at O2 which focused on transforming back office services. From a service provider side, the example of OpusCapita, which provides Business Process Outsourcing (BPO) services, started its journey by focusing on the internal adoption of RPA, and next moved to implementing RPA solutions for its clients [8].

While the promise of RPA has been widely discussed in the popular and professional media [9, 10], there have been numerous reports suggesting that firms struggle to benefit from this technology [11, 12]. A KPMG report [5] has suggested that while firms have high expectations to benefit from such technologies, in reality many firms have developed a relatively low level of readiness to deploy such solutions. Deloitte's [13] study has further stated that intelligent automation will have severe impact on new ways of working, challenging the firm's ability to cope with change needed within the firm, such as, augmenting human work with smart machines. As bots and humans are expected to work together, failing to augment them will have negative consequences for both human and bot performance. Indeed, unlike the implementation of robots in manufacturing where robots' actions are visible thus allowing humans to anticipate collaboration and hence adjust their behaviors according to observed robot's activities, in the case of RPA, software bots operate with very little visibility for the individuals who interact with them, thus making their ability to anticipate action and adjust behavior more challenging. In this regard, the challenges that humans reported about working side-by-side software bots at the workplace is key to understanding human's ability to collaborate and engage with them [14]. The aim of our research is to show how humans and bots interact within the context of a firm's implementation of RPA, based on the following research questions: (i) what challenges employees face when interacting with bots and (ii) how firms can mitigate these risks.

We studied a bot implementation program at KAS Bank, a financial institution based in the Netherlands, with an emphasis on the challenges that humans reported when software bots were introduced in their work environment. We first present our research methodology. Next, we introduce KAS Bank's bots program followed by our analysis of the interactions between humans and bots. Subsequently, we highlight the challenges humans faced in such interactions and conclude with a set of practices assisting individuals to develop a perspective on bots.

2   Research Methodology

Since empirical research related to human-bot interaction is limited the aim of our research is to show how humans and bots interact within the context of a firm's implementation of RPA. As such, we opted for an exploratory, case-study-based research that will gain us a deep understanding of the phenomenon under study [15]. A case study approach does not allow statistical generalization since the number of entities as described in case studies is too small. However, our main objective is to expand and generalize theories (analytical generalization) and not to enumerate frequencies (statistical generalization) [15]. Applying a semi-structured interview method as a research instrument is useful to select data and information for exploratory-descriptive studies that may be extended later [16]. We use two main criteria to select a case study in which humans and bots interact. First, we identify a business process that is transactional by nature and routine-based. Second, we select a type of business process that can be characterized by frequent interactions between humans and bots as these type of processes are perceived to be complex due to interdependencies between actors. We selected a case study in which a client automated various financial-oriented business processes. An independent Dutch Bank was selected that is considered a leading European provider of custodian and fund administration services, offering tailored financial services to institutional investors and financial institutions.

We collected data by conducting in-depth interviews during two visits to KAS Bank based in Amsterdam, The Netherlands. In the first visit, we collected and studied corporate information (website, press releases, RPA presentation, RPA blueprints and process information). In the second visit we collected qualitative interview data from 15 KAS Bank representatives that comprise various roles (see Appendix for the interviewee list). All interviews were recorded and transcribed and discussed by the two researchers. We conducted interviews with client representatives, including business and IT management, audit manager, software programmer, process designers, and business process experts. In this way we avoid 'elite bias'. The interviews were semi-structured and based on a protocol that included open questions on how to identify human-bot interaction challenges. In total we conducted 15 interviews and all interviewed participants had been engaged in human-bot interactions (see Appendix). This was to ensure internal consistency within the business process landscape. The varying hierarchical levels of the interviewed staff members prevent potential limitations of the evolving phenomenon from arising. The interviewees were asked to describe their role in human-bot interactions and specifically how they dealt with challenges. Interviews varied from 30 min to 120 min in duration. Additional information was gathered from company information, business process information, and RPA configurations and reports. All the interviews were then transcribed, and the transcripts were sent to the participants to be confirmed.

When executing our qualitative research concept maps are used to guide us through the process of data analysis. Since knowledge is fairly nonlinear, concepts can be seen as organized networks. By selecting and organizing relevant information we are able to identify links between concepts, so that we can fathom the data [17]. Interview data of the staff members was translated into concept maps. As a result of the coding process we were able to create more insight in relevant concepts and human-bot interactions.

3   KAS BANK Bot Program

KAS Bank is an independent Dutch bank founded in 1806. The bank is considered to be a leading European provider of custodian and fund administration services providing tailor-made financial services to institutional investors and financial institutions. As a response to market developments, KAS Bank decided in 2014 to initiate a cost reduction program to minimize operating costs. A LEAN program was launched to streamline and simplify financial business processes at the bank. However, the results were not sufficient enough to meet the cost reduction program's objective. As a result, KAS

Bank outsourced a number of IT functions to a service provider, a deal that included the transfer of employees and IT assets. The outsourcing program has proven to be successful, delivering both significant costs reductions and flexibility regarding pricing mechanisms (pay per use). The bank's executives were encouraged by these results and sought to explore additional mechanisms through which cost reductions can be achieved. In 2016, KAS Bank's operations department has introduced the RPA program. The RPA journey started with KAS Bank exploring the automation of some standard processes. Candidate processes were analyzed in two steps. First, four main criteria were used to assess which processes were ideal to be included in the RPA program. These revolve around (i) how much transactional oriented the process was, (ii) whether the process was routine-based, (iii) whether these were repetitive tasks, and (iv) whether the process was of low complexity (standardized). As second step, three aspects are used to rank the score corresponding with the (i) degree of feasibility, (ii) impact on service quality and (iii) impact on customer management (see Fig. 1).

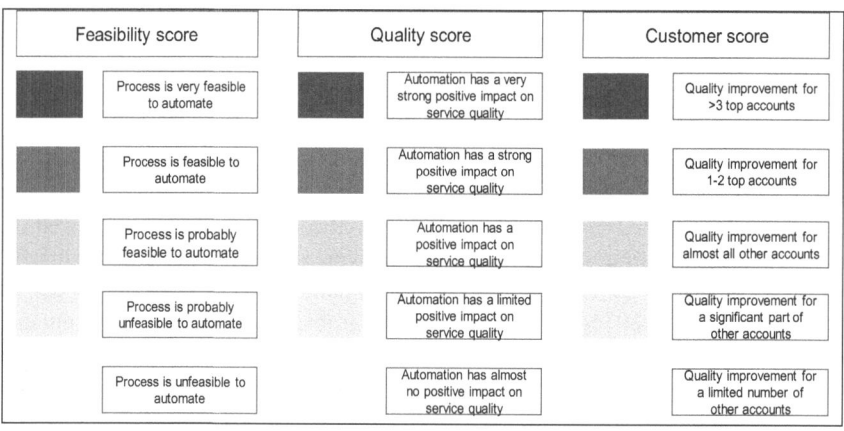

Fig. 1. Overview selection criteria (step 2)

Using this selection method, the operations department assessed numerous business processes. Consequently, a business case was developed per each business process that was identified as promising for automation in which various aspects were analyzed, such as, the impact of automation on the degree of business process improvement, cost involved, the needed support in terms of information systems and people, and the time to market, for instance, for trading services. By indicating the impact on each business process through automation, KAS Bank was able to define the value delivered to their clients and the value provided to KAS Bank in itself. At the start in 2016, two business processes were automated within 6 weeks. This included the development of a planning scheme, build of the bot, and a two-week implementation. More recent bots were introduced over eight weeks that consist of a six weeks development period and two weeks implementation period. In many ways, KAS Bank's bot implementation approach is consistent with [8] in which a four-stage approach (workshop, process assessment, business case proposal, RPA implementation) was pursued. At the time of data collection,

KAS Bank automated 20 financial business processes using five bots. Among the various business processes automated at KAS Bank are treasury operations, obligation payments, calculating and booking, and client data management (e.g. internal invoicing, opening new and changing existing bank accounts). Bots implemented at KAS BANK have taken over manual processed transactions which were carried out by employees using Excel spreadsheets. Many of these employees carried out this line of work for over a decade. While the original introduction of bots was to reduce cost, recent automation projects sought to improve the quality of business processes by removing and skipping rework.

4   Humans and Bots: The Challenges

Although the benefits of using RPA have been addressed in academic literature and practice [18], challenges associated with the visibility of bots' actions and hence humans' reaction have not been addressed so far. Our examination of KAS Bank's bot program suggests that 3 key visibility challenges evolved that led humans to struggle with in their software bots environment. We discuss these three areas of visibility below.

4.1   Challenge 1: The Visibility to the Bot Concept

Based on our interviews at KAS Bank we noticed that employees were struggling with the concept of bots. More particularly, the following questions were raised by employees: what bots are? how do they work? what can they deliver to the firm? and how are they able to fulfil employees tasks? These questions correspond with [19] work who studied the RPA concept and its implications for financial processes. We frame this challenge as the visibility of employees to the bot concept. At KAS Bank, employees were first skeptical about what bots were and their ability to perform tasks previously carried out by humans. Indeed, employees' perception of what bots can or cannot do varied significantly. When the Bot Program was discussed as an option, most operations employees were skeptical about the concept. In fact, some of them challenged the bot's ability to replace them and perform a task they have carried out for a while. They have perceived their unique and often undocumented knowledge and experience to be critical for the completion of the task, despite their work being categorized as rule-based and repetitive.

> *"During the start of the program employees were skeptical as they did not believe that their skills and experience could be copied by a software program. The idea that bots do exact the same things as humans do was not accepted: they did not believe that it could work." (Source: software programmer).*

During KAS Bank's initiation of the bot program employees discussed the concept of applying bots as part of business processes and argued that they did not understand the concept. Actually, the majority of employees were not aware that software is used to fulfill business oriented tasks. By explaining how a bot looks like and what bots can and cannot do, employees were informed about the practical consequences.

> *"Various employees did not understand how the robot works and what type of tasks are conducted. We learned that we have to explain how bots work and how they fit into a business process." (Source: process designer).*

As part of KAS Bank's explanation how bots work employees were informed about the fact that a bot is just a software program and that the IT department will program business rules in the software bot. As a consequence, process managers have to sketch out business process tasks first. Subsequently, an IT department software programmer is able to configure the bot and translate process descriptions into program rules. In doing so, employees created a better understanding of how humans and bots work together.

4.2   Challenge 2: Visibility to the End-to-End Business Process

The introduction of bots to the operations environment also created a process challenge. Operations personnel who were manually performing tasks to be automated have developed over the years a partial understanding of the business process. These personnel have become accustomed to focus on data entry and problem solving of specific process steps, that the big picture of what the transaction represents have become hidden to them. KAS Bank established a development team to implement the bots, however, the team struggled to compose the end-to-end business process as operations personnel could only provide information on segregated steps that involved multiple teams and across departments. As a result, the development team had difficulties in configuring the bots for an end-to-end business process. Bots, therefore, were eventually configured to handle an amalgam of transactions. The following statements reflect on this aspect:

> "We experienced that employees who are fulfilling process steps just focus on their dedicated tasks and have less insights in other process related tasks. In fact, employees have built a specific profile in conducting tasks. Since we introduced bots, we noticed that employees have to understand the process as a whole, which require a more generic profile." (Source: Business Process Manager Finance 1)

> "Previously, employees performed repetitive tasks. Today [after automation], they have to understand process tasks and interpret which tasks they still have to do themselves. This means that employees need to understand the process as a whole to collaborate with a robot successfully." (Source: Business Process Selection Specialist)

As during the introduction of RPA at KAS Bank certain process steps were replaced by bots, employees became confused about 'who is doing what' as they did not have an overall view of the process. Originally, employees knew who to contact in case of unclarities for instance in case of process hand-overs. Now, bots have taken over the majority of process tasks, which increased the unclarity of mutual responsibilities. As a result, employees showed resistant behavior to fulfill their tasks. This corresponds with [20] study who pointed out that RPA solutions require firms to consider the end-to-end process. While firms benefit from integrating sub-processes and tasks into an end-to-end automated process, humans' involvement and understanding of the process can be hindered by the automated process, as demonstrated in the KAS Bank case.

4.3   Challenge 3: Visibility to Solve What Bots Cannot Process

As bots became operational, they processed transactions that previously were manually performed by humans. Bots depend on input data to generate meaningful output. Their output, often in the form of a report, was handed over to operations employees who needed to check it prior to passing it on to an external client. The development team assumed that data provided as input from internal and external sources would be in line with the bots' requirements, thus resulting in the generation of a client report. Operations personnel were consequently informed about their new responsibilities to check the reports before releasing them to clients. At the same, the development team informed operations personnel that their work was affected by bots to identify the impact of bots' implementation and consequently adapt their way of working. Yet, the full impact of robotizing tasks was not assessed as data provided as input was not always complete or accurate.

Bots at KAS Bank were not always able to process tasks they were designed to complete. When a bot failed to complete a task, the incomplete task was flagged as an exception. In most cases, when bots generated exceptions, it was because data was either incomplete or incorrect. For example, a data field which was defined as numeric contained letters and therefore produced an exception by the bot. As an output, the bot produced an exception report to be reviewed and corrected by operations personnel (see Fig. 2 - example of an exception report). As a result, operations personnel have become essential for the completion of tasks that the bot has failed to complete.

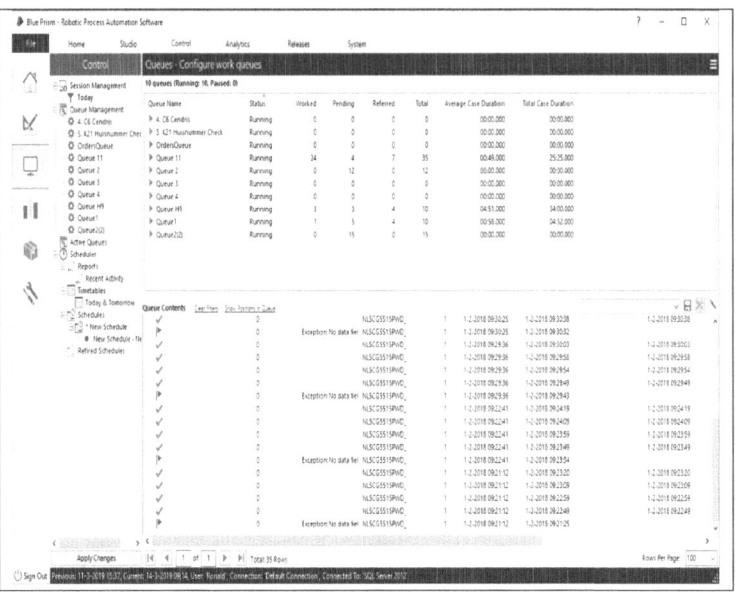

Fig. 2. Example of an RPA exception list

"Within a business process at least 40% of all tasks can be conducted by a bot, but often more. The percentage is influenced by the number of exceptions regarding process tasks. Specifically, the data quality is a real issue as bots are rejecting tasks in case of poor data quality. That's where the humans come in as they have to repair the quality of data first.' (Source: Functional Application Manager).

"A design criterion is a bot has to handle 2000 financial (swift) transactions per week. Based on our conducted proof of concept we experienced that 20% of all transactions were labelled as exceptions. That means that we still need humans to repair bot errors." (Source: Software Programmer)

The observation that not all process steps can be automated correspond to the research of [21] who state that the aim of automation is to replace human manual control by automatic devices and computers. The author's findings suggest that the increased interest in human factors reflects the irony that the more advanced a control system is, the more crucial the contribution of the human operator.

As a result of bot exceptions at KAS Bank, operations personnel needed to engage in work they previously manually performed, however in a different way. Previously they entered data for all the fields, but now they needed to analyze the source of the exception and consequently complete the missing/wrong information. Handling exceptions have changed the operations personnel's' roles in two ways. On the one hand, some operations personnel pursued a root-cause analysis and engaged in redesigning the process by working with the development team to avoid the re-occurrence of these exceptions. These initiatives required KAS Bank to provide operations personnel opportunities to develop themselves further and assume a process improvement manager role. On the other hand, other operations personnel were finding the task of handling exceptions as discouraging. While in the past these individuals were responsible for assessing the quality of the data as input, allocate the data field that the data should be entered and complete data entry, now these individuals are instructed by the bot to decode the nature of the exception and take steps to fix this specific mistake. They have little visibility to the input data, and yet, they require to fix it. Consequently, these operations personnel sought alternative lines of employment.

The three challenges demonstrate that because humans lacked visibility to what bots are, do and fail to do, firms need to address these shortcomings by assisting humans to collaborate with bots. Based on our observations at KAS Bank, we developed practices to overcome such challenges and improve human visibility to what bots are and do.

5   Five Practices to Help Introducing Humans to Bots

We offer five practices the improve visibility of what bots are and do, as well as how humans should engage with bots' outcomes based on observations made at KAS Bank. Two practices relate to the visibility to the bot concept, one to visibility to the end-to-end business process, and one to visibility to solve what bots cannot process.

5.1   Practice #1. Humanize the Bot

Any bot program will encounter behavioral change by employees toward the bot during the implementation stage. At KAS Bank, employees were first skeptical about the impact of bots on their jobs, and the ability of bots to replace them. Gradually, employees became aware of what bots can and cannot do. Interestingly, we noticed that post-implementation, employees referred to bots operating in their environment as if they were another human colleague. They attributed success and failure to the bot, despite the fact that a bot's performance is a direct outcome of the quality of a software program. Further, the development team gave each bot a comic hero name, and insisted on referring to the bot by its name in any communications.

> *"We also use bot names in our internal communications about performance and exceptions. As we inform teams and employees about the progress and benefits of automation, the bot names become familiar." (Source: Head Process Improvement)*

Our observations suggest that as soon as the bots are implemented, employees try to find the human being in the bots. Phrases such as "we have a new co-worker: <name comic hero>" and "<name comic hero> does act strange, we need to help him" were often used. We even noticed that employees praised the bots for fulfilling a lot of work. One business process manager stated that "we need to get the bot out of the humans and get the human into the bot". Indeed, each new bot was registered as a new team member, which included assigning training sessions and clearly defining their tasks, just as for any human worker. Such a practice helps humans to visibility of what the bots are and treat them as co-workers, allowing them to understand the bots' areas of responsibilities and abilities. Our findings are consistent with the research of [22] who studied the integration of robots into a hospital workflow. Indeed, with increased stress levels by caregivers, so the emotional response to the robot increases by humans around the robot.

5.2   Practice #2. Visualize the Bot

Our case at KAS Bank shows that it was important to visualize what bots do. We observed that the design team at the Bank pursued several steps to improve visibility of what bots do and are during the design and implementation stages. First, presentations were organized for all departments and teams as an internal roadshow. Then, the Bank held sessions in which simulations of the bots' functionalities were shared with employees, and what the manually performed tasks would look like in an automated workflow. Lastly, when a bot was implemented, the Bank repeated the workflow presentations to show how the bot operated in the live environment. A workflow chart (see Fig. 3) was placed in operations team offices to ensure that they could clearly see how 'their' bots performed work and assess the junctions where humans could be needed to complete the task.

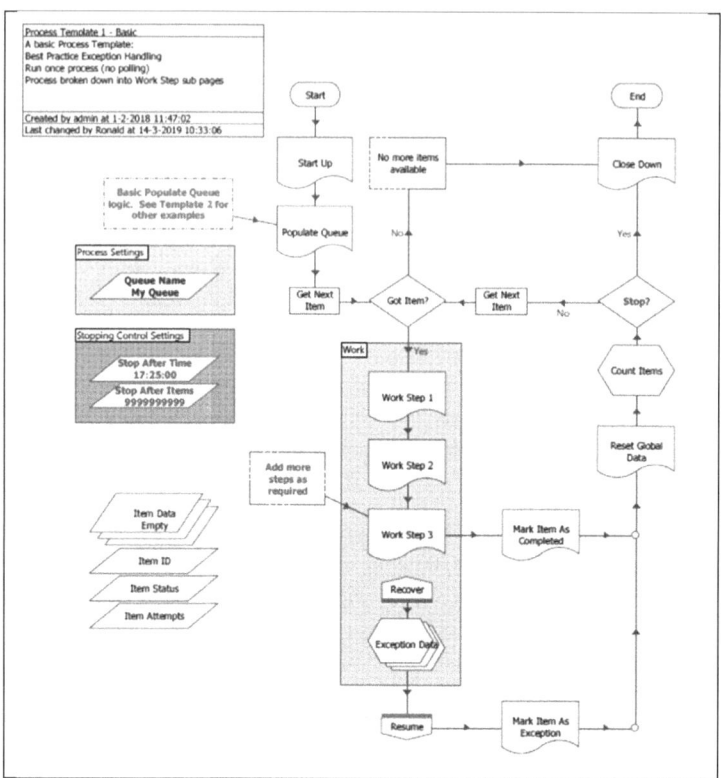

Fig. 3. Example business process visualization

"The process graphics helped to understand what tasks are fulfilled by bots and these insights are helpful for handling exceptions, which in turn is a new task of process experts. Moreover, both the Proof of Concept and the graphics helped to build trust in the bots as we have to rely on them." (Source: Business Process Manager Finance 2)

Showing bots in a live environment stimulated interest and generated discussions within the Bank with regard to the bots' impact on work. Questions such as "How long will it take to program a bot?", "What is the IT view on managing bots?", "Can the bot do other tasks?", and "How does the bot make decisions?" were raised in these meetings, further helping people to understand and further clarity some of bots' abilities and their impact on human work. These findings correspond with [23] work in which they argue that employees involved in accounting processes need to understand how to unpack human-machine interactions. We provide insight into the steps and actions that improve such visibility by humans of bots to allow humans relate to what bots do and how they do that.

5.3   Practice #3. Help Humans Visualize Positive Human-Bot Interactions

One of the challenges we observed was that the lack of visibility to what bots do and consequently the need for humans to 'pick-up' exceptions and complete tasks the bot failed to complete created a sense of frustration and resentment among employees. As such, the true threat of bots was not necessarily in that bots replace humans, but humans losing ownership of the tasks and processes, thus finding themselves as 'fixing' bots issues. We find that after employees became familiar with working with bots they experienced the advantages. One expert stressed the positive impact some employees experienced:

> *"After the implementation of the bots in our business processes some colleagues try to find the human in the robot. The say 'the bot does not work!, we as humans will fix the problem' or 'the robot does act strange, we need to give him a hand.' We also experienced that colleagues are praising the bots to full fil lot of work. Moreover, they state that they have a new co-worker: a bot." (Source: Process Designer 2).*

At KAS Bank, there were hardly any redundancies following the implementation of the bots program, however, several operators, who were previously involved in data entry, sought alternative lines of employment as they struggled to cope with the changing nature of the job. Such an outcome can be mitigated should management offer new career avenues that will re-establish links between humans and bots. For example, we observed that some operations personnel were encouraged and took on developing process improvement skills during robotization. Some used their freed-up time to get training in advanced areas of management and invested in developing relationships with clients. Or as an expert argued:

> *"Business process operators do not necessarily lose their jobs, with only a limited number compared to our original expectations. Instead, they have focused on process improvements and providing services such as financial reporting to our external clients on a regular basis." (Source: Business Process Expert Finance 1).*

Indeed, RPA implementation requires changes in business processes. In this regard, helping individuals become process leaders is therefore key to maintaining human involvement in the bots program. KAS Bank introduced new roles called 'process champions' who were involved in training and educating others about taking ownership of the entire bot business process. Consequently, employees learned when and how to interact with bots, and how exceptions should be handled. Moreover, process champions propagated a LEAN methodology, which encouraged employees to identify process improvements on a daily basis and continue to improve bot operations. One process expert explained:

> *"Process experts create an in-depth understanding of how robots are built and what type of tasks they perform to identify improvement initiatives. By encouraging the use of bots and aligning human-bot interactions, our process champions fulfill a vital role. Through providing examples, answering questions, and discussing process and bot improvements with their colleagues, they accelerate the*

performance of robotized processes." (Source: Business Process Expert Finance 2)

Process champions also conducted two-monthly reviews of bot workflows. The review reports offered a better understanding of how many tasks had been fulfilled by bots and provided root-cause analysis of tasks the bots had failed to complete. The report and the review process created opportunities for stakeholders to engage in improving the bots' workflow and performance. One manager highlighted the advantages of this function:

> *"Employees are encouraged to provide input to tweak/fine tune the robot. The goal is to provide improvement suggestions through which process tasks can be simplified and operate faster. Based on our findings, the robotics development team learned how to optimize process steps and decrease the number of process failures. It's a process itself to train the robot in handling tasks even better and better." (Source: Functional Application Manager)*

As claimed by [24], process skills are essential when applying RPA solutions, not just to improve efficiencies but also to help humans relate and visualize opportunities to be part of the bots program.

5.4 Practice #4. Making Bots Governance More Visible

Humans respond to either formal or informal governance mechanisms but interpreting desired outcomes and anticipating rewards or penalties. However, humans may struggle understanding their interactions with bots should there not be a governing structure for such interactions. In this regard, humans lack visibility of how bots are governed. In our case, KAS Bank established a unique Center of Excellence (CoE) to coherently govern human-bot interactions. The CoE's objectives were twofold. First, it was responsible for governing a wide range of tasks, such as: establishing bot ownership, verifying general audit and IT controls (e.g. authorization), separation of duties, roles and responsibilities, and legal issues. From a control and reporting perspective, the CoE was responsible for KAS Bank fulfilling its obligation to show compliance with financial and IT regulation standards (e.g. ISAE 3402) and report their findings to clients. In addition, the CoE coordinated end-to-end business process, in particular when various sub-processes were managed by a number of departments. This was done in collaboration with the IT department who were responsible for the operational management of the bots. One manager explained:

> *"We are managing one business process end-to-end, which consists of three sub-processes that are all managed individually by various business teams. Per sub-process exceptions are handled, however, one employee coordinates the end-to end process." (Source: Business Process Manager Finance 2)*

In addition to humans governing bots, the governance structure also included the management of data quality, such as completeness, accuracy, integrity and consistency. This aspect in governance is also important for the human-bot interactions as exceptions are generated by the bots are the result of low quality data but have to be resolved by humans. Data management governance allowed humans in the bots program to engage in data quality issues and redesign data structures that improve the bot's performance. One manager explained:

> "As data quality becomes important, in our view business data owners have to guard and improve data quality. KAS Bank's strategy is to become a more data driven company. That means that we definitely have to improve the quality of data if we intend to extend the number of bots in the near future." (Source: Business Process Manager Finance 1)

For humans to be involved in governing bots, multiple aspects of governance should be considered such as roles, process ownership, data management and expected performance.

5.5 Practice #5. Visualize the Bot

The firm's service roadmap should capture the opportunities for collaboration between humans and bots. By developing a tightly coupled bot-human roadmap, firms will ensure that humans and smart automation platforms interact. As a consequence, a bot-human roadmap has to be translated into an operational plan to support business needs by means of an enabling IT landscape. Moreover, a sound architectural view can be seen as a prerequisite to support such an IT landscape. The Bank's enterprise architect explained:

> "A bot-human roadmap consists of IT architectural blueprints, and clear IT boundaries (infrastructure, applications, data) that can be translated into a strategic bot agenda which can be managed by our senior managers. Therefore, we need a roadmap to align KAS Bank's business goals with an adequate IT landscape." (Source: Enterprise Architect).

Identifying the sweet spot between fully human and fully autonomous robotic processes will enable firms to anticipate the hand-over points between automation platforms and humans [25]. By developing a bot-human roadmap firms also pay attention to implement bots as part of an IT landscape. In doing so, interoperability agreements towards existing information systems (applications, middleware, infrastructure) are established which improve the robustness of robotized business processes. We noticed that KAS Bank's architects focus on applying standards to decrease the number of bot exceptions due to failing IT malfunction. Business departments increasing dependency on bots that are capable of handling large volumes of work put additional pressure on the IT department to repair bots swiftly. By using design principles architects aim is to design a coherent IT landscape to increase operational bot performance.

> "In the near future KAS Bank intends to use cognitive solutions which are able to handle even more complex process exceptions. This will result in an additional pressure to our IT departments to sustain their operational performance." (Source: Managing Director Operations)

Next, we have listed the key challenges and related RPA practices in Table 1.

Table 1. Challenges and related RPA practices

Key challenges	RPA practices	
Visibility to the bot concept	1. Humanize your bot	Treat bots as human beings and co-workers to achieve acceptance
		Train bots to do exactly the same tasks as humans do
	2. Visualize the bot	Demonstrate how bots work in practice to explore opportunities
		Visualize process steps to create a better understanding
Visibility to the end-to-end business process	3. Help humans visualize positive human-bot interactions	Develop job rotation opportunities for employees who seek alternative lines of employment
		Encourage process champions to educate collegues about taking ownership of the entire bot business process
Visibility to solve what bots cannot process	4. Making bots governance visible	Establish a Center of Excellence (CoE) to coherently govern human-bot challenges
		Develop a data governance policy and plan to assess and improve the quality of data
	5. Visibility into the bot-human roadmap	Ensure that humans and intelligent automation platforms interact
		Identify the sweet spot between fully human and fully autonomous robotic processes to anticipate the hand-over areas and consequently develop a strategic bot-human roadmap

6 Concluding Remarks

This study is guided by the questions a) how does a firm address the employees' challenges that are associated with RPA deployment, and b) what practices can be developed to overcome these challenges? The introduction of software robotic solutions to support business processes leads to new organizational challenges. In this paper we examined interactions between humans and bots by describing three challenges that a client faced when implementing a bot program. Based on evidence we offered a set of practices that help firms to develop a perspective on what bots can and cannot do as a way to encourage humans' involvement in bot's work. As cognitive and artificial intelligence are likely replace additional areas of work, this article is a stepping stone in preparing humans to accept such solutions while advancing human skills.

Appendix A

Interview Scheme and Interview Questions

Role	Duration
Manager Income and Tax	30 min
Audit Manager	30 min
Managing Director IT	60 min
Functional Application Manager	50 min
Managing Director Operations	30 min
Enterprise Architect	45 min
Software Programmer	45 min
Head Process Improvement	30 min
Process Designer 1	45 min
Process Designer 2	45 min
Business Process Selection Specialist	120 min
Business Process Manager Finance 1	45 min
Business Process Manager Finance 2	45 min
Business Process Expert Finance 1	45 min
Business Process Expert Finance 2	30 min

Category	Interview questions
Generic questions	What was the firm's rationale to start robotizing financial business processes?
	How will the firm's financial business processes change due to robotizing work?
	In general, do you have insights in what type of tasks are executed by bots?
	To what degree are you involved in robotized processes?
Specific questions	What process related tasks do you have to execute?

(continued)

(*continued*)

Category	Interview questions
	What are the efforts of robotization in practice?
	What is the effect of robotization on employees (humans)?
	How is the handover determined and described between humans and bots?
	Who will pick up and execute the process exception list?
	To what degree does binding between humans and bots take place in practice?
	How is your expertise influenced by robotized business processes?
	Who has oversight on the robotized processes in detail (steps, tasks, responsibilities)?

References

1. Leyh, C., Bley, K., Seek, S.: Elicitation of processes in business process management in the era of digitization – the same techniques as decades ago? In: Piazolo, F., Geist, V., Brehm, L., Schmidt, R. (eds.) ERP Future 2016. LNBIP, vol. 285, pp. 42–56. Springer, Cham (2017). https://doi.org/10.1007/978-3-319-58801-8_4
2. Frank, M., Roehrig, P., Pring, B.: What to Do When Machines Do Everything: How to Get Ahead in a World of AI, Algorithms, Bots, and Big Data. Wiley, Hoboken (2017)
3. Wilson, H.J., Daugherty, P.R.: Collaborative intelligence: humans and ai are joining forces. Harvard Bus. Rev. **96**, 114–123 (2018)
4. Lacity, M.C., Willcocks, L.P: Robotic process automation at Telefónica O2. MIS Q. Exec. **15**(1), 21-35 (2016)
5. KPMG report 'Ready, Set, Fail? Avoiding setbacks in the intelligent automation race. https://advisory.kpmg.us/articles/2018/new-study-findings-read-ready-set-fail.html
6. Devarajan, Y.: A study of robotic process automation use cases today for tomorrow's business. Int. J. Comput. Technol. **5**(6), 12–18 (2018)
7. Leopold, H., van der Aa, H., Reijers, H.A.: Identifying candidate tasks for robotic process automation in textual process descriptions. In: PMDS 2018 Working Conference, Tallinn, Estonia, 11–12 June 2018 (2018). http://www.bpmds.org
8. Hallikainen, P., Bekkhus, R., Pan, S.: How OpusCapita used internal RPA capabilities to offer services to clients. MIS Q. Exec. **17**(1), 41–52 (2018)
9. Vernon, D.: Artificial Cognitive Systems. A Primer. MIT Press, Cambridge (2014)
10. Sundar, S.S., Bellur, S., Oh, J., Jia, H., Kim, H.S.: Theoretical importance of contingency in human computer interaction: effects of message interactivity on user engagement. Commun. Res. 1–31 (2014)
11. McKinsey: Jobs lost, jobs gained: what the future of work will mean for jobs, skills, and wages (2017). https://www.mckinsey.com/featured-insights/future-of-work/jobs-lost-jobs-gained-what-the-future-of-work-will-mean-for-jobs-skills-and-wages
12. Forrester Predictions 2019: Artificial Intelligence: No Pain, No Gain With Enterprise AI, 6 November 2018. https://www.forrester.com/report/Predictions+2019+Artificial+Intelligence/-/E-RES144617

13. Deloitte: The robots are ready. Are you? Untapped advantage in your digital workforce (2017). https://www2.deloitte.com/content/dam/Deloitte/nl/Documents/strategy/deloitte-nl-consulting-robots-are-ready.pdf
14. Krämer, A.D., Guillory, J.E., Hancock, J.T.: Experimental evidence of massive-scale emotional contagion through social networks. Proc. Nat. Acad. Sci. **111**, 8788–8790 (2014). 201320040
15. Yin, R.K.: Case Study Research: Design and Methods. Sage Publications, London (2009)
16. Denzin, N.K.: The Research Act: A Theoretical Introduction to Sociological Methods. McGraw-Hill, New York (1978)
17. Orlikowski, W.J., Lacono, C.S.: Research commentary: desperately seeking the 'IT' in IT research- a call to theorizing the IT artifact. Inf. Syst. Res. **9**12(2), 121–134 (2001)
18. Willcocks, L.P., Lacity, M.C.: Service Automation Robots and the Future of Work. SB Publishing, Ashford (2016)
19. Moffitt, K.C., Rozario, A.M., Vasarhelyi, M.A.: Robotic process automation for auditing. J. Emer. Tech. Acc. **15**(1), 1–10 (2018)
20. Kirchmer, M., Franz, P.: Value-driven robotic process automation (RPA). In: Shishkov, B. (ed.) BMSD 2019. LNBIP, vol. 356, pp. 31–46. Springer, Cham (2019). https://doi.org/10.1007/978-3-030-24854-3_3
21. Bainbridge, L.: Ironies of automation. Automatica **19**(6), 775–779 (1983)
22. Mutlu, B., Forlizzi, J.: Robots in organizations: the role of workflow, social, and environmental factors in human-robot interaction. In: Proceedings of the 3rd ACM/IEEE International Conference on Human Robot Interaction, pp. 287–294 (2008)
23. Lehner, O., Leitner-Hanetseder, S., Eisl, C.: The whatness of digital accounting: status quo and ways to move forward. ACRN J. Finan. Risk Persect. 8, Special Issue Digital Accounting (2019)
24. Lamberton, C., Brigo, D., Hoy, D.: Impact of robotics, RPA and AI on the insurance industry: challenges and opportunities. J. Finan. Perspect. **4**(1), 8–20 (2017)
25. Kaivo-Oja, J., Roth, S., Westerlund, L.: Futures of robotics. Human work in digital transformation. Int. J. Technol. Manage. **73**(4), 176–205 (2017)

Designing a Sourcing Ecosystem for Strategic Innovation Through "Big Data" Applications

Kevan Penter[✉], Brian Perrin, John Wreford, and Graham Pervan

Faculty Business and Law, Curtin University, GPO Box U1987, Perth, WA, Australia
kevan.penter@team.telstra.com

Abstract. Published research on innovation from Information Technology and Business Process Outsourcing (ITO/BPO) is rare [1]. Strategic innovation involves high uncertainties better addressed through agile methods and a collaborative approach [1–3]. Key success factors in delivering ITO/BPO innovation are high-quality relationships, trust and collaborative cultures [1–4], and establishing an effective governance configuration. The authors report on longitudinal case studies of a global mining company ("GMC") and a group of its suppliers aimed at understanding how GMC is developing "big data" applications to generate game-changing innovation. This paper describes how GMC has developed a "big data" platform to support internal staff, customers, consultants and third party suppliers to create applications that can transform global mining and smelting industries to deliver a price premium for GMC's products. GMC has encountered a shortage of suitably experienced data scientists in its key operating locations resulting in a significant skills gap in its big data program. GMC's sourcing strategy aims to build an open and collaborative ecosystem that draws upon secondary markets to help fill the skills gap. To create an environment in which open innovation [5] can flourish, GMC established an Analytics Speed Team (AST) as an internal consulting and program management group to drive faster progress with big data applications. A contribution of this research is to identify the role of AST in establishing an effective governance configuration for open innovation. A practical contribution is made by analysing the value of secondary markets for ITO services in a sourcing ecosystem optimised for delivering innovation.

Keywords: Sourcing configuration · Sourcing ecosystem · Cloud services · Innovation in outsourcing/offshoring · Big data · Artificial intelligence · Secondary markets · "Gig" economy

1 Introduction

More than three decades of research and practice in the Information Technology and Business Process Outsourcing (ITO/BPO) industries have seen substantial growth, and the creation of significant business value. While most if not all of the early ITO/BPO initiatives focused on delivering cost savings for client companies, more recent research [1, 3, 4] has identified *innovation* as a possible outcome from outsourcing initiatives,

© Springer Nature Switzerland AG 2020
I. Oshri et al. (Eds.): Global Sourcing 2019, LNBIP 410, pp. 162–192, 2020.
https://doi.org/10.1007/978-3-030-66834-1_10

and have sought to understand the nature of the relationships between client company and suppliers that are most effective in the search for new ideas [3].

Published research on innovation from ITO/BPO, however, is rare and has emerged only recently [1]. Whitley and Willcocks [2] say collaborative innovation in ITO/BPO is an infrequently researched strategic motivation, representing a significant gap in our understanding of outsourcing practice.

In this research paper, the authors report on a series of longitudinal case studies aimed at understanding how a global mining company (pseudonym "GlobalMinCo" or "GMC") is obtaining innovation through ITO/BPO focused on "big data" applications, and how an ecosystem of mining equipment, technology and service (METS) suppliers is also contributing to this innovation. In this context, "big data" is defined as large volumes of extensively varied data generated, captured and processed at high speed by applications within a collaborative sourcing ecosystem using widely available commercial cloud services platforms and open source software tools. This paper describes how GMC uses the "big data" platform and tools to support internal staff, customers, consultants and third party suppliers to innovate and transform global mining and smelting industries and to obtain a price premium for GMC's minerals and metals products and services.

GMC's "big data" strategy built on more than a decade of work on mining automation (referred to by GMC as Mine of the Future ™), involving several billion dollars investment in Information and Communications Technology, systems and applications. Leading global mining companies were early to adopt ITO and BPO (including offshoring), and in common with its competitors and peers, GMC has a mature and successful ITO/BPO portfolio, including offshore captive centres and arms-length contracting relationships with leading global ITO/BPO suppliers.

Building on a decade-long program of developing mining automation including the Mine of the Future ™ technology suite, GMC initially utilised its established ITO/BPO sourcing strategy for the development of big data applications, which were seen as a new and major wave of innovation aimed at maintaining GMC's technology lead and competitive position as the global mining company with the lowest cost of operations. However, as noted by Lacity and Willcocks [4], successful innovation is not an automatic outcome from outsourcing.

After an initial two-year period of limited success, GMC found it was necessary to change its big data sourcing strategy. An initial sourcing strategy based on the use of external consultants together with its existing OBPO captive centre and portfolio of ITO/BPO sourcing contracts was found to be too slow, expensive and inflexible in delivering the business benefits sought from big data applications.

In this paper, we explain how GMC changed its sourcing strategy to develop a more dynamic ecosystem of internal capability and external suppliers. We analyse how this required a radical change in organisation, IT architecture, development methodology, leadership and governance. We identify some successful big data applications that have emerged, and also report on potential challenges to be addressed, possibly by further changes to sourcing strategy.

Appendix 4 provides definitions for key terms and their interrelationships. Section 2 introduces the research problem and research questions while Sect. 3 presents a review of literature relevant to the problem under study. Section 4 outlines the research methods that have been adopted. Noting that in this research paper we are analysing decisions by GMC to change its ITO/BPO sourcing strategy for big data applications, Sect. 5 provides an overview of the mining industry context in which GMC operates, while Sect. 6 provides a brief summary of the company itself, and Sect. 7 presents tentative case analysis and findings. Limitations and opportunities for future research are discussed in Sect. 8 while Sect. 9 suggests tentative conclusions and potential contribution.

2   Research Problem and Research Questions

The research problem that the authors have sought to address in this paper is to investigate whether and how ITO/BPO strategies can contribute to strategic innovation in an industry sector that is undergoing a significant, IT-led transformation [6]. Exploratory research led to a recognition of the significant role in innovation that is played by supplier companies from the METS sector, so in this research we sought to understand the sources of innovation (was it client-led, supplier-led and/or influenced by institutional factors?). As part of the research journey, we also recognised that the open innovation paradigm [5, 7] may offer explanatory power for the phenomenon under study.

As noted by Whitley and Willcocks [2], **innovation** represents a significant gap in our understanding of outsourcing practice. We set out to investigate the extent to which strategic innovation could be obtained through an ITO sourcing strategy. We noted research findings by Oshri et al. [1] that suggested that partnership contracts/relationships, and effective relational governance were critical success factors for achieving strategic innovation through outsourcing.

In keeping with the concept of researching strategic innovation obtained through ITO, we focused on a particular set of applications being developed in an area generically referred to as "big data" as it has been argued (see for example [8]), that few academic papers have been published describing the benefits that are being obtained from big data. We also were aware that GMC was seeking to obtain strategic benefits from its big data initiatives so it fit the requirements as a suitable research setting.

Based on initial exploratory work on the case study, both the model of the global sourcing learning curve presented by Whitley and Willcocks ([2], p. 97) and the process described in Lacity and Willcocks [4] as Acculturation, Inspiration (idea generation), Funding and Injection (change management) seemed likely to offer insights into GMC's managerial intentions, and have a high degree of relevance in the GMC case.

As noted by Jayatilaka and Hirschheim [9], ITO phenomena can be researched and understood as an organisational change phenomenon influenced by institutional processes. That appears highly relevant to the global mining industry which is currently undergoing an IT-led transformation, so we have also sought to understand the institutional forces on management, not only in GMC but also in suppliers to the mining industry and also on GMC's main competitor "Big Australian" (pseudonym).

While mindful of the transformation that is occurring across the global mining industry (refer to Sect. 5) our unit of analysis in this research is primarily at the level of individual companies (e.g. GMC and its METS suppliers). We also recognised a need to narrow the scope of research to make it more manageable with the resources available. Accordingly, we have focused on GMC's portfolio of big data and machine learning applications rather than the full range of GMC's robotics, IoT and mining automation initiatives.

It is acknowledged in the academic literature that a client organisation's goals for its ITO strategy are highly context-specific and these goals are likely to change over time [10, 11]. This leads to frequent recommendations in the literature for more longitudinal case studies of ITO (see for example [12–14]). Hence, in this research the authors have adopted a longitudinal case study approach, with a particular research objective of identifying and understanding the drivers of changes in sourcing strategy.

RQ1:   What are the key success factors that contribute to successful strategic innovation achieved through ITO? How did GMC craft its "big data" sourcing strategy, and how did this change over time?

RQ2:   How does a client company organize for successful innovation when its ITO partners and their contributions are diverse and not known in advance?

RQ3:   How do digital platforms and secondary labour markets facilitate ITO supplier ecosystems that are effective in delivering innovation? How efficient are secondary labour markets in delivering hyper-talents in areas such as data science and artificial intelligence?

3   Literature Review

3.1   Can ITO/BPO Drive Innovation for the Client Company?

It is common to find references in commercial and marketing publications to the potential of ITO to drive innovation for client companies. However, published research on innovation is comparatively rare, and appears to have emerged only recently. ITO/BPO can be viewed as a form of organisational innovation, and innovation can also be viewed as one of the objectives of ITO/BPO [15–18].

The strategic profile of a company or organisation is likely to influence ITO strategy [19], with firms that are classified as "defenders" in terms of their strategic profile [20] likely to be attracted to ITO as a means of reducing costs. On the other hand, firms classified as "prospectors" in the Miles and Snow [20] typology focus on innovation (e.g. new products and services) to meet new and changing customer needs and generate revenue growth. Hence, a firm classified as a "prospector" is likely to place a greater emphasis on achieving innovation from ITO activities. In this research paper, GMC would fit the Miles and Snow [20] definition of a "prospector", in both senses of the word.

Collaborative innovation in ITO/BPO is a strategic motivation that has been infrequently researched, and according to Whitley and Willcocks [2] represents a significant gap in our understanding of outsourcing practice. In a review of ITO literature, Lacity, Khan, Yan and Willcocks, [21] identified only one study that considered innovation as a driver for IT outsourcing while a review of BPO literature [22] identified three studies from a collection of 87 articles that identified innovation as a motivation for BPO.

Aubert et al. [23] suggests that it is not surprising that innovation has been rare in the ITO field where research findings have argued in favour of tight contracts in an environment of low uncertainty. Lacity and Willcocks ([4], p. 40) observe that historically, "innovation and ITO/BPO have been rare bedfellows". The view that offshore ITO/BPO does not present an easy path to innovation was also supported by Levina and Vaast [24] who reported case study findings that innovation came mostly from the client. These authors noted that boundaries of various forms (power distance, organisational boundaries, geographic and cultural distance) could have the effect of reducing collaboration between parties which would lower innovation. This view was corroborated by Straub, Weill and Schwaig [25] who noted that IT-enabled competitive advantage required continuous innovation, and an executive mindset that understood the strategic use of IT. Such an approach and mindset was difficult to achieve when control over an organisation's strategic IT assets was handed over to an external service provider.

While noting that relatively few BPO relationships achieve successful innovation, Lacity and Willcocks [4] conducted case study research that found that in high performing BPO relationships, multiple innovation projects delivered substantial improvement to the client's performance.

These authors (Lacity and Willcocks [4]) conducted case study research on a sample of 24 client and provider pairs (48 organisations in total) that had been identified as working together to foster dynamic innovation. The importance of senior management leadership was emphasised, with effective leadership "pairs" identified as the most important factor in successful BPO innovation. The importance of a high quality relationship and a collaborative culture in delivering innovation from BPO have been identified as key success factors by Oshri et al. [1].

In arm's length contractual relationships, another critical success factor was that client firms provide incentives to BPO service providers to deliver innovation (Lacity and Willcocks [4]). Not discussed in this research study was the performance of captive centres in delivering BPO innovation.

In summary, there appears to be a significant research gap in evaluating the extent to which OBPO can deliver strategic innovation to client companies, and in particular, the performance of captive centres in delivering innovation appears to be a significant research gap.

3.2   ITO Sourcing Strategy

One of the first research articles to begin addressing company strategy for offshore IT outsourcing was Carmel and Agarwal [26] who developed a 4-stage maturation model for US companies sourcing IT work offshore (SITO). The four stages in the SITO model were as indicated in Table 1 below.

Carmel and Agarwal [26] also note the importance of captive centres (which they refer to as "Tech Insourcing") in their survey of offshore practices of US firms, noting that captive centres are more prevalent in companies that are operating at stage 4 in the maturation model.

GMC fits the definition of a company that has been operating at stage 4 of the maturation model, with an extensive offshore ITO/BPO portfolio including arms-length contracting and captive centres. In the ITO domain, Cullen et al. [27] have developed a "configuration framework" which provides a high-level description of the set of choices available to senior management in crafting an IT sourcing model. The model developed by Cullen et al. [27] has a degree of fit with GMC's sourcing options. However, the

Table 1. 4-stage Maturation Model for sourcing IT work offshore (Source: Carmel and Agarwal [26])

Stage	Description	Characteristics
1	Offshore bystander	Domestic sourcing only
2	Offshore experimenters	Pilot testing with non-core IT applications & processes
3	Proactive cost focus	Broad corporate wide efforts to achieve cost efficiencies through offshore work
4	Proactive strategic focus	Offshore sourcing is a strategic imperative to achieve competitive advantage and accelerate time to market

model presented by these authors assumes purely domestic sourcing whereas GMC is committed to a global sourcing strategy, and is also focused on knowledge-intensive services (also referred to by Contractor et al. [11] as relocation of high value company functions).

According to Contractor et al. [11], companies in GMC's situation should craft sourcing strategy on the basis that the company is seeking simultaneously cost efficiencies, new sources of knowledge and expertise and strategic advantage (e.g. through innovation and competitive advantage). In this research, we are addressing a gap identified by Lewin and Volberda [28] who called for studies encompassing the interactions between management intentionality, path dependent experience, knowledge accumulation in the client company and institutional and competitive factors.

3.3 Technology Ecosystem Governance and Open Innovation

It has been argued by Nambisan, Siegel and Kenney [7] that digital platforms and open innovation environments have created new opportunities for managers in a range of established industries, from car manufacturing [29] to mining [30]. However, success with open innovation typically requires that management establish an innovation context (technology ecosystem) in which a dynamic and possibly unpredictable group of actors with diverse goals and motives be harmonised and orchestrated [5]. Effectively governing an open innovation paradigm is a critical success factor because engaging and collaborating with external suppliers often requires managing risks and tensions [31].

3.4 Business Analytics

In reviewing research literature on business analytics and "big data", we encountered two broad streams. Firstly, a rich stream that has developed over several decades and continues to advance, dealing with business analytics and business intelligence (see for example: [32–34]. Secondly, a comprehensive stream based around the implicit (and in some cases explicit) assumption that "big data" is different to what might be called business analytics. Gunther, Mehrizi, Huysman and Feldberg [35] provide a comprehensive review of the second stream of literature.

Seddon et al. [33] provide a useful insight into the evolution of what they describe as business analytics (BA), and provide a number of helpful models and frameworks for conceptualising this area of research. Their focus on how business analytics contributes to business value brings a particular clarity and they present useful models that can be used to bridge the gap between what might be called "traditional" BA and big data.

Shollo and Galliers [32] describe how BA has evolved over several decades from reactive, standardised static reports to proactive generation of personalised interactive reports. The latter state appears to accurately represent what GMC is endeavouring to achieve from their big data initiatives. Successful BA applications typically involve some combination of processes, products and technologies which deliver an evidence/data-based paradigm for making management decisions [32]. It is also noted that BA systems have not always delivered on their promises of supporting decision-making.

Sharma, Mithas and Kankanhalli [36] argue that the shortcomings identified by Shollo and Galliers [32] frequently result from an implicit assumption that organisations can capture value from BA while continuing to function as before, whereas behavioural, organisational and strategic issues need more attention to exploit the potential of BA. It is noteworthy that this perspective on BA aligns with the views of Lacity and Willcocks [4] on change management required to maximise prospects of achieving innovation in ITO/BPO relationships.

3.5 How Is Big Data Different?

Should academics and management practitioners be interested in big data, and if so, why (Wamba et al. [8])? Since Anderson [37, 38] there has been a rapidly increasing stream of articles proposing that "big data" is different (see for expel Davenport, Barth and Bean [39], that it represents a "management revolution" (McAfee and Brynjolfsson [40] and that it can "unleash new organisational capabilities and value" (Davenport et al. [39]. However, as is noted by Wamba et al. [8], despite the concept of "big data" generating tremendous attention worldwide, few academic papers have actually studied business benefits being obtained from "big data", nor is the concept well defined. In reviewing definitions of "big data" found in the academic literature in the period 2008 to 2012, Wamba et al. ([8], page 236) identify fourteen different definitions, albeit a degree of commonality can be found across each of these definitions.

A counter view to the concept of "big data as a management revolution" is to be found in Sharma et al. (2014) where it is argued that while "big data" and "analytics" are recent buzz words, the ideas associated with these concepts have a longer history and build on a long tradition of research into business analytics and business intelligence tools. Support for this view is also found in Shollo and Galliers [32].

A systematic review of big data literature is presented by Gunther et al. [35] who present a convincing argument that big data is different, but also call for more research explaining how companies obtain business value from big data. In this research, we are endeavouring to respond to that call to action.

4   Research Method

The research reported in this paper had its genesis in a larger project over the past decade that examined critical success factors for OBPO, whether through arms-length contracts or via captive centres. In that earlier research, data was gathered through longitudinal case study research across a range of industry sectors at a number of Australian and international companies that are conducting OBPO at locations in India, the Philippines, China, South Africa and Vietnam and also at their OBPO service providers.

Several of the earlier longitudinal case studies identified significant changes in sourcing strategy, including one case (Boeing) that looked at an initially failed strategy to obtain innovation from an outsourcing strategy, where that initial failure was subsequently addressed by bringing responsibility for innovation back into the client company [41, 42]. That earlier case Boeing case study stimulated an interest by the authors to do further research into both strategic innovation from outsourcing, and also the drivers for sourcing changes.

We were also aware of and interested in the emerging research on achieving innovation through ITO, and were aware of the significant IT-led transformation that is occurring in the global mining industry (see for example Deloitte [43]). The opportunity to conduct a longitudinal case study of the implementation of "big data" and analytics at GMC thus presented an opportunity to study both strategic innovation driven through an ITO sourcing strategy that has changed significantly since inception.

Our selection of a longitudinal case study of innovation and transformation in the mining industry was influenced by three factors. Firstly, an important aspect of Curtin University's community engagement is through the mining industry, in part influenced by the School of Mines which has a rich 117-year history of teaching, research and innovation. Secondly, as researchers we were familiar with the technology-led transformation that was occurring in GMC and had access to information about its mining automation and big data initiatives. We also had access to Mining Equipment, Technology and Services (METS) suppliers who were major contributors to the big data initiatives that were underway. Thirdly, the mining industry has mature supply chains and a long history of largely successful outsourcing [30, 44] including ITO and BPO. Therefore, we considered that it offered a fruitful and insightful setting for a longitudinal case study aimed at understanding strategic innovation as one of the outcomes of ITO/BPO engagement.

This research commenced with initial exploratory research at GMC where we first investigated the project known as "head grade of ore into the copper smelter" (refer to Use Case One in Appendix 1). The exploratory phase had the objectives of establishing an overall context and structure for tracking the innovations being pursued by GMC and understanding the organisational and supply chain parameters that were involved. We also were able to review the transformation that was underway in the global mining industry and recognised the importance of secondary markets in this transformation and the contribution to innovation of METS suppliers.

A longitudinal case study methodology [45] was adopted because of its advantages in addressing "how" and "why" questions, and because of the opportunities that it provides for holistic, in-depth investigation of a phenomenon in which business context is critically important (see for example Yin [46], Cullen et al. [10]; Jensen, Larsen and Pedersen [46]). A longitudinal case study enabled the evolution of GMC's sourcing strategy and perceptions of success to be tracked over time, and changes in sourcing strategy identified and analysed.

Data was collected through interviews with staff and senior management in GMC and in several of their METS suppliers. We also attended industry conferences, annual results presentations and engaged with mining industry associations and lobby groups. For a broader perspective, we interviewed a recent Australian Government Minister responsible for the mining and industry portfolio, and now a senior executive in the industry. Further data was collected by attending internal team meetings, contextual observations and reviews of company documents and external presentations. Selection of interview subjects was a collaborative process with the companies that were participating in the case studies and was based on the concept of a *key informant* methodology. Interviewees were considered to be key informants if they were able to provide in-depth understanding and/or deep insights, either because of their detailed involvement in the projects under study or their senior management role or specialist knowledge.

To date, interviews have been conducted with about 30 informants, generating approximately 100 h of interview time. A core group of 6 informants have been interviewed on multiple occasions over an extended period of time. Further interviews will be conducted in the next 1–2 years. The onset of the Covid-19 pandemic has restricted face-to-face interviews.

A three-stage coding process (open, axial and selective) was used to analyse the data which was tested against a research framework and set of propositions designed to provide an understanding of the overall sourcing strategy and the extent to which strategic innovation was being delivered.

5   Automation and Transformation in the Global Mining Industry

It is believed that humans have been mining for at least forty thousand years [6]. Two thousand years ago, the Romans developed large-scale hydraulic and underground mining methods for use in alluvial gold deposits in Spain. Mining in the past has often involved large amounts of manual labour in difficult and dangerous work environments. There has also been a history of ongoing development of new methods and technologies, to improve worker safety and improve environmental and economic outcomes.

The past decade has seen a dramatic increase in demand for minerals and metals, led by industrialisation and urbanisation in China and elsewhere in Asia. This trend is expected to continue. However, miners tend to be price-takers and are exposed to cycles of rapidly declining prices for their commodities whenever demand moderates. Other global challenges for the mining industry include a general process of grade decline, as high-grade ores or those that can be extracted most cost-effectively are mined first. The remaining deposits are of a lower grade, in more remote locations, deeper in the ground, mixed with more impurities or have complex ore bodies making mining more difficult and costly [6].

Mining typically takes place in harsh and often hostile conditions. Traditionally, miners have worked in conditions that are dirty, noisy, usually confined and often in remote locations. The potentially adverse environmental impacts of mining operations are well known and have led to significant changes in how the industry operates and is regulated [6, 43]. In the past decade, governments as well as the mining industry itself have made very significant (and on the whole successful) efforts to improve safety and move towards more sustainable practices. GMC is recognised as a leader in these areas.

Faced with these challenges, industry commentators (see for example Matysek and Fisher [6]) have observed that the global mining industry is moving through a period marked by high rates of innovation, leading to a major transformation, largely led by Information and Communications Technology (ICT), automated operations and robotics.

Four key technologies that are driving the transformation are:

- Autonomous machinery and robotics (including drones), equipped with dense fields of sensors;
- Widespread adoption of leading edge communications, data analytics, machine learning and artificial intelligence applications;
- Connected and wearable worker technologies such as virtual reality head sets and smart devices that facilitate real-time decision-making;
- Development of a global mining industry technology ecosystem, based on standard IT tools, applications and systems, to facilitate seamless communication between mining companies, their suppliers and customers and to coordinate all activities across the value chain.

Various mining industry reports [43] forecast that new large mines will be fully automated by 2030, with autonomous drill and blast systems, autonomous trucks and rail systems, site monitoring via drones and operations managed from remote operations centres.

Wireless and satellite communications systems will send out alerts if capital plant equipment fails or requires repair and servicing. Maintenance and inspection staff will attend sites only when urgently required, while virtual reality heads sets will enable these on-site teams to simulate the required repair tasks, monitor fatigue levels while on site and improve safety performance [43].

6   GlobalMinCo (GMC) Overview

Formed through a complex series of mergers and acquisitions, GMC is now regarded by most measures as the world's second largest mining company by US dollar value of commodities sold to customers. In the financial year ending on 30 June 2019 (FY19), GMC generated revenues of $45 billion USD, Earnings before Interest, Tax and Depreciation of $10.3 billion and return on capital invested of 20%. Listed on three major stock exchanges (London, New York and Australia), GMC has a market capitalisation of approximately $35 billion USD.

GMC commenced operations in 1874 and brought capital and management expertise to the task of transforming one of the mines of antiquity into (for the next two decades) the world's number one copper producer. For 145 years, GMC has been pioneering the production of materials essential to human progress. The minerals and metals produced by GMC play a vital role in making modern lifestyles work. GMC now operates on six continents and in thirty five countries.

From its formation, a consistent theme in GMC's purpose and business operations has been to seek better and more productive ways to extract minerals, while improving safety and reducing environmental impacts. GMC's business strategy involves prioritising value created over volume. Hence, it has a focus on identifying and acquiring world-class mineral deposits with multi-decade life spans as sources of essential materials, and optimising the effective management and lifecycle of those assets. GMC is generally regarded as the global leader in mining automation, in which it has invested several billion dollars in IT-driven improvement in productivity, and as the world's lowest cost producer across the range of materials that it supplies (Table 2).

Table 2. Partial list of GMC minerals and metals production

Base minerals	Key applications	Description of GMC position in value chain
Bauxite, alumina, aluminium	Aluminium metal for a wide range of applications	Horizontally integrated producer of aluminium metal – involved in all stages from mining ore to smelting
Iron ore	Key ingredient for steel making	Supplier of iron ore as a feedstock to steel mills located around the world
Titanium dioxide	Used as a pigment in paint & other applications	Supplier of titanium dioxide to manufacturers
Diamonds	Jewellery and industrial cutting	Extraction, polishing and marketing of diamonds
Copper	Wide range of applications, especially electrical	Horizontally integrated producer of copper metal to 99.999% purity – involved in all stages from mining ore to smelting and refining
Borate	Wide range of industrial applications	Key supplier of high quality borate to industrial customers, especially in North America
Gold	Precious metal	Supplier to global markets
Silver	Precious metal	Supplier to global markets
Molybdenum	Steel making ingredient	Supplier of refined metal to steel-making customers
Salt	Chemical processes and manufacturing	Supplier of high quality salt to chemical manufacturers
Nickel	Steel making ingredient	Supplier of refined metal to steel-making customers

In common with other mining companies, GMC's business comprises much more than extracting ore. For GMC, the value chain includes extraction, processing, beneficiation, infrastructure, domestic transport (often through its own rail networks), logistics, ports and international shipping. GMC depends on world class ICT, data analytics, machine learning, robotics and artificial intelligence. Without seamless, integrated and highly efficient infrastructure, logistics, IT systems and communications networks, GMC cannot sustainably generate value and meet expectations of shareholders, governments and the communities in which it operates.

7   GMC Case Analysis

7.1   Evolution of GMC's Big Data Sourcing Strategy

GMC launched its big data portfolio of initiatives in the first quarter of calendar year 2015. The initial sourcing strategy was based on one of GMC's offshore captive centres located in India, together with contributions from its established portfolio of ITO/BPO suppliers who were well versed in the established IT architecture. Thought leadership for the big data initiatives was provided by two leading global consultancies recognised for their capabilities and leadership in the application of cutting edge IT solutions.

Initial results were disappointing. Applications took a long time to be developed and engagement by GMC's operating business units was limited. Recognising that its initial big data sourcing strategy was not delivering the results that had been expected, and after two years that saw only limited success, GMC embarked upon a change in sourcing strategy and also made related organisational changes.

7.2   Role of the Analytics Speed Team (AST)

From 2017 onwards, the Analytics Speed Team (AST) was established as an internal consulting group to drive faster progress with big data applications and to be closer to the main operating divisions. Nodes of big data internal expertise (referred to internally as "hubs") were built up, based in Perth, Brisbane, Montreal and Singapore, with a view to building collaborative relationships respectively with the Iron Ore, Bauxite/Alumina, Copper and Marketing operating businesses. The current organisational structure for AST is described in Appendix 2.

Two important early decisions by AST were to adopt a specialised and open IT architecture for big data applications (referred to as the Open Data Environment (ODE)), and to utilise an agile development methodology. Drivers for establishing the specialised big data IT architecture were to provide secure Application Programming Interfaces (API) and standard tools to enable a larger number of internal GMC staff as well as third party suppliers and customers to have secure access to GMC's big data "lakes" and big data applications.

In establishing AST, GMC was acknowledging that its initial big data IT environment was very challenging for METS suppliers seeking to provide analytics applications. To establish each new data science project typically required several months and extensive staff resources. As a result, cycle time in bringing analytics applications to the point where business benefits were delivered to GMC was too long. The ODE was established to provide an ecosystem in which both internal and external parties could deliver analytics applications to GMC in an efficient and transparent manner.

By providing an Open Data Environment (ODE) which allowed secure working with both internal and external staff and partners, AST was able to tap into secondary markets for specialised talent and expertise. Described internally as the ODE, the aim was to provide a software platform allowing rapid development and deployment of data analytics, machine learning, artificial intelligence and automation across GMC.

The intention was two-fold; external parties such as suppliers and customers could access data and applications developed within GMC, and these external parties could also put forward applications and data sources that GMC could utilise. As an example, external suppliers of autonomous vehicles and autonomous drill and blast platforms were themselves generating massive volumes of data and applications that could be shared with GMC if a common big data architecture and standards could be agreed. Within the Mining Equipment, Technology and Services (METS) industry, a consensus was emerging around cloud-based approaches to big data with Amazon Web Services (AWS) widely adopted. Accordingly, AST adopted the IT architectures that are described in Appendix 3 and engaged with key external parties including METS suppliers and consultants to promote adoption of both AWS as a big data cloud solution and GMC's preferred IT architecture. The adoption of the AWS platform to create an Open Data Environment was instrumental in mobilising secondary markets to contribute solutions that enabled more rapid progress.

AST decided to utilise an agile software development methodology in order to promote engagement by and collaboration with the operating business units and to dramatically increase the speed with which big data applications were made available. The terminology "agile development" refers to a group of software development methodologies based on iterative development, where business requirements and solutions evolve through collaboration between self-organising cross-functional teams. Key principles of agile development are to satisfy the end customer (in this case, the customers were the operating divisions in GMC), to welcome changes in business requirements, to agree upon business requirements through face-to-face time between customer representatives and developers, and frequent deliveries of capability.

Utilising the agile methodology required that "sprints" and "hackathons" were arranged at key hub locations. These sessions were attended by a combination of representatives from AST, the relevant operating business unit and third-party suppliers.

The AST is staffed by a combination of data scientists, business professionals and what has been referred to by Fontaine, McCarthy and Saleh [47] as "analytics translators" – a relatively new role that bridges between data scientists and engineers from the technology domain and staff from the operating business domain, such as marketing professionals, process engineers, operations managers, geologists and mine planners. Translators also make a significant contribution in bridging the business and analytics domains by identifying high value use cases, communicating business needs to technology experts and generating buy-in with business users.

The AST team is organised around two streams of work:

a. Conceptualisation, development and deployment of analytics applications
b. Consulting across the GMC business units

A fundamental objective for the AST Consulting group is to take successful applications development for one business unit, and seek opportunities to deploy that application, perhaps with minor modifications, in another product group. For example, an application to optimise ship berthing and loading for GMC's iron ore business unit may find also application in the Bauxite/Alumina/Aluminium business unit. The Consulting group is also expected to identify potential opportunities for new applications and bring these back to the Applications group for assessment and proof of concept.

Lacity and Willcocks [4] have developed a set of four principles for achieving innovation through ITO. One of these principles – Injecting – essentially involves strong and effective change management to transition individuals, teams and business units from the current status quo to the desired future state. This is clearly one of the roles of the AST Consulting Group.

A key marker of the success of AST occurred in July 2019 when GMC's global CEO presented his 2019 annual award for pioneering excellence to AST for the Machine Learning Model to Predict Head Grade Ore into the Copper Smelter (refer to Use Case One in Appendix 1).

7.3   AST Governance and Resourcing

At time of writing (December 2019), the AST was fully occupied, had a backlog of potential opportunities waiting for assessment and proof of concept, and was engaged in conversations with GMC senior management about expanding the size of the AST team, and also a possible change in outsourcing strategy. AST considered that to some extent it was a victim of its initial successes, and that there was a need for an internal discussion about whether it had simply "picked the low hanging fruit" and that future business benefits would be harder to generate, or whether there was still a significant number of new ideas for big data applications that could be converted to business value with additional resources. There was also an acknowledgement that GMC could not recruit, induct and train enough skilled data and analytics staff in its key hub locations to keep pace with current demand for its services and internal expectations.

The main governance forum for AST was conducted on a monthly basis with representatives from AST, each of the product/business units and GMC senior management. Status of each of the big data applications underway was reported and discussed, business units had an opportunity to bid for resources for new projects and overall priorities were agreed. Consistent with agile methodology, if priorities were changed, some projects might be moved to a temporary backlog for periods of 1–2 months while key priorities were addressed.

Within AST, each application team conducted an internal weekly show case to which all AST members were invited. Show cases consisted of brief presentations on each application or project that was underway and an open discussion that sought to identify any blockers and obstacles and also generate ideas.

7.4   Possible Future Changes in Big Data Sourcing Strategy

Noting the governance and resourcing challenges referred to above, the head of AST was considering establishing a panel of external suppliers with proven skills in the areas where GMC was facing staff shortages, and use these external suppliers to perform proof of concept developments.

GMC considered that its cloud-based big data architecture was a key enabler in establishing a panel of external suppliers, and thus maximising the opportunities to take advantage of secondary markets.

8   Limitations and Future Research

This research paper has a number of significant and obvious limitations, including those that are well-documented as inherent in qualitative case study research. These include a bias towards success in case study research, as noted in Penter, Pervan and Wreford [48], as it has been easier to obtain access to senior executives and to corporate information in cases where there is a general acknowledgment that [the sourcing strategy] has been successful and has delivered results. Given fulsome CEO praise of the success of GMC's big data initiatives, it is likely that many of the key informants for this GMC case study will have a bias towards success.

On the other hand, the research team was aware of the transformation that is occurring in the global mining industry, and the potential of big data to deliver significant business benefits. One of our objectives was to understand emerging best sourcing practices, and GMC is recognised by competitors and industry consultants as a global leader; hence, we were purposefully seeking to research high-performing sourcing approaches that were successful in delivering strategic innovation.

The incomplete nature of our longitudinal case study also gives rise to limitations. We anticipate that a further two years of data collection may be required before we have a sufficient portfolio of verified successful use cases that would enable definitive conclusions to be drawn that may confirm the success of GMC's sourcing strategy for big data and associated innovation. We know that successful outcomes from ITO/BPO is not a static construct, nor is success certain [4]. Hence, there are also advantages for our research in being able to observe over time further changes that may be required in GMC's sourcing strategy or governance approach.

Another key limitation arises from the focus on sourcing strategy and big data applications in one main case study (GMC) and in a series of METS (mining equipment, technology and services) suppliers in one major industry (i.e. mining). Hence, the ability to generalise from the findings of this research has that inherent limitation. However, as noted by Lacity and Willcocks ([4], p. 66), in ITO/BPO, researchers have under-examined the more strategic drivers of outsourcing, including innovation. Thus this research contributes to scarce literature on strategic innovation obtained through outsourcing.

With respect to data collection via interviews and review of company documentation, the interviews conducted to date have not been selected according to any systematic or randomised method. Rather they have been arranged on an opportunistic and convenience basis that has reflected availability, willingness to be interviewed, and in some measure, enthusiasm for the topic being researched.

Interview subjects were initially identified and approached on the basis of a key informant methodology. Interviewees were approached and their cooperation requested on the basis that they had in-depth understanding and/or insights into the sourcing strategy or big data objectives, either because of their senior management role or detailed involvement in the subjects being researched. It was common for interviewees to recommend approaches to other colleagues who had relevant experience and knowledge. Unsolicited offers to contribute were also received from enthusiastic participants in big data applications and use cases.

The disadvantage of such an approach to selection of interviewees is that it may incorporate sampling bias, particularly towards a "rose-tinted glasses" view of the business benefits from big data, and the overall success of the sourcing strategy.

The choice of case study method is supported by Eisenhardt [49] as highly suitable for the circumstances applicable to this research project (i.e. it is a relatively new and under-researched area). However, Eisenhardt [49] also notes that case study methods often yield large volumes of rich data and hence there is a temptation to build theory that captures every idiosyncratic factor revealed in the data and observations. Such theory may lack an overall perspective and may not highlight the most important relationships in a particular theoretical framework. We are conscious of already having a rich data set, and would acknowledge that we are to a certain extent struggling with the challenges identified by Eisenhardt [49].

Data was gathered primarily from informants who were working in Australia, USA and Canada, and all interviews and data collection have been in the English language. Hence there is possible cultural and English language bias. We see an opportunity for similar research in other environments (e.g. Brazil, Middle East, etc.) to compare with the results found so far in this research.

Future research on strategic innovation from ITO/BPO might also focus on seeking insights from a broader range of industries, companies and geographic locations.

9   Conclusion and Potential Contribution

Having noted the transformation that is occurring in the global mining industry, we have sought in this research to understand the sources of innovation, and the extent to which ITO sourcing strategies can be designed to deliver strategic innovation. We were motivated by earlier papers that suggested that strategic innovation was possible from ITO, and that high-quality relational governance was a significant factor contributing to success [1, 4]. By conducting longitudinal, in-depth studies at GMC, and some of its METS suppliers, we observed successful innovation in big data applications being delivered through a collaborative sourcing ecosystem. Preliminary responses to the research questions are indicated in the Table 3 below.

Table 3. Research questions and preliminary conclusions:

Research questions	Preliminary conclusions
What are the key success factors that contribute to successful strategic innovation achieved through ITO? How did GMC craft its "big data" sourcing strategy, and how did this change over time?	GMC has invested in a specific platform AWS in which third-party contributors have a high-level of trust. By dealing with external suppliers in a manner seen as commercially fair, GMC has encouraged generativity by semi-autonomous partners. GMC's AST organisational unit has addressed the factors identified by Lacity and Willcocks [4] as Acculturation, Inspiration, Funding and Injection (change management)
How does a client company organize for successful innovation when its ITO partners and their contributions are diverse and not known in advance?	Technology ecosystem governance principles proposed by Wareham et al. [50] provide a helpful foundation. GMC organisational change and especially the establishment of AST (refer to Appendix 2) has been a critical success factor. GMC senior leadership support, although indirect and subtle, overcame internal resistance to change
How do digital platforms and secondary labour markets facilitate ITO supplier ecosystems that are effective in delivering innovation? How efficient are secondary labour markets in delivering hyper-talents in areas such as data science and artificial intelligence?	We found that the principles of Open Innovation [5] have explanatory power for the innovation delivered for GMC via big data applications. Secondary labour markets have proved remarkably effective in the past two years, but may be approaching their limits as GMC continues to expand its big data portfolio

The results of our research so far indicate that in an industry with mature and well established third party supply chains [43], including the extensive and largely successful use of ITO, strategic innovation is being achieved by GMC through its current sourcing strategy. We build on the findings of Oshri et al. [1] about the importance of relational governance by observing that the adoption of common cloud-based architectures (e.g. AWS) and well established secondary markets appears to replicate effective relational governance.

By establishing an ODE and by dealing with METS suppliers in an open and transparent manner, GMC has established a high degree of trust and "opaque indifference" [51, 52] with its third-party contributors to its big data portfolio. We have also observed that secondary labour market efficiencies reduce the effects of customary behaviours which, in turn, support a reduction in cultural differences when sourcing; as culture consists of a framework of customary behaviours. A reduction in cultural differences provides support for offshore sourcing as the cultural differences between nations is of less importance in secondary markets.

A contribution of this research is to identify that the establishment by GMC of an internal consulting group (AST) to drive faster progress with data analytics and AI has been an important success factor and has to a certain extent replicated the findings of Lacity and Willcocks [4] about the importance of special governance for innovation. We find evidence in GMC's success to date and the role of AST for the principles for delivering innovation referred to by Lacity and Willcocks [4] as *Acculturating, Inspiring, Funding and Injecting*. These principles have important implications for management that is seeking to create an environment in which open innovation can succeed. The role of AST is also consistent with the concept of *Orchestration* of innovation as identified by Nambisan et al. [5], which in turn appears to be aligned with the *Acculturating* concept in Lacity and Willcocks [4].

In our findings to date, we have observed that the development of the secondary markets for consulting and third party ITO suppliers facilitated the development of an open and flexible sourcing ecosystem, and reduced GMC's set up costs and overheads while eliminating some of the hysteresis effects of a sub-optimal initial choice of sourcing configuration [53]. This research provides a practical contribution to our understanding by critically analysing the extent to which the emergence of secondary markets for consulting and third-party suppliers of cloud services, Industrial Internet of Things (IIoT), machine learning and open source software facilitate sourcing ecosystems optimised for delivering innovation and the realisation of value through cost and price performance.

In this research paper, we have sought to make a contribution to scarce literature on strategic innovation achieved through ITO, and we are seeking to provide guidance to managers as to actions that can be taken to strengthen the prospects of successful innovation. We have also identified opportunities for future research that may encourage more investigation of innovation being achieved through ITO relationships.

A further contribution that we are seeking to make is through analysing why and how client companies make changes to their ITO/BPO sourcing configurations. Our investigations are in the context of what Gerbl, McIvor, Loane and Humphreys [54] and Mudambi and Verzin [55] classify as more complex business process (aka "knowledge-intensive services"). Such knowledge-intensive services are hard to codify and require the transfer of significant tacit knowledge. There are also a number of interdependencies between different stakeholders involved in the processes. To deliver innovation in this context requires effective communication, integration and coordination of actors located in different countries and cultures. The cost of coordinating all parties involved so that they operate in a coherent and efficient manner can be very high [46, 56]. We find that the emergence of secondary markets and standardised cloud-based tools can significantly reduce the overheads and costs of coordination.

Appendix One: Selected Big Data Use Cases at GMC

Use Case One: Managing the Head Grade of Ore Delivered into the Copper Smelter

One of GMC's premier assets is a combined open cast copper mine, smelter and refinery located in the USA. The copper operation is contracted with GMC's end customers to deliver 99.99% pure copper metal for premium industrial applications.

Producing highly refined and pure copper metal requires a four-stage process of extracting the copper ore, increasing its concentration in the materials at each stage in the processing process and also recovering other precious metals (silver, gold, molybdenum, platinum) from the mined ore.

Traditionally, managing the flow of material from the mine through the various processing stages has been more art than science, and owed a great deal to decisions and judgements by experienced plant operators who had developed an intuitive "feel" based on patterns, relationships and outcomes they had observed. The development of autonomous mining operations and the increased use of sensors (e.g. to build up a 3D model of the mine and ore body accurate within centimetres, forecasting in advance grades in ore being mined) enabled a large data "lake" to be built up, and machine learning and artificial intelligence algorithms were then developed to predict in advance the so-called "head grade of ore" being delivered into the smelter.

By predicting in advance the "head grade" of ore being delivered into the smelter, GMC is able to optimise the smelting and refining process and make better decisions about the reagents required, thereby lowering production costs and energy consumption and improving environmental outcomes. The benefits in terms of cost reductions are estimated at tens of millions of dollars per annum.

Use Case Two: Materials Handling at the Mine Face – Optimising Crusher Performance

In the global mining industry, ore stocks in favourable locations (e.g. close to the surface, near major industrial concentrations) are depleting, forcing mining companies to move to more remote locations, to dig deeper and to crush more ore to maintain recovery rates of past years. Miners are seeking to reduce energy and water consumption and reduce carbon dioxide emissions. About 3% of global energy consumption was attributed to ore and rock crushing so greater productivity and efficiency in these operations can make a big contribution to emissions reductions.

Crushing and grinding equipment and processes at mining sites are often not working to optimal efficiency. Most of the processing and beneficiation at remote mine sites is done without prior knowledge of ore grades, rock sizes and rock hardness or the presence of "sticky" ore (mined below the water table) that clogs and jams crushing circuits. Autonomous mining processes (e.g. automated drill and blast) are enabling large "lakes" of data to be collected about parameters that impact on crushing efficiency. GMC has developed machine learning and AI applications that forecast and predict factors such as rock size, hardness or "sticky" ore prior to material entering crushing circuits. This has been shown to greatly reduce breakdowns and downtime in crushing circuits because unsuitable material can be prevented from entering the circuit in the first place. Similarly, applications that provide accurate ore grade prediction enable mining operations to be directed towards sectors in the orebody with the highest grades, thus reducing the handling of material in the crushing circuits that has little or no value.

The traditional model for processing and beneficiation in the mining industry is that heterogeneity at the mine face goes through many energy and capital intensive processing stages to achieve homogeneous feedstock's for downstream customers and their processing plants. Data and analytics combined with machine learning and analytics can exploit specific knowledge of heterogeneity at the mine face to reduce this need for processing (e.g. by improving ore to waste extraction ratios, by targeting mining operations on highest grade and easy-to-extract components of the ore body, by managing particle size and rock hardness, by blending "sticky" ore with drier "fines" ore).

Use Case Three: Delivering Precise Ore Grades and Blends to End Customers

To optimise parts of its mining business and to add value to its raw material outputs, GMC has committed to deliver high quality materials with low variability to customers and to ensure long term consistent and reliable supply. To achieve these goals requires that ore grades extracted from mines can be tracked, and that particle sizes (e.g. lumps and fines) are controlled and managed through the supply chain, and that the chemical composition and impurities (e.g. silica, phosphates) in ore shipments are accurately recorded and reported to customers. Commencing with its iron ore business, GMC has developed a branded ore blend that enables customers to select from and specify five different types, depending on the nature of their steel-making processes and the specialty steels that they are producing.

The benefit to end customers is that they can optimise their smelting and processing operations because they know in advance the nature of the raw materials that are being delivered and will be loaded into their furnaces and steel mills. There are also benefits to end customers in terms of ship-scheduling and management of stockpiles and logistics.

To deliver precise ore grades and blends on a consistent basis requires GMC to manage large amounts of data relating to ore extraction from multiple iron ore mines together with its own logistics, stockpiles and shipping.

In the future, GMC will extend the process of managing iron ore grades and blends for its customers to the joint management of scope three carbon dioxide emissions (emissions generated by customers).

Use Case Four: Measuring and Assessing the Risk of Musculoskeletal Injuries (MSK) in Mining Industry Workers

MSK injuries are the most common and most expensive to manage [57] in the mining industry. The solution is comprised of wearable sensors, a personal App connected to cloud-based data analytics and machine learning algorithms. The sensors monitor the wearer's alertness, providing feedback on their readiness to perform complex tasks and helping the wearer manage fatigue which is one of the main causes of accident and injury where heavy mobile equipment is in operation [43].

The wearable sensors use analytics to measure patterns of human movement and load bearing that contribute to the risk of potential injuries. A personal App warns the worker immediately if they are at risk of MSK, and coaches them on techniques to reduce risk. In certain situations (e.g. working at heights or on complicated machinery) virtual reality glasses are utilised to simulate the task and brief the worker on potential hazards and how these can be avoided.

A big data application provides the mining company with insights into the MSK risk profile of their overall workforce, as well as identifying potentially hazardous work sites, activities and scenarios in near real-time, and in some cases forecasting circumstances in which potential safety hazards may arise. This analytical capability provides a foundation for continuous improvement in health and safety practices.

A leading supplier of MSK injury monitoring solutions advised that this technology is rapidly diffusing globally in the mining, logistics, retail and construction industries.

Use Case Five: Using Drones to Improve Mine Safety Through Early Detection of Hazards

One of GMC's best assets is an open cast copper mine located in the USA. Working closely with the Federal Aviation Administration, GMC built a customised drone program to create 3D models of the constantly changing rock walls and rock benches in the open cast mine from which copper ore is extracted. Autonomous drill and blasting equipment regularly excavates ore from within the open cast mine, thus changing the configuration of the rock walls on a daily basis.

By using drones to map and model the changing contours within the mine, people can be removed from harm's way. Data from the drones is examined through machine learning and artificial intelligence algorithms to identify faults in rock walls that may become potentially hazardous (e.g. future locations of rock falls or wall collapses). Drones are also used to inspect mining infrastructure and to perform land surveys, thus enabling 3D models of the mine to be created that are accurate within centimetres.

The benefits of the program are improved safety of the workforce, and improved productivity from the mine site. The 3D models of the ore body also contribute to Use Case One described above.

Use Case Six: Optimising Ship Berthing and Loading

A significant component of GMC's value chain is the logistics associated with transporting ore and processed products from mines to the end customers' processing facilities. Often this involves the transport of ore from remote mines via railways to ports for loading onto very large ships (bulk carriers) for onward seaborne transport to end customers.

Ports for seaborne transport of ore and processed materials are expensive to set up and operate, and are frequently bottlenecks in the supply chain. Improved port performance can significantly improve operating performance by lowering costs per tonne shipped, and by obtaining premium prices through reliable delivery to end customers of precise ore blends and materials.

When a ship is approaching port, ore loading facilities including stockpiles and conveyors need to be configured and moved into precise position for the ship's arrival. Traditionally, ships have reported their position on a 12-hourly basis and have estimated their time of arrival in port and at the loading berth. Historically, such estimated arrival times (ETAs) have lacked precision, as crews are usually not familiar with local weather, tides and channel depths and may not understand the costs and inefficiencies associated with providing an inaccurate ETA.

If there is a significant gap between forecast and actual times of arrival, expensive port loading facilities sit idle waiting for a ship to arrive, and this triggers delays for other ships that are in the queue of arrivals waiting to be loaded. As port handling facilities are extremely capital-intensive and stockpiles occupy large amounts of space, usually only 2 or 3 ships can be simultaneously loaded. So delays in ship loading are costly and represent a significant loss in productivity.

GMC built a big data application based on historical data on ship movements, daily weather and tide information and automatically generated data from its own pilot boats that are sent to meet the large ore carriers as they approach the port and loading berths. This has allowed sophisticated data analytics and pattern matching, reducing gaps between actual arrival time and mobilisation of loading facilities. Detailed tidal information also enables the loading of the ship to be optimised and in some cases, payloads of ore carrying ships can be safely increased.

GMC believes that better utilisation of port loading facilities, optimisation of ship payloads and reduced queuing time for ships waiting to load has already reduced its costs by tens of millions of dollar per year. The application was first developed for GMC's iron ore loading ports and is now being rolled out for all of its global port facilities in all product groups that have significant seaborne loads and logistics.

Use Case Seven: Deciding When to Sell Iron Ore into Spot Markets Based on Customer/End User Sentiment
Much of the iron ore mined by GMC is committed through long term contracts of sale with steel manufacturers located in north Asia (i.e. Korea, China and Japan). However, GMC also retains a proportion of its iron ore for sale through the spot market, and its mines and logistics operations have some flexibility to "surge" volumes if required to supplement volumes for sale on the spot market.

Spot markets for iron ore respond to a variety of economic "signals" including global economic activity and forecasts, geopolitical events, disruptions to iron ore supply chains including those of GMC's competitors and major weather events (e.g. typhoon creating a rain event that disrupts operations at a major mine site).

Consistent with its philosophy of "value over volume", GMC has developed a big data and AI application that analyses data from a variety of largely published sources to measure and predict changes in customer sentiment about the iron ore spot price. If customer sentiment in a particular market suggests that the iron ore spot price is about to surge, GMC can flex its iron ore supply chain to make more ore available in the spot market.

It is also taking action to make its information available to customers and consultants with a view to better matching its production to periods of strong demand from its customers for additional supplies through the spot market.

Appendix Two: GMC Current Organisation for Analytics ("Big Data")

Appendix Three: GMC "Big Data" Architecture utilising AWS

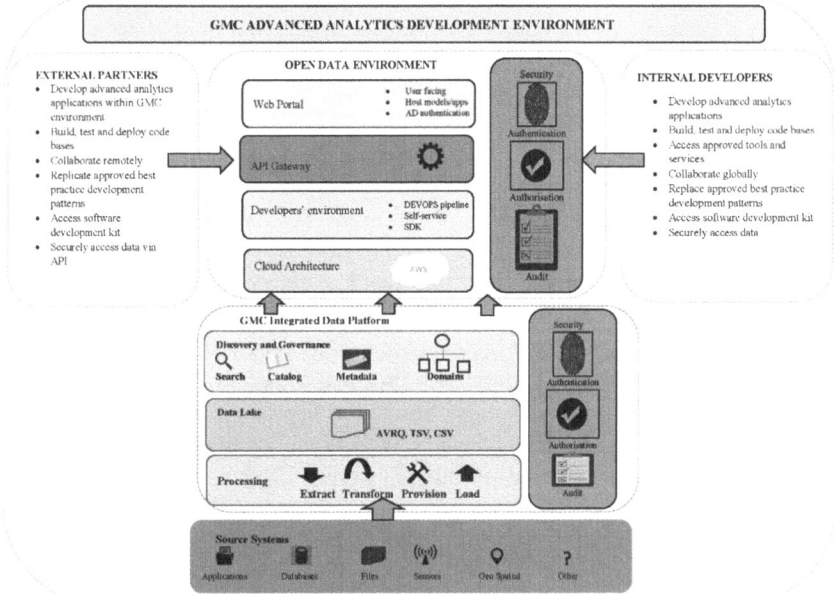

Appendix Four: Key Definitions, Relationships and Acronyms

The purpose of this section is to define carefully the phenomenon under study and its boundaries. Otherwise, there is likely to be ambiguity in any conclusions reached, and the identification of research gaps may be insufficiently precise to allow a significant contribution.

i. Offshore ITO and BPO

This paper fundamentally is considering *outsourcing* which can be conducted in the home nation of the client company (in this case GMC is the client company) and also to foreign locations (*offshore outsourcing*), and involves a decision by the client company to delegate responsibility to external service providers [11]. Offshoring represents restructuring of the client company's value chain along a different dimension, that of geography, and can be further categorised into near shore and far shore outsourcing [58–60].

In broader context of offshore outsourcing, activities can be classified as either offshore ITO or BPO (OITO/OBPO). For the purposes of this paper, it should be noted that the activities being outsourced are a combination of both Information Technology and Business Processes, and can be described as Knowledge-intensive services, hence at the most creative and skill-intensive end of the continuum of ITO/BPO services.

For the purposes of this paper, the acronym ITO is henceforth adopted, and readers are asked to note that this acronym is used to cover predominantly offshore outsourcing, and the outsourcing activities that involved data "lakes", machine learning, and artificial intelligence and associated IT architectures (aka "big data").

GMC is a pseudonym for one of the world's largest and most successful mining companies, operating in thirty five countries and six continents. "Big Australian" is a pseudonym for one of GMC's strongest competitors.

ii. Big Data

According to Jones [61], the meaning of the term "big data" is highly contested in academic literature. It has been argued by Anderson [37] that big data represents a revolutionary change in how we know the world, a view supported by McAfee and Brynjolfsson [40] who refer to big data as a management revolution. Others have argued that the benefits to be gained from big data are evolutionary rather than revolutionary, and build on a rich tradition of research and practical application of business analytics and business intelligence see for example Shollo and Galliers [32].

In the mining industry, the term "big data" typically refers to the use of large datasets for predictive analytics or other advanced applications (such as machine learning and artificial intelligence) as a means of extracting value from the data, including improved accuracy, greater operational efficiency, cost reduction, better decision making and lower risk.

Through the use of automated plant items equipped with networked sensor technology (e.g. autonomous drill and blast, autonomous trucks and trains), aerial remote sensing, and workers using information sensing mobile devices, every phase in GMC's value chain is generating vast amounts of data on a daily basis.

iii. METS Suppliers

The acronym METS refers to an industry segment made up of companies (often small and medium businesses) specialising in Mining Equipment, Technology and Services. The scope of this sector includes manufacture, supply and maintenance of equipment used in the mining sector, technology applications for exploration, mine development, minerals processing, handling and transport, consulting and contract services. It is often reported that the METS industry segment is a very important source of innovation in the global mining industry [32].

iv. Sourcing Strategy

Senior executives are faced with a "dizzying set of choices" in terms of sourcing locations, engagement models, service offerings from ITO suppliers, and the need to maintain and enhance in-house capabilities [62]. Companies face an "inestimable number of choices", and advice from consultants and third parties becomes "a source of constant conflict" [27], [62].

Sourcing strategy is therefore defined for the purpose of this research as a set of management actions designed to seek simultaneously cost efficiencies, new sources of knowledge and expertise and strategic advantage (e.g. through innovation and competitive advantage). In this research, we are addressing a gap identified by Lewin and Volberda [28] who called for studies on strategic sourcing encompassing the interactions between management intentionality, path dependent experience, knowledge accumulation in the client company and institutional and competitive factors.

Three assumptions underpinning this definition of sourcing strategy need to be stated. *Firstly*, it is assumed that client companies conducting ITO have a series of motivations or drivers for conducting ITO, and these drivers are translated into management intentionality. *Secondly*, management intentionality leads to a series of actions and decisions that are aimed at achieving ITO success and/or improving outcomes. This second component could be characterised as "the offshoring organisation in action" [63]. *Thirdly*, that over time as management in both the client company and its ITO service providers gain knowledge from experience with company-specific ITO activities, that there will be dynamic adaptations aimed at increasing gains and/or responding to changes in business context.

v. Innovation

There is a very substantial body of academic literature on the subject of innovation (see for example Jansen, Van Den Bosch and Volberda [64]). Innovations can be classified as incremental, radical or revolutionary (Davenport, Leibold and Voelpel [65]). In the context of outsourcing, Weeks and Feeny [3] identify three different types of innovation, of which *strategic innovation* is defined as significantly enhancing product and service offerings, or enabling a firm to enter new markets. The type of innovation sought by GMC through its big data strategy probably comes closest to this definition of strategic innovation, and also has the intent of achieving elements of game-changing (i.e. radical and revolutionary) innovation identified by Davenport et al. [65].

vi. Open Innovation

Open innovation (OI) has been defined by Chesbrough and Bogers [66, p. 17] as "a distributed innovation process based on purposively managed knowledge flows across organizational boundaries, using pecuniary and non-pecuniary mechanisms in line with the organization's business model". OI builds on the RBV theory of how organizations create value and competitive advantage by exploiting complementarities, and thus moving value creation beyond an organization's boundaries to the ecosystem level [67].

In the context of open innovation, Wareham, Fox and Cano Giner [50] define a technology ecosystem as comprised of a digital platform that supports and facilitates the activities of an extended community of semi-autonomous actors each of whom contributes to *generativity* (i.e. new outputs, ideas, products, etc.).

vii. Secondary Markets

Related to the concept of Open Innovation is the secondary labour market. Primary and secondary labour markets operate differently. A primary labour market, essentially an internal labour market for an organisation, is governed by employment rules, industrial agreements and customary behaviours. A secondary labour market is the antithesis of the primary labour market with few employment rules, no industrial agreements and competitive behaviours reducing the effect of customary behaviours in the search for competitive advantage. This relative freedom or the absence of constraints and competitive behaviours makes for a more conducive environment for innovation.

According to McKinsey Global Institute [68], online talent platforms have already attracted hundreds of millions of users around the world. As they grow in scale, they inject momentum and transparency into job markets. McKinsey [68, 69] defines the "gig economy" as contingent work that is transacted on a digital market place (e.g. LinkedIn). The "gig economy" is particularly effective in mobilising hyper talent in hard to source skill areas such as data science, machine learning and artificial intelligence [70]. Hyper talent is often attracted to the idea of working on a task-by-task basis for different employees concurrently. This trend is termed the "gig economy". In Australia, the largest "gig economy" category is web, mobile and software development (44%) followed by design and creativity (13%); more than 4.1 million Australian workers (32%) had participated in the gig economy between 2014 and 2016 [70].

viii. **Table of Acronyms**

Acronym	Definition
AI	Artificial intelligence
API	Application Programming Interface
AST	"Analytics Speed Team" – pseudonym for data science organisational unit inside GMC
BPO	Business Process Outsourcing
GMC	Global Mining Company – pseudonym for the company that has been the subject of a longitudinal case study reported in this paper
ICT	Information & Communications Technology
IOT	Internet of Things
ITO	Information Technology Outsourcing
METS	Mining Equipment & Technology Services
MSK	Muscular-skeletal – a common form of workforce injury in the mining industry
ODE	Open Data Environment
OBPO	Offshore Business Process Outsourcing
OITO	Offshore Information Technology Outsourcing
SITO	Sourcing Information Technology [Work] Offshore (reference Carmel and Agarwal 2002)

References

1. Oshri, I., Kotlarsky, J., Gerbasi, A.: Strategic innovation through outsourcing: the role of relational and contractual governance. J. Strat. Inf. Syst. **24**(3), 203–216 (2015)
2. Whitley, E., Willcocks, L.: Achieving step change in outsourcing maturity: toward collaborative innovation. MIS Q. Exe. **10**(3), 95–107 (2011)
3. Weeks, M., Feeny, D.: Outsourcing from cost management to innovation and business value. Calif. Manag. Rev. **50**(4), 127–146 (2008)
4. Lacity, M., Willcocks, L.: Business process outsourcing and dynamic innovation. Strat. Outsourcing Int. J. **7**(1), 66–92 (2014)
5. Nambisan, S., Lyytien, K., Majchrzak, A., Song, M.: Digital innovation management: reinventing innovation management research in a digital world. MIS Q. **41**(1), 223–238 (2017)
6. Matysek, A., Fisher, B.: Productivity and Innovation in the Mining Industry. BAE Economics, April 2016
7. Nambisan, S., Siegel, D., Kenney, M.: On open innovation, platforms, and entrepreneurship. Strateg. Entrepreneurship J. **12**, 354–368 (2018)
8. Wamba, A., Akter, S., Edwards, A., Chopin, G., Gnanzou, D.: How "big data" can make big impact: findings from a systematic review and longitudinal case study. Int. J. Prod. Econ. **165**, 234–246 (2015)
9. Jayatilaka, B., Hirschheim, R.: Changes in IT sourcing arrangements: an interpretive field study of technical and institutional influences. Strat. Outsourcing Int. J. **2**(2), 84–122 (2009)
10. Cullen, S., Seddon, P., Willcocks, L.: IT outsourcing success: a multi-dimensional, contextual perspective on outsourcing outcomes. Paper presented at the 2nd Information Systems Workshop on Global Sourcing: Service, Knowledge and Innovation, Val D'Isere, France (2008)
11. Contractor, F., Kumar, V., Kundu, S., Pedersen, T.: Reconceptualising the firm in a world of outsourcing and offshoring: the organizational and geographical relocation of high-value company functions. J. Manage. Stud. **47**(8), 1417–1433 (2010)
12. Parkhe, A.: International outsourcing of services: introduction to the special issue. J. Int. Manag. **13**(1), 3–6 (2007)
13. Hirschheim, R., Dibbern, J., Heinzl, A.: Foreword to the special issue on IS outsourcing. Inf. Syst. Front. **10**(2), 125–127 (2008)
14. Busi, M., McIvor, R.: Setting the outsourcing research agenda: the top-10 most urgent outsourcing areas. Strat. Outsourcing Int. J. **1**(3), 185–197 (2008)
15. Hirschheim, R., Dibbern, J.: Outsourcing in a global economy, traditional information technology outsourcing, offshore outsourcing and business process outsourcing. In: Hirschheim, R., Heinzl, A., Dibbern, J. (eds.) Information Systems Outsourcing: Enduring Themes, Global Challenges and Process Opportunities, pp. 3–21. Springer, Heidelberg (2009). https://doi.org/10.1007/978-3-540-88851-2_1
16. Jayatilaka, B.: Reaching across organisational boundaries for new ideas: innovation from it outsourcing vendors. In: Hirschheim, R., Heinzl, A., Dibbern, J. (eds.) Information Systems Outsourcing: Enduring Themes, Global Challenges and Process Opportunities, pp. 255–275. Springer, Heidelberg (2009). https://doi.org/10.1007/978-3-540-88851-2_12
17. Lacity, M., Willcocks, L.: Outsourcing business processes for innovation. MIT Sloan Manage. Rev. **54**(3), 63 (2013)
18. Aubert, B., Kishore, R., Iriyama, A.: Exploring and managing the "innovation through outsourcing" paradox. J. Strat. Inf. Syst. **24**(4), 255–269 (2015)
19. Aubert, B., Beaurivage, G., Croyeau, A.M., Rivard, S.: Firm strategic profile and IT outsourcing. In: Hirschheim, R., Heinzl, A., Dibbern, J. (eds.) Information Systems Outsourcing: Enduring Themes, Global Challenges and Process Opportunities, pp. 217–240. Springer, Heidelberg (2009). https://doi.org/10.1007/978-3-540-88851-2_10

20. Miles, R., Snow, C.: Organizational Strategy, Structure and Process. McGraw-Hill, New York (1978)
21. Lacity, M., Khan, S., Yan, A., Willcocks, L.: A review of the IT outsourcing empirical literature and future research directions. J. Inf. Tech. **25**(4), 395–433 (2010)
22. Lacity, M., Khan, S., Yan, A.: Review of the empirical business services sourcing literature: an update and future directions. J. Inf. Tech. **31**(3), 269–328 (2016)
23. Aubert, B., Iriyama, A., Ondelansek, K., Kishore, R.: Investigating the relationship between outsourcing and innovation. In: Hirschheim, R., Heinzl, A., Dibbern, J. (eds.) Information Systems Outsourcing Towards Sustainable Business Value, pp. 23–36. Springer, Heidelberg (2014). https://doi.org/10.1007/978-3-662-43820-6_2
24. Levina, N., Vaast, E.: Innovating or doing as told status differences and overlapping boundaries in offshore collaboration. MIS Q. Executive **32**(2), 307–332 (2008)
25. Straub, D., Weill, P., Schwaig, K.: Strategic dependence on the IT resource and outsourcing: a test of the strategic control model. Inf. Syst. Front. **10**(2), 195–210 (2008)
26. Carmel, E., Agarwal, R.: The maturation of offshore sourcing of information technology work. MIS Q. Executive **1**(2), 65–79 (2002)
27. Cullen, S., Seddon, P., Willcocks, L.: IT outsourcing configuration: research into defining and designing outsourcing arrangements. J. Strat. Inf. Syst. **14**(4), 357–387 (2005)
28. Lewin, A., Volberda, H.: Coevolution of global sourcing: the need to understand the underlying mechanisms of firm decisions to offshore. Int. Bus. Rev. **209**(3), 241–251 (2011)
29. Svahn, F., Mathiassen, L., Lindgren, R.: Embracing digital innovation in incumbent firms: how volvo cars managed competing concerns. MIS Q. **41**(1), 239–253 (2017)
30. Westergren, U., Holmstrom, J.: Exploring preconditions for open innovation: value networks in industrial firms. Inf. Organ. **22**, 209–226 (2012)
31. Whelan, E., Conboy, K., Crowston, K., Morgan, L., Rossi, M.: Editorial: the role of information systems in enabling open innovation. J. Assoc. Inf. Syst. **15**(Special Issue), xxi – xxx (2014)
32. Shollo, A., Galliers, R.: Towards an understanding of the role of business intelligence systems in organisational knowing. Inf. Syst. J. **26**, 339–367 (2016)
33. Seddon, P., Constantinidis, D., Tamm, T., Dod, H.: How does business analytics contribute to business value? Inf. Syst. J. **27**, 237–269 (2017)
34. Ain, N., Vaia, G., Delone, W., Waheed, M.: Two decades of research on business intelligence system adoption, utilization and success – a systematic literature review. Decis. Support Syst. **125**, 1–13 (2019)
35. Gunther, W., Mehrizi, M., Huysman, M., Fedberg, F.: Debating big data: a literature review on realizing value from big data. J. Strat. Inf. Syst. **28**, 191–209 (2017)
36. Sharma, R., Mithas, S., Kankanhalli, A.: Transforming decision-making processes: a research agenda for understanding the impact of business analytics on organisations. Eur. J. Inf. Syst. **23**, 441–443 (2014)
37. Anderson, C.: The Petabyte age: because more isn't just more – more is different. Wired, 23 June 2008
38. Anderson, C.: The end of theory: the data deluge makes the scientific method obsolete. Wired, 23 June 2008
39. Davenport, T., Barth, P., Bean, R.: How "big data" is different. MIT Sloan Manage. Rev. **54**(1), 43–46 (2012)
40. McAfee, A., Brynjolfsson, E.: Big data: the management revolution. Harv. Bus. Rev. **90**(10), 60–66 (2012)
41. Shenhar, A., Holzmann, V., Melamed, B., Zhao, Y.: The challenge of innovation in highly complex projects: what can we learn from Boeing's dreamliner experience? Project Manage. J. **47**(2), 62–78 (2016)

42. Tang, C., Zimmerman, J., Nelson, J.: Managing new product development and supply chain risk: the boeing 787 case. Supply Chain Forum Int. J. **10**(2), 74–86 (2009)
43. Deloitte: Innovation in Mining. Deloitte in association with Diggers and Dealers and Australian Association of Mining and Exploration Companies (AMEC). Perth (2016)
44. Baatartogtokh, B., Dunbar, W., van Zyl, D.: The state of outsourcing in the Canadian mining industry. Resourc. Policy (2018). https://doi.org/10.1016/j.resourpol.2018.06.014
45. Yin, R.: Case Study Research: Design and Methods, 3rd edn. Sage Publications, Beverly Hills (2003)
46. Jensen, P., Larsen, M., Pedersen, T.: The organizational design of offshoring: taking stock and moving forward. J. Int. Manag. **19**(4), 315–323 (2013)
47. Fountaine, T., McCarthy, B., Saleh, T.: Building the AI-powered organisation. Harvard Bus. Rev. July-August 2019
48. Penter, K., Wreford, J., Pervan, G., Davidson, F.: Offshore BPO decisions and institutional influence on senior managers. In: Oshri, I., Kotlarsky, J., Willcocks, L.P. (eds.) Global Sourcing 2013. LNBIP, vol. 163, pp. 93–116. Springer, Heidelberg (2013). https://doi.org/10.1007/978-3-642-40951-6_6
49. Eisenhardt, K.: Building theories from case study research. Acad. Manag. Rev. **14**(4), 532–550 (1989)
50. Wareham, J., Fox, P., Cano Giner, J.: Technology ecosystem governance. Organ. Sci. **25**(4), 1195–1215 (2014)
51. Wreford, J., Penter, K., Pervan, G., Davidson, F.: Opaque indifference, trust and service provider success in offshore business process outsourcing. In: Paper presented at the Proceedings of the 22nd Australasian Conference on Information Systems (ACIS), Sydney, Australia (2011)
52. Wreford, J., Penter, K., Pervan, G., Davidson, F.: Seeking opaque indifference in offshore BPO. In: Kotlarsky, J., Oshri, I., Willcocks, L. (eds.) The Dynamics of Global Sourcing. Perspectives and Practices: 6th Global Sourcing Workshop 2012, Courchevel, France, 12–15 March 2012, Revised Selected Papers, pp. 175–193 (2012). Springer, Heidelberg. https://doi.org/10.1007/978-3-642-33920-2_11
53. Augustin, J., Heinzl, A., Dibbern, J.: Unlocking path dependencies in business process outsourcing decision making. In: Paper presented at the 4th Global Sourcing Workshop, Zermatt, Switzerland (2010)
54. Gerbl, M., McIvor, R., Loane, S., Humphreys, P.: A multi-theory approach to understanding the business process outsourcing decision. J. World Bus. **50**(3), 505–518 (2015)
55. Mudambi, R., Venzin, M.: The strategic Nexus of offshoring and outsourcing decisions. J. Manage. Stud. **47**(s2), 1510–1533 (2010)
56. Elia, S., Narula, R., Massini, S.: Disentangling the role of modularity and bandwidth in entry mode choice: the case of business services offshoring. Henley Business School Discussion Paper, JDF-2015-06 (2015)
57. Zhou, V.: Roy Hill's industry collaboration to reduce risk of injury. Australian Mining, 26 September 2019 (2019)
58. Carmel, E., Abbott, P.: Why nearshore means that distance matters. Commun. ACM **50**(10), 40–46 (2007)
59. Gerbl, M., McIvor, R., Humphreys, P.: Making the business process outsourcing decision: why distance matters. Int. J. Oper. Prod. Manage. **36**(9), 1037–1064 (2016)
60. Aubert, B., Rivard, S., Templier, M.: Information technology and distance-induced effort to manage offshore activities. IEEE Trans. Eng. Manage. **58**(4), 758–771 (2011)
61. Jones, M.: What we talk about when we talk about (big) data. J. Strat. Inf. Syst. **28**, 3–16 (2019)
62. Lacity, M., Willcocks, L., Rottman, J.: Global sourcing of back office services: lessons, trends and enduring challenges. Strat. Outsourcing Int. J. **1**(1), 13–34 (2008)

63. Schmeisser, B.: A systematic review of literature on offshoring of value chain activities. J. Int. Manag. **19**(4), 390–406 (2013)
64. Jansen, J., Van Den Bosch, F., Volberda, H.: Exploratory innovation, exploitive innovation, and performance: effects of organizational antecedents and environmental moderators. Manage. Sci. **52**(11), 1661–1674 (2006)
65. Davenport, T., Leibold, M., Voelpel, S.: Strategic Management in the Innovation Economy. Wiley, Boston (2006)
66. Chesbrough, H., Bogers, M.: Explicating open innovation: clarifying an emerging paradigm for understanding innovation. In: Chesbrough, H., Vanhaverbeke, W., West, J. (eds.) New Frontiers in Open Innovation. Oxford University Press, Oxford (2014)
67. West, J., Bogers, M.: Open innovation: current status and research opportunities. Innov. Organ. Manag. **19**(1), 43–50 (2017)
68. McKinsey Global Institute: Independent Work: Choice, Necessity and the Gig Economy, McKinsey & Company, October 2016
69. Bughin, J., Mischke, J.: Exploding myths about the Gig Economy, McKinsey Global Institute, 28 November 2016
70. Australian Industry Group (AiGroup): The Emergence of the Gig Economy, AiGroup Workforce Development, August 2016

Author Index